ERNEST'S WAY

ERNEST'S WAY

An International Journey
Through Hemingway's Life

CRISTEN HEMINGWAY JAYNES

PEGASUS BOOKS
NEW YORK LONDON

ERNEST'S WAY

Pegasus Books Ltd.
148 W 37th Street, 13th Floor
New York, NY 10018

First Pegasus Books edition December 2019

Interior design by Maria Fernandez

Interior maps © Gema Alava and Óscar Quadrado Mendoza

Library of Congress Cataloging-in-Publication Data is available.

ISBN: 978-1-64313-207-5

10 9 8 7 6 5 4 3 2 1

Printed in the United States of America
Distributed by W. W. Norton & Company

*For my family
and John Boisonault*

WHEN I HAVE FEARS THAT I MAY CEASE TO BE

When I have fears that I may cease to be
Before my pen has glean'd my teeming brain,
Before high piled books, in charact'ry,
Hold like rich garners the full-ripen'd grain;
When I behold, upon the night's starr'd face,
Huge cloudy symbols of a high romance,
And think that I may never live to trace
Their shadows, with the magic hand of chance;
And when I feel, fair creature of an hour!
That I may never look upon thee more,
Never have relish in the faery power
Of unreflecting love!—then on the shore
Of the wide world I stand alone, and think
Till love and fame to nothingness do sink.

—John Keats, 1818

CONTENTS

FOREWORD

HILARY HEMINGWAY

Author of *Hemingway in Cuba*

I t's rare to find a Hemingway biography that tells the story of Ernest Hemingway's life in a new way. Recently, there have been some novels that use Hemingway as a fictional character, but to discover a new biography, one that gives the reader new insights into many of the special places where Hemingway roamed, and that shares thoughts about these cities and countries by Hemingway's friends and family, is a true pleasure. That said, *Ernest's Way* is far more than just a collection of Hemingway haunts. Cristen Hemingway Jaynes takes us on a journey, exploring how her great-grandfather, Ernest Hemingway, viewed the world around him. Through *Ernest's Way* we travel back in time to learn what was happening in Oak Park society during Hemingway's childhood, to read the details of the day Ernest's father, Dr. Clarence, committed suicide, to learn how the Spanish Civil War changed Hemingway's view on war, to visit the place in Italy where Ernest first fell in love, and to discover how Paris turned Hemingway-the-journalist into Hemingway-the-author. *Ernest's Way* is both a detailed account of Hemingway's life journey, and a look at what stirred him emotionally to write of these locations and the people who lived and died there. It is a map of both the man and the writer.

It is not widely known that Ernest liked to drink sherry in Spain, but by the end of this book we learn just what were Ernest's favorite drinks, and where the bars he preferred are located in Italy, Toronto, Paris, Madrid, Key West,

Havana, Bimini, London, and Sun Valley. We also discover where Papa lived, ate, explored, and enjoyed life to the fullest; where he fished, who he boxed with, and which women he loved. *Ernest's Way* details the history and architectural description of the buildings, as well as Hemingway's favorite meals and the current chefs who make them. We learn what streets Hemingway's Mob strolled, and who the artists, writers, and musicians were whom he called friends. Moreover, Cristen details her great-grandfather's real-life experiences in these locations and how Papa found inspiration there for his literary works. *Ernest's Way* is a guide not only to where Papa went, but how that location changed him and contributed to his growth as a writer. We discover the beginning of this development when Hemingway was knocking out newspaper stories for Toronto's *Star Weekly*, during which time he was also a hired companion and mentor to the son of a wealthy Toronto couple. While staying in the Connable family mansion, Ernest made good use of their extensive library, where he discovered the works of Joseph Conrad and a book on *Erotic Symbolism*. This, among other things, introduced Ernest to the idea of gender swapping hairstyles that he would later use in his novel *Garden of Eden*.

Ernest's Way is fit-bit-breaking marathon walking tour of Hemingway's stomping grounds. The rich details put the reader firmly on the cobblestone streets of Paris and the wine-soaked avenues of Madrid, alongside the canals of Venice, and on the white sands of Bimini. You can almost hear the rattle of cocktail shakers in Key West bars and smell the cigars along the back streets of Havana. This is more than just a chronicle of Papa's experiences and what he wrote about them. Cristen explains the psychology behind Hemingway's decisions to travel and write about these locales—places where, even a half-century after Hemingway's death, we find he is still adored by locals. Why? Because he made the struggles and courage of their compatriots known.

Ernest's Way has an honesty that Papa would have appreciated. This is not Ernest the superman, but a man whose body was noticeably marked by shrapnel, his bones broken by accidents, his skin tracked by mishaps that left scars. Life has a way of leaving marks on us all, but Hemingway found inspiration in such wounds. In one such case, Cristen explains an injury Papa got in Paris: *"In March of 1928, Ernest rose in the middle of the night in his and Pauline's flat on rue Férou to use the bathroom. When he tried to flush the toilet, he accidentally pulled the cord of the damaged skylight instead of the toilet chain, and glass came crashing down onto his head. He suffered a deep gash, was knocked unconscious, and was taken to the American hospital, where they sewed him up with nine stitches. By then he was so well-known that his mishap was widely reported on both sides of the Atlantic. When Ezra Pound heard about the incident, he sent Ernest a cable: 'Haow the hellsufferin tomcats did you git drunk enough to fall upwards thru the blithering skylight!!!!!!!.'"* Cristen points out that the head wound, perhaps combined with the smells and sounds of the hospital, triggered a memory in Papa's brain. He began a new writing project, one that featured his love affair with nurse Agnes von Kurowsky during the first World War, *A Farewell to Arms.*

Ernest's Way tells us where the cafés, bars, museums, and various Hemingway residences and monuments are, as well as when they are open to the public. One of my favorites is the Cuban restaurant, La Terraza de Cojímar. This, like many of the other Hemingway haunts, still looks much as it did when Ernest was a frequent customer. During Hemingway's time, there were two main docks in Cojímar. One was a large cement dock where Papa would tie up his sport fishing boat, *Pilar.* The other was the small wooden dock beside La Terraza Restaurant. On the first floor of the building was the town's icehouse, so all the fishermen would bring in their catch to that dock. It's where Santiago is teased by the other fishermen at the opening of *The Old Man and the Sea,* and where Santiago ties up his skiff with the remains of his Noble Fish at the end of the book. Though the icehouse has long since moved, La Terraza Bar and Restaurant remains open on the top floor. Today, you can dine on some fine seafood and enjoy the same corner table with its waterside view that Papa so loved. Looking down from a wall of windows, you can still see the stumps of pilings that once held up the wooden dock where the Cojímar fishermen brought their catch. It's easy to imagine the skeleton of Santiago's great marlin tied to his skiff, with the fish's long white spine and huge tail swaying in the waves below. Cristen also tells us about the Hemingway monument in Cojímar, with its bust of Papa that was the first memorial built to honor him after his death in 1961. The monument is made extra special by the fact that the brass sculpted into the bust is comprised of donations of brass propellers and cleats from the fishermen of Cojímar.

Finally, some of the nicest things about this book are the personal stories of Cristen's own adventures while learning about her great-grandfather. Sharing drinks and trading stories with the great-granddaughter of Spanish matador, Juan Belmonte, a dear friend of Ernest; watching a boxing match judged by Papa's friends and former sparring partners in Key West; spending the night in Paris's most famous bookstore; and sharing her own thoughts on seeing her great-grandfather's grave in Idaho. I remember watching Cris on the evening she describes in Key West, at a semi-pro boxing match held at the Hemingway House during the Hemingway Days Festival. It was remarkable to hear from two men who had been Ernest's young sparring partners. Kermit "Shine" Forbes and "Iron Baby" Roberts were all grins talking about Papa's strong jab and his willingness to teach others. I was surprised to learn that Cris had spent the night at Shakespeare and Company bookstore. Sylvia Beach closed her original bookshop after the end of the Second World War, but in 1958, over dinner with George Whitman, Beach decided to give Whitman the use of the name, Shakespeare & Company, for his own bookshop, because, like her, Whitman had welcomed and encouraged writers and artists. Whitman even offered writers, artists, and students a free bed upstairs while staying in Paris. Cristen, who had just finished a French intensive program at Avignon, became one of the lucky ones to spend a few nights at Shakespeare and Company.

Most touching was Cristen's memory of visiting Ernest's Sun Valley grave. At eight years old, it's hard to think about one's dead relative, or to put international fame into perspective, but what got through to her wasn't Papa's lifestyle, or the thousands of photographs that seem to document every moment of this man's life. No, what Cristen took to heart was her great-grandfather's work. Staying up till midnight to finish *The Old Man and the Sea*; learning about her great-grandfather through his own words in *The Sun Also Rises* and *A Moveable Feast*. That's how Ernest would have wanted it. And he would have warned his great-granddaughter that it's none of their business that we must learn how to write. Let them think you're born that way. In truth, there is nothing easy about writing, regardless of DNA. You have only done well when the story ends and the reader feels and understands the journey as if they had walked the path themselves.

Cheers to sore feet and fine champagne with *Ernest's Way*.

ERNEST'S WAY

1

THE WOODS: PART I

OAK PARK, MICHIGAN, AND CHICAGO

D uring the last Ice Age, what is now the city of Chicago was covered by a glacial lake. Stands of oak trees carpeted the shores of prehistoric Lake Chicago—the predecessor to Lake Michigan—and were eventually home to the Potawatomi, Sauk, and Meskwaki Native American tribes. In 1835, Betty and Joseph Kettlestrings of Yorkshire, England, purchased 172 acres—referred to as "Oak Ridge" by the area's first settlers—on which they built a house, established a farm, and eventually opened a tavern and inn for travelers. More settlers arrived when the Galena and Chicago Union Railroad became the first train to run west of Chicago in 1848. The village was named "Oak Park" when the post office was established, as "Oak Ridge" had already been claimed by another Illinois post office. Most of the Lake Michigan Potawatomi—meaning "those who tend the hearth-fire"—were forced to relocate to Nebraska, though some bands held their ground and established what are now federally recognized tribes. The Sauk and Meskwaki tribes were forcibly relocated to Oklahoma in the 1870s and are now known as the Sac and Fox Nation.

During the 1870s, so many churches were built in Oak Park that it was referred to as "Saints' Rest."[1] After the 1871 Chicago Fire, the village experienced a development boom when many Chicagoans moved into the surrounding areas and the streetcar lines were expanded. In 1872, Oak Park got its own railroad depot on the Chicago and Northwestern Railway, and that same year the Illinois Temperance Act banned the sale of alcohol in Oak Park—a law that was in force for a hundred years. Until 1902, when Ernest Hemingway was three, Oak Park was still an unincorporated part of Cicero Township.

Like Asheville, Bozeman, and other fine, smaller cities in America, the village nine miles west of Chicago has the hushed, expectant quality of Edward Hopper's 1930 painting, *Early Sunday Morning*. In many ways, Oak Park hasn't changed much since then, or even since Hemingway was nurtured by its close-knit community. One can still stroll down the oak-lined sidewalks and feel the austere hum of an erstwhile age.

At eight o'clock on the morning of July 21, 1899, Ernest Miller Hemingway was born in the south front bedroom of the gabled Victorian at 439 North Oak Park Avenue. Of the sunny and hot first day of her son's life, Grace Hall Hemingway wrote, "The robins sang their sweetest songs to welcome the little stranger into this beautiful world."[2] Ernest's love of words became apparent before he was two when he began giving everyone nicknames—he was "Bobby-the-squirrel" and could correctly identify seventy-three birds in his mother's *Birds of Nature* book.[3] He seemed to live legitimately in two worlds; the stories he'd invent were just as real as his surroundings. After Ernie told a tale of how he'd single-handedly caught a runaway horse, his maternal grandfather and namesake, Ernest Hall, said to Grace, "Chumpy dear, this boy is going to be heard from someday. If he uses his imagination for good purposes, he'll be famous, but if he starts the wrong way, with all his energy, he'll end in jail, and it's up to you which way he goes."[4]

Hemingway's Birthplace Museum

439 (now 339) North Oak Park Avenue.
Open Weds.–Fri. & Sun. 1–5 P.M.; Sat. 10 A.M.–5 P.M. Closed major
holidays. Tel. (708) 445-3071. General information: info@ehfop.org.
Group tour bookings: grouptours@ehfop.org. Tours begin at the top of
each hour with the last tour at 4 P.M.

Grace and Clarence Hemingway's first home was with Grace's father, Ernest Hall, in his Queen Anne-style Victorian at 439 North Oak Park Avenue. Their first four children—Marcelline, Ernest, Ursula, and Madelaine ("Sunny")—were born while the family was living here. The house has three stories and six bedrooms, with one upstairs bath. It was the first house in Oak Park to have electricity—at the rate of twenty dollars per year—and one of the first to have indoor plumbing and a telephone. Clarence's parents, Anson and Adelaide, lived across the street at **444 North Oak Park Avenue**.

With its wraparound porch and grand turret, the elegant residence was designed by architect Wesley Arnold and built for Grandfather Hall in 1890. Ernest lived here until he was six, within walking distance of nature trails and preserves that kept him connected to the woods while he was away from *Windemere*, the family's summer cottage. Hemingway's birthplace home was restored beginning in 1992, and displays furnishings, photographs, writings, and memorabilia from Hemingway's earliest years in Oak Park.

A short walk from Hemingway's birthplace and childhood home is the **Frank Lloyd Wright Home and Studio** at 951 Chicago Avenue. Wright—who was known as an "organic architect"—built the house in 1889 and lived there until 1909, and it is where he and his wife Catherine Tobin raised their six children. Wright designed more than one hundred structures in a studio added to the home in 1898. Wright's first public commission, the **Unity Temple** at 875 Lake Street, was built between 1905 and 1908, and is said to have been one of his favorites. Oak Park contains the largest collection of homes designed by Wright in the world. When Ernest's little brother, Leicester, enrolled in a Saturday art class at the Frank Lloyd Wright Home in 1922, it sparked his mother's interest in painting. Grace asked if she could enroll in the class and the instructor allowed her to sit in alongside the children. Soon after, Grace enrolled at the **Art Institute of Chicago** and began her painting career.

By the summer of 1900, the summer cottage on Walloon Lake in Northern Michigan that Grace had designed was finished. With two bedrooms and a large fireplace, it sat amongst the maples and hemlocks near the shore. Grace would name the cottage *Windemere* for Lake Windermere, near her ancestral home in Cumbria, England. Cupped by green hills and facing the lake, it would be the family's gathering place each summer, where the rules of city life were tossed aside. The children could wear overalls, swim all day, and play without chores or obligations. For a woman as insistent on discipline and decorum as Grace was, this loosening of the rules was remarkably modern. But Grace was a wild card. Though dedicated to raising her children with the Christian principles of selflessness, discipline, and sacrifice, she placed a high priority on independence and solitude, and made sure they were exposed to as much culture as possible. She took them to the opera, symphony, and to the Art Institute of Chicago, where Ernest was first exposed to the sorts of great works of art that would influence his sensibilities as a writer.

Independent from a young age, Grace was the first girl in Chicago to ride a bicycle. Her brother Leicester had been given a "high-wheeler," which in the 1880s was seen as inappropriate for women to ride. Incensed, Grace put on a pair of her brother's trousers—another *no-no*—and rode his bicycle around the block. "People rushed to their windows, shopkeepers in their aprons stood in doorways gaping in wonder at the sight," Ernest's older sister, Marcelline, recalled Grace telling her. "To my mother's great delight she heard people calling to each other, 'Come quick and look! It's a *girl* on a bicycle!' . . . She was always proud that she had dared to be the first girl in Chicago to ride a boy's high bike."[5] In later years, Ernest's little sister Sunny recalled that her father had said he'd fallen in love with Grace's voice and her audacity to ride a bicycle.

Windemere cottage was where Ernest got his first taste of many things that would become lifelong enjoyments—taking long hikes through the woods, storytelling, fishing, and being out on the water. The first craft he ever manned was the family rowboat, *Marcelline of Windemere*. Returning to the cottage each summer, Ernie found that he was most comfortable barefoot and roughing it—using the skills his father taught him to make fires, build lean-tos, fish for trout, and hunt small game. In the woods he was at home with his instinctual self, and he would seek out and reclaim that unrestrained feeling of freedom at every opportunity—whether in Spain, Idaho, or the vastness of the Gulf Stream—for the rest of his life.

Harbor Springs Train Station
111 West Bay Street, Harbor Springs, Michigan.

When the Hemingway family traveled north by steamship from Chicago to spend the summer at *Windemere* cottage, they disembarked at Harbor Springs and transferred their luggage and other belongings to the nearby train station, where it was loaded onto a "dummy" train to begin the journey to Petoskey and Walloon Lake Village. In 1874, the Grand Rapids and Indiana Railroad built a line to service Petoskey, with a branch line to Harbor Springs added in 1882. The depot, designed by Grand Rapids architect Sidney J. Osgood, was constructed in 1889, and was in use as a passenger station until 1962. The interior of what was once the passenger area retains its original maple flooring, and most of the baggage storage is elevated to the height of a wagon to facilitate loading. Between the passenger area and the baggage room is the original ticket office, containing a large bay window. As of 2016, the building houses the members-only Depot Club & Restaurant.

Taylor Horton Creek Nature Preserve
Horton Creek Road, Boyne City, Michigan. Tel. (231) 347-0991.

Growing up, Hemingway loved to fish for trout on Horton Creek, and refers to it in several stories. It was likely the model for the creek mentioned in the Nick Adams stories "Summer People" and "The Last Good Country," and the terrain is reminiscent of the backcountry Hemingway and two high school friends encountered along the East Branch of the Upper Peninsula's **Fox River** during the 1919 camping trip that inspired "Big Two-Hearted River." Combined with the **Schultz Working Forest Reserve** and three other nature preserves—**Horton Creek Wetlands**, **Taylor Horton Creek**, and **Nick Adams**—Horton Creek Nature Preserve is made up of 325 acres, including 2.25 miles of Horton Creek frontage. Nearly three miles of trails wind through mature hardwood forests and stands of pin cherry brushed with clusters of bull thistle and white clover, while hemlock and yellow birch grow along the edge of Horton Creek.

When Ernest wasn't practicing his survival skills, he was participating in the chorus of small-town life in Oak Park, where he was reluctantly being civilized by his parents. Grace Hall and Dr. Clarence Edmonds Hemingway each had their own passions and values, which they instilled in the members of their growing family. Underneath their churchgoing and somewhat conventional exteriors were deeper selves of extraordinary character. Grace was a gifted singer who had studied opera in New York and debuted at Madison Square Garden, been offered a contract with the Metropolitan Opera, and been invited to sing for Queen Victoria—all before she was twenty-five. She'd turned down the opportunity for a career in the opera to return to Oak Park and start a family with the young man who lived across the street.

"Dr. Ed," as Clarence was known, was a general medical practitioner, collector, and lover of everything having to do with the outdoors. His home office was full of animals preserved by his own taxidermy techniques or in a solution of formaldehyde. He collected stamps and Native American arrowheads, and could usually be found either out making house calls to his patients, fishing, hunting, chopping wood, or in the kitchen, as cooking was one of his passions.

Always generous with his time, Clarence loved teaching his children and their friends about the wilderness, with which he seemed to have a spiritual connection. He organized Marcelline and Ernest's class into an Agassiz Club, named for the Swiss-born naturalist, Louis Agassiz. "He . . . taught us to be quiet in the woods," Marcelline wrote. "He would cock his head sideways, raise his index finger in the air, saying 'Sh-sh-sh' and whisper 'Listen.'"[6] During the Michigan summers, Clarence taught his children how to build fires in wet and dry weather, how to make shelters out of boughs, how to stay afloat in deep water, how to tie flies, and how to dress game and cook it over a campfire. He taught them gun safety and the ethics of shooting game, saying, "It takes kindness to kill cleanly, and it takes a wise man never to shoot more than he can use to eat."[7] Clarence never killed animals for sport, only out of necessity or for food, and he insisted that any animals his children killed were eaten. This was proven in the summer of 1913 when the dog belonging to their neighbor, Henry Bacon, got into a tussle with a porcupine. Ernest and his friend, Harold Sampson, thinking they were doing the right thing avenging the dog's mouthful of quills, went after the porcupine and shot it. Even though he had to pull each quill from the dog's mouth individually and painfully, Clarence didn't feel that the boys' revenge was justified. As punishment, they were required to eat their kill, which Harold reported was "about as tender and tasty as a piece of shoe leather."[8] While Clarence believed all edible animals, including raccoon and squirrel, should be consumed if shot, the same didn't apply to predators. This philosophy offers an at least partial explanation for Ernest's intense relationship with the natural world, and why, as he moved from post-Victorian, small-town America and its surrounding wildlands into the wider world, his relationship with animals ultimately appeared shocking as concepts of conservation and cruelty evolved.

Dr. Ed donated his time and services wherever needed and often didn't charge patients who couldn't afford to pay. Always busy, he had no tolerance for idleness in others, especially his children. Physical activity *was* leisure, not sitting in a chair thinking or "relaxing." His father's work ethic rubbed off on Ernest, who was disciplined with his writing and believed physical activity was the best way to right the mind. As friendly and generous as Dr. Ed was, he had an unpredictable temper, which may have been caused in part by unchecked diabetes. He was prone to the same drastic mood changes that would later plague Ernest, and both father and son's black moods often appeared without warning.

Grace Hall was born in a house on Fulton Street in Chicago on June 15, 1872. Her parents, Ernest Hall and Caroline Hancock, had both come from England to America in their youth. Although the family had lost most of what they owned in the Chicago Fire of 1871, Ernest Hall's cutlery business did well enough that he was able to recover and prosper. The Halls were a notably musical family. Grace's father sang baritone, her Uncle Tyley Hancock sang tenor, and she and her mother sang contralto and soprano, respectively, in the St. Paul's Episcopal Cathedral choir, and soloed at Chicago's Apollo Club. Grace was introduced to opera as a baby and was humming arias before she could talk. She had an uncanny ear, and developed the ability to play complex pieces from memory. Grace's mother made it clear that developing her talent would always take precedence over any housework or cooking, and Grace carried this practice into her adult life, explaining to Marcelline, "I pay out of what I earn in my professional life for the cook and the laundress and the nursemaid who do the work that other girls' mothers have to do."[9]

When Grace was in high school, the Halls moved to Oak Park, and it was during her sophomore year at Oak Park High School that she met Clarence Hemingway. They were not high school sweethearts, however, as the interests that became their lifelong passions meant they had little in common as friends. Besides that, Grace told Marcelline later, her future husband "seemed to her to have very large wrists and ankles because his coat sleeves were too short and his long trousers stopped too far above his shoe tops."[10] Sounds similar to the casual mode of dress of a certain Ernest Miller Hemingway. Although Grace and Clarence had lived across the street from each other on Oak Park Avenue for years, it wasn't until Grace's mother became sick with cancer that they became close. Young Clarence had left Oak Park to attend Oberlin College in Ohio, followed by Rush Medical College in Chicago, and had returned in 1894 to become the assistant of Dr. William R. Lewis, Caroline Hall's doctor. During her mother's illness, Grace leaned on Clarence, and by the time her mother died on September 5, 1895, their relationship had become romantic.

That fall, Grace Hall studied with opera coach, Madame Louisa Cappianni, in New York and lived at the Art Students League. Madame Cappianni arranged for Grace to audition with the Metropolitan Opera, and they offered her a contract. Grace debuted at Madison Square

Garden, earning a thousand dollars, but hesitated to sign a contract with the opera for the following year. Convinced to return to Oak Park by both Clarence and her father—who wanted her to go to Europe with him that summer—Grace came home. She and Clarence were married at the **First Congregational Church** of Oak Park on October 1, 1896, leaving her operatic career behind.

Though Grace had chosen not to pursue opera professionally, she continued to give concerts, solo in the church choir, and teach voice to more than fifty pupils at a time on Chicago's West Side. This sometimes earned her a thousand dollars a month—an enormous sum at the turn of the twentieth century—while Clarence earned about twenty times less when they were first married. Grace was always singing and composing, and would often get up in the middle of the night when a melody came to her and go down to the piano to play it through so as not to forget.

Grace's father, Ernest Hall, was born and educated in London, but even after moving to the midwestern United States, he retained the dress and habits of an Englishman. Marcelline recalled him "wearing immaculate gray gloves and a black derby or a high top hat . . . walking along the street, with his little white woolly Yorkshire terrier, named Tassle, by his side."[11] Grace and her father were close, sharing a love of books, music, and humor. The family attended Grace Episcopal Church and shared family prayers in the parlor after breakfast. Ernest Hall was fond of his son-in-law Clarence, calling him "dear boy" and "the blessed doctor."[12] At the breakfast table, Grandfather Hall told the children stories of his life in London, where he said he'd spotted Charles Dickens while on a walk. Ernest Hall had served in an Iowa regiment during all four years of the Civil War, but though he'd been shot and a bullet remained in his body for the rest of his life, he'd refused the pension offered to him by the U.S. Government.

On Ernest's third birthday, he and his father went fishing together for the first time and Ernest landed his own catch, which included the biggest fish of the day. According to his mother, young Ernest was sensitive to the suffering of animals, "crying bitterly over the death of a fly he had tried to revive on sugar and water."[13] In the summer of 1905, the Hemingways bought forty acres across the lake from *Windemere*, which they named

Longfield Farm. The spirit of expansion had begun in Oak Park, where Grace had decided to design and build a bigger, finer, and more modern home after her father had passed away from Bright's Disease in May.

Oak Park Public Library (formerly the Scoville Institute)
834 Lake Street.

From 1905 to 1906, the Hemingways lived in a rented house on Grove Avenue, next door to the Oak Park Public Library, while their new house on Kenilworth Avenue was being finished. Then known as the Scoville Institute, the library was founded in 1903 and also served as a civic and cultural center where a variety of the town's clubs met. In the fall of 1905, Ernest and Marcelline began first grade together at the **Lowell School**, founded in 1859 and also on Lake Street. Marcelline had been held back in kindergarten so that she and Ernest could be in the same class together once Ernest turned six. Grace had wanted twins and to a certain extent raised Marcelline and Ernest as such. The "twins," who had just begun to read, would often go to the children's room at the Scoville Institute after school, until the librarian sent them home for supper. The Hemingways moved into their new house in the fall of 1906, and Ernest and Marcelline were transferred to the **Oliver Wendell Holmes Elementary School** down the street on Kenilworth Avenue.

Hemingway's Second Home
600 North Kenilworth Avenue.

In April of 1906, the Hemingways moved into their brand new, three-story, eight-bedroom home designed by Grace. The house, on the corner of Kenilworth Avenue and Iowa Street, had a bigger kitchen, an office for Dr. Ed, and a room with an indoor balcony for Grace to compose, teach, and perform music. The Kenilworth house is not open to the public, but in 1974 The Historical Society of Oak Park and River Forest placed a plaque out front that reads: "In this home Ernest Hemingway, novelist and journalist, lived his boyhood years and created his first literary efforts, 1906–1920."

Oliver Wendell Holmes Elementary School
508 North Kenilworth Avenue.

Ernest and Marcelline attended grammar school at the Oliver Wendell Holmes School from second through eighth grade. On April 7, 1911, Ernest wrote one of his first short stories, "My First Sea Vouge [*sic*]," for his sixth grade English class. The story was inspired by a trip his great-uncle, Tyley Hancock, had made with Tyley's father to Australia, and evinced the kinds of details suggestive of the understated allegory that would mark Hemingway's later fiction. To his mother's disappointment, Ernie wasn't as musically gifted as Marcelline—who sang and played violin and viola—though he did sing in the **Third Congregational Church**'s vested choir during his elementary school years and played cello for two years in the high school orchestra. In March of 1912, Ernest tried his hand at acting in the Holmes School's seventh grade production of *Robin Hood*, for which he wore a costume complete with wig, poofy hat, velvet tunic, and bow and arrow. Marcelline and Ernest graduated from the Oliver Wendell Holmes School in 1913.

During his teenage years, Ernest began to distance himself from his parents by sleeping outside in a tent behind *Windemere* and going on extended excursions alone in the surrounding woods—experiences that would be the basis for several of his Nick Adams stories. In the summer of 1913, Ernest confronted the Christian ideals his parents often referred to when he and Sunny went fishing at the western end of Walloon Lake. As their boat, *Ursula of Windemere*, came ashore, a blue heron flew up out of the reeds. On impulse, Ernest shot and killed the rare bird, telling his family afterward that he'd wanted it for the high school's museum. The spot where he'd killed the heron happened to be near the game warden's house, and though the warden wasn't home, his teenage son was. When the warden's son saw what Ernest had done, he told Ernest and Sunny that his father would arrest them. They made a run for it in the boat, and, after dropping Sunny off at *Windemere*, Ernest headed across the lake to Longfield Farm. He hitched a ride with Wesley Dilworth to Boyne City, where Wesley phoned the local magistrate and arranged for Ernest to confess and pay a fine. When Ernest came home a day or two later, his father reprimanded him. Ernest reminded his father that he himself sometimes hunted out of season when he was in the mood to eat restricted game. Clarence tried to maintain his hard-nosed expression, but couldn't do it for long. "But I don't get caught,"[14] he smiled.

Oak Park High School
201 Scoville Avenue.

In the fall of 1913, Ernest began his first year in the austere brown building that housed Oak Park and River Forest High School, built in 1907. Ernest loved English and liked chemistry and ancient history well enough, but Latin, music theory, and plane geometry gave him trouble. His mother empathized, having had a hard time with Latin herself, and hired a tutor for her son. Overall, Ernest did well, earning mostly As. He took part in many of the clubs, sports, and artistic activities offered at Oak Park High School, including the Burt Club debate society, the boys' Rifle Club, the Hiking Club, and, with Marcelline, the Glee Club. English classes were taught by the head of the department, Frank J. Platt, and met in the English Club—a lounge-like room with leather-backed chairs.

Other notable alumni of Oak Park High School include poet Charles Simic; actor and the voice of Homer Simpson, Dan Castellaneta; documentary photographer Bruce Davidson—best known for his coverage of the civil rights movement; actress Mary Elizabeth Mastrantonio; actor and rapper Ludacris; and comedian Kathy Griffin.

All of the Hemingway children received a weekly allowance, computed as one penny for each year of their age, and Ernest earned extra money mowing lawns, shoveling snow, and delivering *Oak Leaves*, the local weekly. When he began attending Oak Park High School, Ernest was fourteen and only five-feet-four inches tall. Self-conscious about his lack of height, he grew only an inch during his freshman year. But by the following summer at Walloon Lake, he'd hit a growth spurt and began to grow an inch or more a month. To compliment his height, Ernest spent the summer he turned fifteen adding a bit of brawn by working at Longfield Farm with Harold Sampson.

During Ernest's sophomore year, two milestones occurred. The first was that he started taking an active interest in girls. That fall, he began walking home with fellow classmate, Dorothy Davies, and in the winter he took her to a basketball game. This thrilled his mother and sent his friends into fits of teasing. When spring came, Ernest finally got the little brother he'd been hoping for since he was three. Leicester Clarence Hemingway, named for their father and Grace's brother, was born on April Fool's Day, 1915. When big brother Ernest came back from the war in 1919, he brought three-year-old Lessie—as his sisters called him—an Italian cape, which he would don and run around the house. This inspired one of the nicknames the whole family would adopt for the baby of the Hemingway clan, "The Baron." Nearly sixteen years apart, Ernest and Les missed growing up together, but as adults they would fish the Gulf Stream in Ernest's *Pilar* and were both in London during the Second World War.

When Leicester was thirteen, he would be on the front line of a tragedy at the family home on Kenilworth Avenue. On December 6, 1928, he was recovering from a cold and had stayed home from school. After Clarence returned from his morning rounds, he went to check on his son, who had become increasingly important to him after Ernest left home. Clarence comforted Les, telling him he was going to be alright and that he loved him. He asked if the mail had come. Les told his father that the mail was on the table by the front door, but Clarence didn't bother to check. He'd been worrying over some parcels of land that he and Grace had bought in 1925 in Sarasota, Florida, as an investment and for their planned retirement. They'd spent their savings and taken out a mortgage on the Kenilworth house to buy the land. The payments and interest on the mortgage, the $700 they owed in property taxes, plus the expense of still having two children at home had become too much to handle. Times were tough for many Chicagoans, and Clarence still frequently treated his patients without charge, or on the barter system. He'd asked his brother, George, a bank director who owned a real estate company, for a loan to cover the property taxes, but George had advised Clarence to sell some of the land while it could still be sold instead of shouldering another debt. Humiliating as it was for him, Clarence had even written to Ernest about a loan. Not having heard back and figuring his son wasn't keen on the idea, Clarence felt that he had run out of options.

That December morning, Clarence's foot had been hurting, which he knew was likely related to the poor circulation and nerve damage from his untreated diabetes, and might mean eventual amputation. He had never been truly ill before and didn't want to live as an "invalid." Clarence told Grace he was going upstairs to lie down until lunchtime. He closed and locked their bedroom door. The brief blast rang through the midday still of the house. Clarence had shot himself with his father Anson Hemingway's Smith and Wesson .32 Civil War pistol. A panicked Grace was unable to open the locked door, and Leicester got a hammer and screwdriver to take it off at the hinges. After finding Clarence on the bed, Leicester tried to calm his mother, who was hysterical. If Clarence had opened the mail, he would have found a check from Ernest for the $700 owed in property taxes.

Leicester wrote about his father's suicide in his World War II novel, *The Sound of the Trumpet*. Ernest told him the section was so good he wished he'd written it himself. Ernest carried an enormous amount of guilt over the death of his father, both for having left home and for having delayed in sending the check, and this guilt translated into bitterness toward his mother.

In the summer of 1915, Ernest and Lew Clarahan made the annual trip to *Windemere* by boat, wagon, and on foot, fishing for trout along the way. It took them between four and five days to get to **Horton Bay**, where they stopped in at Pinehurst Cottage for one of family friend Liz Dilworth's famous chicken dinners. In a sixteenth birthday letter sent to Ernest from Oak Park, Clarence wrote that when he joined Ernest at *Windemere*, they would go trout fishing together.

Ernest became more involved in sports and extracurricular activities during his second year of high school, going out for lightweight football and swimming. As he grew more confident, his camaraderie with his fellow classmates—with whom he shared an affection for nicknames—grew, and they dubbed him "Hemingstein." In one of his classmate's memory books, Ernest signed his name with the couplet, "I've never guzzled Beer nor wine / and yet they call me Hemingstien [*sic*],"[15] accompanied by a sketch of a frosty beer mug springing with condensation. Marcelline and Ernest entered a Bible reading contest put on by the adviser of the Third Congregational Church's Christian Endeavor Society, Fred Sweeney. The first member of the group to read every word of the King James Bible would get a prize. Harold Sampson completed the challenge first, but despite missing out on the prize, Marcelline and Ernest continued reading, finishing the entire bible and passing a test Mr. Sweeney gave on it.

As a member of the boys' Hiking Club, Ernest went on treks of twenty-five- and thirty-plus miles. On one expedition with Paul Haase, Harold Sampson, and Proctor Gilbert, Ernest walked from Oak Park to Lake Zurich, Illinois—more than thirty-five miles—in his bare feet. As a testament to his physical endurance and determination, he also ran in the ninth annual cross-country run in heavy rain, coming in forty-third out of forty-six contestants.

Ernest's early interest in being a writer was evident in a May 5, 1915, note that he wrote to Marcelline after she was one of twelve out of one hundred whose manuscripts were chosen for the Story Club:

> *Hey, how in the name of all things just and un-*
> *just did you get in the Story Club? If I couldn't*
> *write a better story than you, I'd consign myself*
> *to purgatory. Congratulations!*
>
> > *Thine eternally,*
> > *Ernestums*[16]

First Congregational Church (First United Church of Oak Park)
848 Lake Street.

By the fall of 1915, the Hemingways had left the Third Congregational Church on Chicago's West Side to join Ernest's paternal grandparents, as well as his aunt, Grace Hemingway, in services led by Dr. William E. Barton at the First Congregational Church. Ernest and Marcelline were active in the Plymouth League, the church's Sunday afternoon youth group, where Ernest acted as chairman, treasurer, and occasional speaker. Ernest and Marcelline also played in the church's orchestra and took part in amateur plays, picnics, and socials organized by the church's youth director.

With 1916 came Hemingway's first literary and journalistic publications. In January, he saw his first byline on a piece covering a Chicago Symphony concert for Oak Park High School's weekly newspaper, *The Trapeze*. In February, his first short story, "The Judgment of Manitou," was published in the school's literary magazine, the *Tabula*. Set in the Michigan woods, the story recounts the tale of half-Cree Indian, half-French Pierre and his mistrust of his white friend, Dick Haywood—both fur trappers. Pierre, thinking Dick has stolen his wallet, sets a trap for him. After Pierre discovers that a red squirrel is the culprit, he tries to save his friend, but it's too late—the wolves have gotten him. The story ends with Pierre about to shoot himself after stumbling into a bear trap. Simple as the story is, it evinces the dark realism of Hemingway's future fiction.

Residence of Tom Cusack
822 North Euclid Avenue.

Hemingway's lifelong passion for boxing began in 1916 when he attended his first professional prize fight and went to watch boxers train at a downtown Chicago gym. From then on, Ernest challenged his schoolmates to sparring matches in Grace's music room. When she inevitably disapproved, the boys moved the ring to Tom Cusack's basement gymnasium and to the open prairie behind his house. In April of 1916, Hemingway's short story, "A Matter of Colour"—a boxing tale in the style of his hero, Ring Lardner—was published in the *Tabula*.

Hemingway's first significant love affair went unrequited, but it wasn't with nurse Agnes von Kurowsky in Milan. During his junior year at Oak Park High School, Ernest was captivated by Frances Elizabeth Coates, an elegant and talented opera singer. Coates was a year older than Hemingway, and they were both on the staff of the *Tabula*—he as a writer, she as the music editor. At the end of May 1916, Ernest, Frances, Harold Sampson, and Marcelline took a canoe trip on the Des Plaines River. It was clear that there wasn't much romantic interest on Frances's end—a disappointment not only to Ernest, but to Grace, as she liked the thought of her son dating such a talented and poised young woman (and an opera singer to boot). In 1920, Frances married John Grace, another former classmate from Oak Park High School. Although Coates hadn't reciprocated Ernest's romantic interest, she kept his high school picture in a little gold frame in her dressing room, held onto snapshots of him, and followed his life and career through newspaper clippings. Ernest remembered her, too, naming the Horton Bay waitress in his story, "Up in Michigan," "Liz Coates."

Once school let out in the summer of 1916, Hemingway went on another camping and fishing expedition with Lew Clarahan before the annual trip to *Windemere*. They set off on the afternoon of June 10 on a route that would take them forty-eight miles south of Oak Park to **Frankfort**, Illinois. The trip would provide Ernest's maturing mind with the material for some of his Nick Adams stories. He chronicled the trip in his diary in the succinct and detailed style of his forthcoming fiction: "Camped in dandy spot on bank of stream. Many trout. . . . Killed water moccasin on R.R. track. Many trout jumping. Great fighters."[17] The following night, Ernest and Lew took refuge from a rainstorm in an abandoned lumber dam, then took the train to **Kalkaska**, Michigan. They hiked to **Rapid River** and stayed up all night fishing. After lunch at a greasy spoon in Kalkaska the next day, Ernest and Lew parted ways—Lew heading back to Oak Park and Ernest bound for Walloon Lake.

Stafford's Perry Hotel
100 Lewis Street, Petoskey, Michigan. Tel. (231) 347-4000.

Built in 1899 by Dr. Norman J. Perry, a former dentist, the Perry Hotel is the last of twenty-one hotels that were in operation in Petoskey in 1900. Hemingway was a guest here following his 1916 fishing and camping trip with Lew Clarahan. Back then, the Perry featured a lively dinner orchestra with dances at least once a week. Due to its popularity, the hotel doubled its capacity by adding a four-story, forty-six-room wing in 1926.

Breakfast and lunch are offered in the elegant **H.O. Rose Dining Room**, which has a panoramic view of **Little Traverse Bay**. Guests can enjoy pizza with a selection of beers from the "Hall of Foam" collection in the **Noggin Room Pub**, or al fresco summer grill dining on the **Rose Garden Veranda**.

While waiting for the train in **Mancelona**, Michigan, Ernest recorded notes on the river and creek where he and Lew had fished, and on several of the people he'd seen. He also made more specific notes evocative of his first Nick Adams story, "Indian Camp": "Tough-looking lumberjack. Young Indian girl. Kills self and girl."[18] Originally published in 1924 in Ford Madox Ford's *Transatlantic Review*, "Indian Camp" is the story of a country doctor, based on Hemingway's father, called to a Native American camp to tend to a woman who has been in labor for days. The doctor and his son, Nick Adams, find the woman and her husband in a cabin sharing a bunk bed, the man on the top bunk with an injured foot. In order to save the woman's life, the doctor performs an emergency cesarean section using a jack-knife. Nick, who is just a boy, holds a basin for his father during the operation. Once the excruciating procedure is over, the body of the woman's husband is discovered, still in the bunk above his wife, his throat slit from ear to ear with a straight razor. "Indian Camp" was the first of Hemingway's stories to introduce the recurring themes of birth and fear of death, which Hemingway experienced during the births of all three of his children. He wrote "Indian Camp" only a few months after the birth of his first son, Bumby, which he had not been present to experience; the death of Catherine Barkley in *A Farewell to Arms* was inspired by his second wife Pauline's near-death in giving birth to their first son Patrick in 1928.

Greensky Hill Indian United Methodist Church
08484 Greensky Hill Road, Charlevoix, Michigan. Located at the junction of U.S. Route 31 and CR 630. Tel. (231) 459-8067.

A Michigan Historic Site, Hemingway wrote about this Native American sacred place in several of his Nick Adams stories, including "Indian Camp," "The Doctor and the Doctor's Wife," "Ten Indians," "The Indians Moved Away," and "Fathers and Sons." Prudence Boulton, who may have been the model for the character of Prudie in "Ten Indians," and Trudy in "Fathers and Sons," is said to be buried in an unmarked grave at Greensky Hill. Founded in 1844 by Peter Greensky, also known as Shagasokicki, a Chippewa chief who had become a Christian preacher, the first services were held in makeshift buildings of bark and boughs until the 1850s, when a church was constructed from lumber brought by canoe from Traverse City. Surrounding the church was a circle of "council trees," where the Indian chiefs met to discuss tribal issues. The church has been preserved with its original woodwork and is still used by a congregation that celebrates both Christian beliefs and Native American customs. Greensky Hill Indian United Methodist Church was added to the National Register of Historic Places in 1972.

At the start of Hemingway's senior year of high school, he found that he'd grown too big—almost six feet tall and 150 pounds—for lightweight football. Though he still wasn't coordinated enough to be first-string, he joined the varsity team. His extremely large feet posed a problem both in finding football shoes that fit and in playing the game. Despite his struggles, he earned his varsity letter and was elected captain of the new water basketball team.

During their final year of high school, Marcelline and Ernest both took English V and VI, electives taught by Miss Fanny Biggs. English V was a course in short story writing. For his early stories, Ernest drew upon tales he'd heard from the Native Americans and other residents around Walloon Lake. English VI was a journalism course conducted as though it were a newspaper office, where students took turns being editor-in-chief and writing features and advertising copy, as well as news, sports, society, and personal columns. Developing a distinctive writing style was required by Miss Biggs, and she advised her students to put the most important information first so that, if necessary, an editor could easily cut that which was least important. Marcelline and Ernest were both chosen to be on the eight-student editorial board of the *Trapeze*, which came out weekly and had a monthly rotating editor-in-chief. Ernest continued writing journalism and features for the *Trapeze*, averaging more than a story per week.

After football season ended, Ernest's third short story, "Sepi Jingan," was published in the November 1916 issue of the *Tabula*. The story was based on Ernest's Ojibway acquaintance, Billy Tabeshaw, and Tabeshaw's dog. In the story, the main character is in pursuit of revenge against another Native American, Paul Black Bird, who had killed his cousin. On the Fourth of July, Black Bird knocks him down, planning to kill him and his dog, Sepi Jingan. But it's the dog who has the final revenge. In Hemingway's use of nature, short sentences, and the rhythmic reiteration of words are stirrings of his later work.

Little Traverse Historical Museum
100 Depot Street, Petoskey. Tel. (231) 347-2620.
Open Mon.–Sat. 10 A.M.–4 P.M.

The Victorian Shingle-style building that now houses the Little Traverse Historical Museum was completed by the Chicago and West Michigan Railroad in 1892. The building served as the Pere Marquette Railroad station, which Hemingway refers to in "The Indians Moved Away" and "Sepi Jingan." The Grand Rapids and Indiana Railroad began service to Petoskey in 1874, and was the only railroad in the area. In 1891, a second railroad, the Chicago and West Michigan Railway, began constructing a line between Elk Rapids and Petoskey. The railway purchased this land on the shore of Little Traverse Bay on which to place their Petoskey Depot. In 1899, the Chicago and West Michigan Railway and its Petoskey station were absorbed into the Pere Marquette Railway. The Pere Marquette was merged into the Chesapeake and Ohio Railway in 1947. The Petoskey station was abandoned in the 1950s, and in 1970 the Little Traverse Regional Historical Society began leasing the depot and some of its surrounding land. In 1971, the station was converted into a museum that was later named the Little Traverse Historical Museum and now houses a permanent exhibit on Hemingway. The building was placed on the National Register of Historic Places in 1970.

During his final year at Oak Park High School, Ernest the writer became Ernest the actor. In *Beau Brummell*, the 1917 senior play, Ernest's friend, Morris Musselman—who became a Hollywood screenwriter of *The Three Musketeers* fame—had the lead, Marcelline was in the orchestra, and Ernest played Richard Brinsley Sheridan, the second-biggest part. Always the architect of adventure, Ernest came up with a fake group for the *Trapeze* to cover, called the Shotgun Club. Each week he'd report on what the Shotgun Club was up to and how it was coming in first place in the invented competitions in which it had entered. Of the members of this fictitious six-member club, which included Musselman, Hemingway was the only one who had ever used a gun.

In an undated high school notebook, Ernest recorded some basic information about himself: his favorite authors were O. Henry and Rudyard Kipling, his favorite flowers were the Lady Slipper and the Tiger Lily, and trout fishing, hiking, and boxing were among his favorite sports. He noted that two of the subjects he most enjoyed were English and zoology, and in a mostly erased line at the bottom of the page, he stated prophetically: "I intend to travel and write."[19]

As Ernest was gearing up to graduate in the spring of 1917, he did intend to travel and write, but he also planned to attend college. Grace's brother, Leicester Hall, had graduated from Amherst, and both of Ernest's paternal grandparents had attended Wheaton. It was expected that Marcelline and Ernest would follow in the Oberlin tradition of their father. Ernest floated around the idea of attending either Cornell or the University of Illinois, which was recorded as his official choice in the Oak Park High School yearbook. But in April of 1917, President Woodrow Wilson had given up the United States's neutrality in the First World War, and when graduation rolled around in June, joining the war effort was at the forefront of Ernest's mind. Instead of deciding which college to attend, he turned his attention to finding a summer job. Clarence asked his brother, Alfred Tyler Hemingway, who lived in **Kansas City** and was friends with Colonel Nelson of the *Kansas City Star*, whether Ernest might be able to find summer employment there. As it happened, there would be an opening as a cub reporter, but not until September. This left Ernest free for one more Michigan summer.

Marcelline and Ernest graduated from Oak Park High School on June 13, 1917, the month before Ernest's eighteenth birthday. Commencement week, which began on June 8, had a patriotic theme. Hemingway's literary achievements were celebrated by his being named "class prophet," for which he delivered a rousing and witty commencement speech to his graduating class of

150. The commencement exercises included five student speakers—Marcelline gave a speech called "The New Girlhood"—as well as prayers, the singing of hymns and school songs, and the presentation of diplomas.

Following graduation, Grace, Clarence, Leicester, and Ernest drove the 487 miles, including detours, from Oak Park to Walloon Lake in the family's Ford touring car. The trip took more than five days over rough roads that were sometimes nothing but sand. The family camped or slept in the car, frying eggs over a fire for breakfast. That summer at *Windemere*, Ernest and his father worked at Longfield Farm, removing an old tenant farmhouse and building a new icehouse, tending the vegetable garden, cutting hay, and planting new fruit trees. In the fall of 1917, Ernest moved to Kansas City to try his hand as a cub reporter for the *Kansas City Star*. On May 28, 1918, he sailed to Italy to serve as a Red Cross ambulance driver in the war.

Once the war was over, a wounded Hemingway headed home to convalesce, arriving in New York on January 21, 1919, on Transatlantic American's *Giuseppe Verdi* from **Genoa**. The harbor was swarming with reporters there to cover the soldiers' arrival, and they singled Hemingway out as the first American wounded on the Italian front. That cold and snowy night, Clarence and Marcelline met their limping hero at La Salle Street train station in Chicago to bring him home. Ernest spent the first half of 1919 recuperating from his injuries and receiving visitors who were interested in seeing the souvenirs he'd brought back from Italy in a trunk. After his intense wartime experiences, Oak Park felt more provincial than ever. Holed up in his room much of the time with a secret stash of Italian spirits, it didn't take long before Ernest was depressed and lonely for his sweetheart, Red Cross nurse Agnes von Kurowsky, and his friends overseas.

In the spring of 1919, after days of hoping for a letter from Agnes, one finally came. Once Ernest had digested its contents, he became physically ill and went to bed with a fever. Agnes had thrown him over for an Italian officer, Tenente Domenico Caracciolo. In June, she would write again to let Ernest know she'd fallen out with her Major. As Ernest wrote in a letter to Howell Jenkins, Agnes was "in a hell of a way mentally" and said Ernest should "feel revenged for what she did to me."[20]

Following his rejection by Agnes and months of convalescing in Oak Park, Hemingway wasn't writing much fiction and still had no interest in college. He joined his family at *Windemere* for the summer and decided to stay on through the fall and winter to turn his energies toward writing. Once the cold set in over Walloon Lake and the cottage's fireplace wasn't enough to keep him warm, Ernest rented a second-floor room at **602 State Street** in Petoskey, where he continued work on his fiction. His early stories were overwritten, with titles like "Wolves and Doughnuts," but as he continued to distance himself from his family post-war, he began to have the sorts of adult experiences necessary for literary growth.

Carnegie Building (formerly the Petoskey Public Library)
451 East Mitchell Street, Petoskey.

For many years, the Carnegie Building was the location of the Petoskey Public Library—the interior of which features black ash woodwork and a fireplace—where Hemingway could frequently be found while he was living in Petoskey during the winter of 1919–1920. In December of 1919, he was asked to give a presentation on his wartime experiences to the Ladies' Aid Society in the library's basement assembly room, which was created for meetings of an "educational and patriotic nature." Designed by the Grand Rapids architectural firm of Williamson & Crow, the building is an example of the neoclassical revival style and was constructed in 1908 and dedicated in 1909. In 1908, Andrew Carnegie donated $12,500 to the City of Petoskey for the library, with $5,000 in additional funds raised through taxation.

City Park Grill
432 East Lake Street, Petoskey. Tel. (231) 347-0101.
Dining room open Sun.–Thurs. 11:30 A.M.–9 P.M.; Fri. & Sat. 11:30 A.M.–10 P.M. Bar open Sun.–Thurs. 11:30 A.M.–10 P.M.; Fri. & Sat. 11:30–1:30 A.M. Daily happy hour 4–6:30 P.M.

Constructed by Alanso McCarthy in 1875 and known then as **McCarthy Hall**, 432 East Lake Street was an exclusively male billiards parlor offering cigars and "intoxicating beverages." In 1888, the building was purchased by

Frank J. Gruclich, who changed the establishment's name to **The Annex**. Dining and entertainment was available at the adjacent **Cushman Hotel**, where a secret underground tunnel was installed to circumvent Prohibition, which began in Michigan in 1917. The Annex was a favorite summertime haunt of young Hemingway, who could often be found writing in the second seat from the end of the bar. He also enjoyed billiards and watching bare-knuckle boxing matches at nearby **Pennsylvania Park**. The Annex is mentioned in Hemingway's short story "Gentleman of the World." In 1932, The Annex's name was changed to the **Park Garden Café**, and in 1997 to City Park Grill, which offers dishes like House-Made Potato Gnocchi and Blackened Walleye, as well as daily and seasonal specials.

After spending the rest of the winter and most of the spring of 1920 in Toronto, Ernest returned to Oak Park during the last week of May. He'd been planning a trip to Asia with Bill Smith, Jack Pentecost, and Ted Brumback, and hung around Horton Bay that summer. Upon his return to *Windemere*, Ernest received a letter from his father, dated June 4, 1920: "Do hope dear Ernest that you will think more of what others have done for you and try to be charitable and kind and gentle. . . . I want you to represent all that is good and noble and brave and courteous in manhood, and fear God and respect Woman."[21] Despite his father's admonitions, Hemingway went back to what his parents regarded as a slovenly life of drinking, fishing, and carousing with friends, both male and female.

Later that summer, after an incident involving Ernest, Sunny, Ursula, Ted Brumback, two young neighbor girls, and a midnight picnic that turned into an all-night scandal, Grace banished Ernest from *Windemere*. She refused to finance any of his trip to Asia, and wrote him a letter just before his twenty-first birthday saying that he must stop lazing around and sponging off his parents. In the letter, she summarized what she saw as the symptoms of his misdirection: not living within his means and spending too much time on hedonistic pursuits. She likened his lifestyle to a bank account with insufficient funds. Ernest had not grown out of the "summers are for leisure" philosophy that he'd been raised with, nor would he ever cease to make the pursuit of pleasure more of a priority than his parents had. In this way, as with his writing, he was embracing a more modern age.

Ousted from his boyhood paradise, Ernest retrieved his clothing and a few belongings from Oak Park and moved in with Y. Kenley Smith and his wife in Chicago. In the 1920s, Chicago was experiencing a literary renaissance and its downtown streets, coffee shops, and bars were teeming with journalists, editors, publishers, and writers like Sherwood Anderson and Carl Sandburg. H. L. Mencken referred to Chicago during this time as "the literary capital of the United States."[22] One night Hemingway is rumored to have read aloud to Sandburg—who was known for his own bardic bravura—from *The Rubaiyat of Omar Khayyam*. In December, Hemingway answered a want-ad in the *Chicago Tribune* for a job as a writer and editorial assistant for the Cooperative Society of America's monthly magazine, *Cooperative Commonwealth*. The editor, Richard Loper, started him out at $40 per week writing for the 100-page publication.

Ernest was doing plenty of writing—both his own fiction and free-lance features for Toronto's *Star Weekly*—but try as he might to get his first short stories published, he was met with rejection after rejection. The *Star*'s managing editor, John Bone, had begun a side scheme of borrowing the work of unknown feature writers and selling them to other American as well as British newspapers under his own byline, and he began doing this with some of Hemingway's work. However, knowing that these papers would be more interested in stories from a more stimulating locale than Toronto, Bone offered Hemingway a job as *Star Weekly*'s first European correspondent. At first, Hemingway turned down the offer. His job at *Cooperative Commonwealth* wasn't much, but he didn't want to leave it without the guarantee of a substantial raise. Always one to shoot for the moon, he proposed $85 per week to Bone—a startling increase from his starting salary of half a cent per word as a reporter for the *Star*, or the $40 a week he was earning at *Cooperative Commonwealth*. Bone didn't bite.

While staying with the Smiths, whose apartment was referred to by their group of friends as the "Domicile," Ernest's first poem was published in a small literary magazine. His parents were pleased with his efforts at becoming more responsible and were supportive of his writing. At one of the Domicile's frequent Sunday afternoon parties, Ernest met "a tall, auburn-haired girl from St. Louis"[23] named Elizabeth Hadley Richardson, referred to warmly by her friends as "Hash." Hadley played the piano, and the Domicile's bright parties were buoyant with song and dance. Hadley was soon giving Ernest her opinion on his short stories across the kitchen table. She encouraged him in his writing, and they corresponded regularly after she returned to St. Louis.

Hadley and Ernest were married on a warm September 3, 1921, in a small white church in Horton Bay. At the time of their marriage, Ernest had not yet sold a single short story. Their reception was held across the street in the home of Beth Dilworth. Grace had the floors of *Windemere* polished and offered up the cottage for the newlyweds' two-week honeymoon.

Walloon Lake Public Access and Boat Launch
Travel southeast of Horton Bay on the Charlevoix–Boyne City Road for one mile, then turn left to the end of Sumner Road.

Offering a panoramic view of Walloon Lake, this is where Hemingway's fictional character Nick Adams and his new wife Helen row across to the cottage where they will spend their honeymoon in the story "Wedding Day," just as Hadley and Ernest did on theirs. To the right is the private property that was once Longfield Farm, purchased by Grace in 1905 with part of the inheritance from her father. The Hemingways improved upon the forty-acre farm by planting fruit trees, hay, and vegetables with the assistance of the Sumner and Washburn families, and it was where Ernest frequently set up camp during the summer months. The property was also the site of Grace's own private cottage, built in 1919.

Horton Bay General Store
05115 Boyne City Road, Boyne City. Tel. (231) 582-7827.
Open Mon. & Tues. 8–10 A.M.*; Weds.–Sun. 8* A.M.*–2* P.M. *Garden patio open for lunch seven days a week and for tapas Fri.–Sun. by reservation.*

The church where Hadley and Ernest were married in 1921 once sat next to Horton Bay General Store, established in 1876, which displays Hemingway photos and memorabilia. Ernest frequented the General Store growing up, and he describes it in his story "Up in Michigan." It was also the model for Mr. Packard's store in "The Last Good Country." Horton Bay General Store was the center of the small lumbering community and surrounding farms, and local farmers would bring in beans to be weighed and shipped or milk to be separated. In the evenings, families would gather in the store to discuss crop prices while their children played outside. In 1879, the first Horton Bay Post Office opened inside the General Store. The first floor of the Late Victorian-frame building has the original board ceiling, shelves, flooring, one sales counter, and several carbide and kerosene lamps. The store once carried groceries, hardware, clothing, and other products, while the second floor served as the proprietor's living quarters, which have been extensively remodeled and have served as a bed and breakfast since 2001. Today, the store has a soda fountain offering traditional malted ice cream, as well as a garden patio tavern out back. The building was placed on the National Register of Historic Places in 1991.

Red Fox Inn
05081 Boyne City Road, Boyne City. Tel. (253) 988-6297.

Next door to the Horton Bay General Store is the Red Fox Inn, a bed and breakfast with a restaurant and store specializing in Hemingway titles and memorabilia. Built in 1878, the building was one of the earliest homes in Horton Bay. The inn is mentioned in "Up in Michigan," and Vollie Fox, the inn's original proprietor, gave a teenaged Ernest fishing tips. In 1919, Fox and his wife Lizzie founded the Red Fox Inn restaurant, where Hemingway and his family enjoyed many family-style meals. John Kotesky, a local farmer who supplied the inn with fresh vegetables, is remembered for having driven Hadley and Ernest from Horton Bay to Walloon Lake at the beginning of their honeymoon. The building's interior has three large dining rooms on the first floor and four guest rooms, a parlor, and a bathroom on the second floor. The entire structure retains its original woodwork, paneled doors, and hardware. Vollie Fox passed away in 1947 and Lizzie became sole owner of the property. In 1955, she sold it to her daughter, Marian Ruth Fox Hartwell. In the 1970s, the building was converted to a bed and breakfast operating only during the summer months and remains in the Hartwell family. It was listed on the National Register of Historic Places in 1995.

Despite Hemingway's attempts to reject his upbringing, who he became was in great part how his parents raised him to be—the artist and the man of the woods. Grace and Clarence's intelligence and respective passions complemented Hemingway's brilliance and strong will in a rare way. Without the creativity of his mother and the discipline of both his parents, Hemingway would not have become Hemingway.

Hadley and Ernest's Chicago Apartment
1239 North Dearborn Street.

Ernest and Hadley's first home was a cold and dingy top-floor flat in a brownstone in the Near North Side neighborhood of Chicago, less than half a mile from Lake Michigan. The apartment was so unappealing, especially to Hadley, that the couple spent as little time there as possible. While living in the Dearborn Street apartment, Ernest found out that the Cooperative Society of America was corrupt and headed toward bankruptcy and quit writing for *Cooperative Commonwealth*. Unemployed and with no reason to stay in Chicago, Ernest's nostalgia soon got the better of him and he convinced Hadley that they should move to Italy.

Originally built as a single-family dwelling around 1890, the Dearborn Street building had been converted into apartments by its second owner—a person by the name of Gorman—by the time Hadley and Ernest moved in during the fall of 1921. The current owner has turned the building back into a single-family residence and assembled a collection of Hemingway photos, clippings, film posters, books by and about the author, and memorabilia chronicling Hemingway's time in Oak Park, Chicago, Paris, Key West, Africa, and Spain.

In the fall of 1921, Sherwood Anderson—who had been a frequent visitor to the Domicile—and his wife, Tennessee, returned from Paris and invited the Hemingways to supper. Sherwood advised Ernest that Paris was the best place for a writer to live, not Italy. The dollar went a long way and the Left Bank was full of artists and writers overflowing with visionary ideas. He recommended that Hadley and Ernest stay at Hôtel Jacob et d'Angleterre—where he and Tennessee had stayed—until they found a flat of their own. He also offered to write letters of introduction to Gertrude Stein, Sylvia Beach, Lewis Galantière, and Ezra Pound. Inspired by Anderson's suggestion, Hemingway approached John Bone about his previous job offer as a foreign correspondent. This time he used a more humble tone and they came to an agreement. Hemingway would write freelance features for *Star Weekly* while based in Paris. He would be paid standard rates for his regular articles, and $75 per week when sent on special assignment. The Hemingways donated all of the canned goods they'd accumulated at their North Dearborn Street apartment to the Andersons, and, in December of 1921, boarded the *Leopoldina*, bound for Paris.

ADDITIONAL PLACES OF INTEREST

Art Institute of Chicago
111 South Michigan Avenue, Chicago.
Open every day 10:30 A.M.–5 P.M.; Thurs. until 8 P.M.

Grace Hall Hemingway frequently took her children to the Art Institute of Chicago, one of the oldest and largest art museums in the United States. When she turned fifty and the quality of her exquisite contralto voice had begun to fade, Grace took classes at the Art Institute for two years. She turned the music room of her home into an art studio and took to driving her Ford all over the country, from Nantucket to California, with her painting supplies. She covered thousands of miles, parking with the windshield facing a particular vista she wished to paint, cracking the window, and working with her canvas on the steering wheel. She was one of the founders of the Oak Park and River Forest Art League, which hosted a one-woman show of her paintings, as did Marshall Field's in Chicago and the Illinois Art Society, among other venues. Grace signed her paintings "Hall Hemingway."

Newberry Library
60 West Walton Street, Chicago.
Open Mon., Fri. & Sat. 8:15 A.M.–5 P.M.*; Tues.–Thurs. 8:15* A.M.–7:30 P.M.

Established in 1887, the Newberry is an independent research library specializing in the humanities. The library has a collection of Hemingway-related material, including items of original correspondence, an original photograph of Hemingway, items related to the World War I Red Cross ambulance service, a typescript of the 1939 eulogy Hemingway wrote for Gene Van Guilder, and a photostat of Hemingway's 1961 will. Located in Washington Square, the Newberry was named in honor of its founding bequest by the estate of philanthropist Walter Loomis Newberry. The Newberry offers meet-the-author lectures, exhibitions, continuing education classes, concerts, and other programs related to its collections.

2

MILAN AND VENETO

Veneto: *A region of Northeast Italy on the Adriatic Sea, with the Dolomites mountain range in the north and a fertile plain in the south; crossed by the Rivers Po, Adige, and Piave. Capital: Venice.*

L ove and death were intertwined in Hemingway's life and writing, and he was introduced to both on his first trip abroad at eighteen, as an ambulance driver for the Red Cross. From then on, he would associate tragedy and rapture with the effervescence of Milan, with the imposing majesty of the Dolomites, and, later, with the watery jewel of Venice.

When Hemingway graduated from Oak Park High School in 1917, he and many of the young people of his generation felt that there were bigger priorities than starting college. Ernest was desperate to get in on the most exciting thing he could imagine: a war overseas. After trying to join the Army, Navy, and Marines, but being turned down by each because of poor sight in his left eye, he was resolute; one way or another, he was going to get in on "the show." He took a job as a cub reporter for the *Kansas City Star*, at first staying with his Uncle Tyler and Aunt Arabell on Walnut Street in Kansas City, but soon finding a room of his own downtown near the *Star* offices. Ernest's work covering "fires, fights, and funerals"[1] thrilled him so much that he wrote to his family in Oak Park telling them that he'd decided not to go to college.

1918

In early 1918, the *Kansas City Star* assigned Hemingway to interview a group of Italian Red Cross officers who had come to the United States to recruit volunteers for their ambulance corps. The officers informed Hemingway that the corps was accepting men in good health who had otherwise been unable to pass the physical requirements for the armed services. Hemingway signed up immediately. He was so excited that he told several of his friends who'd also been ineligible, and some of them joined up too. Hemingway's last day as a reporter for the *Kansas City Star* was on April 30, 1918. Before shipping out, he and his friends, including Ted Brumback, went on one last fishing trip in Canada while awaiting the telegram with their sailing itinerary. They left **New York Harbor** on the SS *Chicago* bound for **Bordeaux** on May 23, reaching **Paris** and **Milan** in early June.

When Hemingway arrived in Milan, **Teatro alla Scala**, **San Siro** racing track, and the **Galleria Vittorio Emanuele II** were buzzing with uniformed young men. On his first night in Italy, Hemingway stayed at **Hotel Vittoria**, near the city center. His first duty with the Red Cross came almost immediately when a munitions factory exploded in the countryside at **Bollate**. Hemingway's gruesome task was to search for the bodies and fragments of the factory workers—mostly those of women—and carry them to a makeshift morgue. The brutal initiation shocked and moved Hemingway, and the images would stay with him.

The Red Cross volunteers were divided into groups, and Hemingway and Brumback were assigned to Section Four of the Ambulance Unit. On June 9, the volunteers boarded the train for **Vicenza**. From Vicenza they were driven fifteen miles northwest to **Schio**, in the foothills of the Dolomites. Hemingway spent his first night in Schio at the **Albergo Due Spadi** hotel on Via Carducci. The Due Spadi had a restaurant in a garden-like trattoria under a wisteria bush where Hemingway would frequently drink beer with his Section Four comrades. Today, the restaurant is called **Osteria Due Spade** and displays a plaque with a portrait of Hemingway.

Section Four's base of operations was in an abandoned wool warehouse, **Lanificio Cazzola,** next to the *torrente* Leogra, a creek flowing through the middle of town. A fleet of ambulances stood at the ready in the garages and the volunteer drivers bunked in a large room on the second floor. The young men of Section Four nicknamed their spare accommodations—the north window of which had a fine view of the Dolomites—the "Schio Country Club." They put together a newspaper called *Ciao*, printed in Vicenza. Hemingway banged out Ring Lardner–inspired pieces in epistolary form on a borrowed typewriter. Three ambulances were on call at a time—Hemingway's was an unwieldy Fiat—each making one run per day to evacuate the wounded. The men dined in the mess hall downstairs, where there was plenty of spaghetti, rabbit stew, and wine. Today, what was once the Schio Country Club has been converted into apartments, with a plaque expressing gratitude for the "work demonstrated by Ernest Hemingway and the other drivers of Section IV."

While driving his ambulance in the town of **Dolo** on the river Brenta, Hemingway met fellow Chicagoan, John Dos Passos. Dos Passos had begun his service as an ambulance driver for the Norton-Harjes Ambulance Corps in France, been transferred to Italy, and was about to leave to join the U.S. Army's Ambulance and Medical Corps in Paris. The two young writers talked for a couple of hours, but Dos Passos wouldn't remember Hemingway's name until they met again in Paris.

Restless and eager to be near the front, Hemingway volunteered to man one of a series of emergency canteens being set up along the **Piave** river. He arrived at his new post on June 14 and reported to his commanding officer, Capt. Jim Gamble. Before beginning their canteen service, the new volunteers were given leave in **Mestre**, where some of them visited **La Villa Rosa**. Hemingway describes the Italian officers' bordello in his story, "How Death Sought Out the Town Major of Roncade," discovered in 2004 in the Hemingway archives of Boston's Kennedy Library. La Villa Rosa is also portrayed in *A Farewell to Arms*.

While volunteering with the canteen service at the front, Hemingway's headquarters were at **Fossalta di Piave**. The first week was quiet, and supplies were slow in coming. Ernest rode his bike out to visit fellow volunteers Bill Horne and Warren Pease in the nearby village of **Monastier di Treviso**. Horne and Pease were staying on the second floor of **Villa Albrizzi**, a silkworm-breeding operation. Hemingway would later describe the sound of the silkworms chewing their mulberry leaves as he tried to sleep.

Despite the initial hush at the front, Hemingway could at last feel the breath of war. On the sweltering night of July 8, an exchange of fire across the Piave had begun to intensify. Hemingway was out on his bicycle delivering chocolate, cigarettes, and postcards to the soldiers in the trenches. "Some of them he had met before and for a while they talked in pidgin Italian. His pronunciation amused them."[2] Midnight came. It was so hot that Hemingway had left off his underclothes and was sweating through his uniform. The air was quiet as a premonition when a mortar shell came swinging toward them through the still air. Hemingway later described the flash and his sudden inability to move or breathe. The man next to him, twenty-six-year-old Fedele Temperini of the 69 Reggimento Fanteria, Brigata Ancona, lay lifeless. A native of the medieval city of Montalcino in Tuscany, Temperini had taken the brunt of the blast that would otherwise surely have killed Hemingway. It doesn't escape me that this also means that if it weren't for Fedele Temperini, I would not exist. What happened next has been debated, but the traditional telling of events—based on Hemingway's own accounts—is that another soldier nearby was sobbing in pain. Hemingway put the man over his shoulder, ignoring the desire of his own body to fold, and lurched himself forward away from the trenches. All at once, he was arrested by a jolt of pain as a machine gun bullet cut through his right knee, causing his legs to buckle. Nearly unconscious but still moving under the inertia of his own will, Hemingway crossed the last several yards to the outpost. While there's no way to know exactly what happened that night on the Italian front a century ago, it is certain that my great-grandfather was young, he was badly wounded, and he was brave. Two men carried him on a stretcher to the nearest dressing station, but it had been evacuated. While they waited for two hours inside a roofless shed for an ambulance, Hemingway prayed.

Just before dawn, the ambulance came to take Hemingway to a first-aid station in a converted schoolhouse near **Fornaci**. In Fornaci, he and the other wounded men were given the blessing of the sick by Florentine chaplain Don Giuseppe Bianchi of the 70th Brigata Ancona. Hemingway had previously met Don Bianchi when he dined with Italian officers at the front. In *A Farewell to Arms*, Hemingway describes the priest based on Don Bianchi as a young man from the Abruzzi. Years later, when he was preparing to ask permission of the Catholic Church to marry his devout second wife, Pauline Pfeiffer, Hemingway would call the anointing by Don Bianchi an act of "extreme unction," citing it as the moment he became a Catholic.

After Hemingway was given morphine and a tetanus shot, doctors removed twenty-eight *scaggia*, or shell fragments, from his legs and feet, leaving hundreds of smaller, deeply embedded bits of shrapnel to work their way out slowly from under his skin. After these initial procedures, Hemingway was taken to **Villa Toso**, a field hospital in **Casier**, just outside of **Treviso**. On July 15—less than a week before his nineteenth birthday—the young ambulance driver from Oak Park was put on a sluggish hospital train headed west through **Venice**, Vicenza, **Verona**, past majestic **Lake Garda**, and on through **Brescia** to Milan. From his position in his berth, Hemingway was unable to watch the receding Northern Italian countryside.

At six o'clock on the morning of July 17, 1918, the train carrying Hemingway pulled into the same station in Milan where he'd begun his tour only six weeks earlier. He was taken to the **Ospedale Croce Rossa Americana**, on the third and fourth floors of 10 Via Alessandro Manzoni, which had been a pensione before the war. Hemingway occupied top-floor room 106, overlooking the yellow acacias and maples. The stone palazzo that housed the American Red Cross Hospital was originally **Palazzo Anguissola**, built between 1775 and 1778. The palace, which Hemingway describes in *A Farewell to Arms*, is two blocks from **Piazza del Duomo**, the Galleria, and **Piazza La Scala**. There is a plaque commemorating Hemingway's wartime presence in Milan at 6 Via Armorari that reads: "In summer 1918, this building was a hospital operated by the American Red Cross, where Ernest Hemingway, wounded on the front line on the Piave, received care and treatment. Thus was born the true story behind *A Farewell to Arms*."

There were only three patients in the Red Cross Hospital when Hemingway was admitted, with eighteen nurses to care for them. His first nurse was Elsie MacDonald—known to her friends as "Mac." Hemingway was relieved to find out from the surgeon, Capt. Sammarelli, that his wounds weren't infected. X-rays showed two machine gun slugs—one embedded behind his right kneecap and one in his right foot—which Capt. Sammarelli planned to remove shortly after Hemingway's birthday. Ted Brumback came from Schio to check on his friend and wrote to Ernest's family describing the events that had befallen their newly-minted war hero. On his birthday, Ernest himself wrote to his parents telling of the first-rate treatment he was receiving at the Croce Rossa, as well as the news that he'd received a recommendation for Italy's Silver Medal of Valor.

When I was sixteen, my uncle and I were invited to represent our family at a ceremony honoring my great-grandfather at the Kennedy Library in Boston. While I was attempting to socialize with the adults, a dignified man approached me. He seemed excited and said he recognized me as a relative of Hemingway. I was stunned. It was Henry Villard, a former United States ambassador and Hemingway's roommate at the Ospedale Croce Rossa Americana in Milan. He'd recognized something in me that reminded him of Ernest when he was barely older than I was. Not only that, but Ernest's sweetheart, Agnes von Kurowsky, had been the nurse on duty when Villard was brought to the American Red Cross Hospital in Milan in 1918.

Agnes Hannah von Kurowsky was born in Philadelphia in 1892. First trained as a public librarian in Washington, D.C., she graduated from the

Bellevue Nurses Training Program in New York City in 1917. In June of 1918, she sailed to Europe with the American Red Cross, where her first assignment was at the Ospedale Croce Rossa in Milan. Agnes, who liked night duty and often volunteered for it, was in charge on the evening of August 1 when a young ambulance driver from Manhattan, Henry Serrano Villard, was brought in with malaria and jaundice. After a rough train trip, during which Villard was plagued by constant nausea and dry heaves, the clean hospital with the friendly nurses was divine. Agnes gave him "a hot bath, a dose of castor oil, a cocktail, and an eggnog. In the comfortable bed, with real sheets and pillowcases, he drifted away into his first sound sleep in months."[3]

In those days, it was frowned upon for the Red Cross nurses to go on unchaperoned dates, but, on August 10, Agnes accepted a dinner invitation from Capt. Enrico Serena. Capt. Serena—who wore a patch over one eye and called Hemingway "Baby"—was the prototype for one of Hemingway's most charming characters in *A Farewell to Arms*, Capt. Rinaldi. Capt. Serena took Agnes to the **Sempioncino** restaurant on Corso Sempione, but when she discovered that he'd reserved a private room with a couch, she escaped by saying that she had to return to the hospital for night duty. The morning of Agnes's date with Capt. Serena, Ernest's operation to have the bullets removed from his knee and foot—zipped up with twenty-eight stitches—had been successful. Elsie MacDonald wired Ernest's family to let them know the good news. The Chicago newspapers were already carrying the story of his heroism as the first American to be wounded in Italy.

August was a stifling month to be stuck in bed, but Ernest received many well-wishers. He passed the time by drinking cognac and hiding the empty bottles in his closet, pulling out the smaller *scaggia* fragments from his leg with a penknife, and telling stories to Capt. Serena and the other Italian soldiers. Ernest's friend, Bill Horne, who was hospitalized with gastroenteritis, kept him company for three weeks. Ernest had gained confidence through his service and was no longer the shy kid who was awkward with girls. He and Agnes got to know each other over the course of the long summer nights, during which Agnes was frequently the only nurse on duty. Although she didn't take the affair as seriously as he did, Agnes encouraged

Ernest by referring to him as "Kid" and herself as "Mrs. Kid," and kept his photograph in the pocket of her uniform.

By September, Ernest was walking with crutches and had been promoted to First Lieutenant, but he was forbidden to drive an ambulance for six months. After his new stripes had been sewn onto his uniform, he and Agnes rode with Mac and two aviation lieutenants named George to the San Siro racetrack to bet on the horses. Hemingway would describe the fresh holiday feeling of being at the races, as he would many of the places he went that fall in Milan, ten years later in *A Farewell to Arms*. He and Agnes attended the opening night of Renzo Bianchi's *Ghismonda* at La Scala opera house, as well as *Il Carillon Magico*, which Agnes wrote in her diary was the most delightful ballet she'd ever seen. Hemingway references La Scala in his short story "My Old Man."

That fall, Marcelline got a surprise when she went to the movies one night. The newsreels were all about the war, and the one before the movie she'd gone to see featured her brother Ernest smiling from a wheelchair on the hospital terrace in Milan. Marcelline asked the projectionist to replay it after the film, and she rushed home to tell the family, who followed the newsreel around to several Chicago movie theaters. They wrote to Ernest asking if the nurse in the film was Agnes, the young woman he'd written them about. He replied that she wasn't, but that "Ag is prettier than anybody you guys ever saw. Wait till you see her!"[4]

In late September, Tenente Hemingway took convalescent leave to go with fellow ambulance driver, Minnesotan Johnny Miller, to the **Grand Hôtel des Iles Borromées** in **Stresa** on **Lake Maggiore**. Ernest and Johnny went rowing on Lake Maggiore and rode up to the top of the **Mottarone** to view the region's seven lakes. In the opulent surroundings of the Grand Hôtel, the Americans were befriended by Conte Emanuele Greppi, the inspiration for Count Greffi in *A Farewell to Arms*. They played billiards with the exquisitely dressed Count with the old-world manners, who treated them to several bottles of champagne. It was Ernest's first brush with the bright and elegant lifestyle of nobility, and he was smitten.

Today, the rooms where Hemingway stayed at the Grand Hôtel des Iles Borromées in 1918 and when he returned in 1948 with his fourth wife Mary—rooms 105 and 106—make up the **Presidential Suite**. The snowy mountains of Switzerland can be seen from its windows, and much of the furniture is the same as it was during Hemingway's time. The Grand Hôtel makes an appearance in *A Farewell to Arms* when Lieutenant Frederic Henry takes a room looking out over Lake Maggiore. The hotel lounge is where Lieutenant Henry orders a dry martini and obtains the rowboat that will take him and Catherine Barkley to the safety of Switzerland. The elegant Grand Hôtel des Iles Borromées has hosted many luminaries since it opened in 1861, and its leather-bound "Golden Book" contains the signatures of the King of Italy, the Queen of Romania, Arturo Toscanini, John Steinbeck, Clark Gable, Andrew Carnegie, and—from October 1, 1948—Ernest Hemingway, who added "an old client" next to his signature.

When Hemingway returned from Stresa, Agnes gave him the news that she'd volunteered to help with an outbreak of influenza in **Florence**. They wrote to each other often, and the endearments and nicknames in Agnes's letters belied any implication that their relationship was only to be a wartime romance. In a letter to his father, Ernest said that he planned to stay in Italy until the war was over, though he still couldn't drive or walk without a cane.

In late October, Ernest returned to the Schio Country Club in search of his Section Four comrades, but found that many of them had gone to the front at **Bassano**, a walled city near **Mount Grappa**. When Hemingway arrived, there was a tremendous firefight going on, ringing the valley in a flashing glow. Bassano del Grappa is home to **Ponte Vecchio**, a covered wooden bridge spanning the Brenta River, and the causeway next to it has been named **Lungobrenta Hemingway**. This golden town in the foothills of the Dolomites pays further tribute to Hemingway's presence during World War I with the **Museo Hemingway e della Grande Guerra**. In Bassano, Hemingway came down with a bad case of jaundice and returned to Milan to recuperate. He was mostly well by November 3, the day the Italian-Austrian Armistice of Villa Giusti was signed.

Hemingway was at the **Anglo-American Officers' Club** in Milan when the news of the armistice came. Eric "Chink" Dorman-Smith, a twenty-three-year-old Irish major in the British Army, was sitting nearby, and he and Ernest used the moment of jubilation to strike up a conversation.

Ernest was impressed to learn that Chink had been wounded three times and had received the Military Cross for extraordinary heroism. Both young men were voracious readers and had a similar misanthropic humor, and they got along like brothers. They took to dining together at **Biffi's** in the Galleria and going for drinks at the **Cova**.

In the middle of November, Agnes returned from Florence, but was promptly sent away again, this time to Treviso, where there was another flu outbreak. She still wrote to Ernest almost every day, and on December 9, he went to visit her. One of his friends from the Schio Country Club, Capt. Jim Gamble, had offered to provide the funds for Ernest to stay another year in Italy, but Agnes discouraged it, worrying that he would become no more than a malingering layabout. While she felt Ernest should return to America, she also talked of missing the States herself and entertained the idea—at least in the abstract—that they might be married someday.

With Agnes still tending the sick in Treviso, Ernest and Chink toured the holiday party circuit, capped by a Christmas Day dance at Caffè Cova. In Hemingway's story "In Another Country," he describes the dim, smoky warmth of the Cova. He had booked passage on the SS *Giuseppe Verdi* for just after the new year, and must have felt the dying firelight of the first romantic period of his adulthood. On January 21, 1919, Tenente Hemingway stepped off the giant steamship in New York Harbor a celebrity and a war hero, and was immediately interviewed by the *New York Sun*. After spending the night at the house of his Section Four comrade, Bill Horne, in Yonkers, Ernest boarded the train for Chicago, further recuperation, and a new kind of anguish.

1922

In April of 1922, Hadley and Ernest were living in Paris, where Ernest was working as a foreign correspondent for the *Toronto Star*. He was eager for Hadley to see Italy and wanted to show her the places that had transformed him from a naïve midwestern boy into a veteran and expatriate. By the middle of May, the Hemingways found that between Ernest's lucrative dispatches on the Genoa Conference and Hadley's trust fund, they finally had enough money for a month-long trip to Italy. Chink met them in **Chamby**, Switzerland, for a trek through the Alps. The comrades ascended the 7,000-foot **Cap au Moine** to **Aigle**, where they drank robust lager, read at the inn, and Ernest fished the **Rhône Canal**. On May 30, the buoyant party hiked over **St. Bernard Pass** in the deep snow, Hadley wearing a totally unsuitable pair of flat shoes that were on the verge of splitting. That night was spent in a hospice run by monks who were bewildered by Hadley's presence. By the time the party reached **Aosta** the next day, Hadley was suffering like a marathon runner in pointe shoes. From Aosta, they took the train to Milan, where the Hemingways said their goodbyes to Chink, who'd taken a furlough for the trip.

In Milan, Ernest took Hadley to the building that had housed the Red Cross Hospital during the war. They went to the **Duomo** and drank Capri wine with peaches, wild strawberries, and chipped ice at Biffi's, as Ernest had done with Agnes in 1918, and as he would later describe in *A Moveable Feast*. Ernest was anxious to return to Schio with Hadley, which he viewed as the last seat of his unsullied youth. But when they arrived on June 13, he was shocked by the postwar look of the town. Without the nervous intimacy of combat, it had lost its feeling of refuge. The Schio Country Club was once again a wool factory, and the Hemingways spent the night at the Albergo Due Spade, where Ernest had stayed in 1918, but which no longer had the wisteria creeper he so romanticized.

The Hemingways headed northwest to **Rovereto** in a hired car, winding around **Lake Garda** to the resort town of **Sirmione**, where they spent the evening. They took the train from Verona to Mestre, where they hired another car to Fossalta. In "A Veteran visits the Old Front," an article written for *Star Weekly*, Ernest recounted his impressions of Fossalta as a washed-over wasteland where all evidence of the war had crumbled to dust. Later he would recreate the biblical chaos of the Italian front in his second novel, *A Farewell to Arms*.

1923

In February of 1923, the Hemingways had been skiing at Chamby since before Christmas. While they were still in the snug and safe environment of their chalet, Hadley gave Ernest the news that he was going to be a father. It was another blow. In November, Hadley had lost nearly all of his manuscripts at the Gare de Lyon in Paris, and since then his confidence had dried up. He was too young and they were too poor for a baby; it would be another hindrance to his writing. Soon after, they were invited to join Dorothy and Ezra Pound at **Rapallo** on the Italian Riviera, where Hadley felt the sea air and warmth of the Mediterranean would be good for her pregnancy. Descending into **Montreux**, Hadley and Ernest curved around Lake Maggiore to Stresa, through **Gallarate**, and into Milan, where they had dinner at **Campari's** before joining the Pounds at Rapallo. Artist Mike Strater, whom Ernest had been hoping to box and play tennis with, was on hand with his wife and new baby, but had sprained his ankle. Ernest found the environment leaden after the invigorating tonic of the Alps. Strater did portraits of the Hemingways, and Ernest tried to write, but it still wasn't coming. He appealed to Gertrude Stein for advice in a letter, truly fearing that his talent was gone for good.

It was at the lowest point of his depleted resolve that a fortuitous meeting helped raise Ernest from the mat. The poet and anthologist Edward O'Brien was staying in the hills two thousand feet above Rapallo at the **Sanctuary of Our Lady of Montallegro**. The editor from Boston was compiling material for *The Best Short Stories of 1923*, and asked Ernest if he had anything to contribute. Ernest brought out "My Old Man," an unpublished story about a jockey and his son, with the tepid lack of confidence of someone who's just had their œuvre stolen. It was the only story other than "Up in Michigan" that had not been lost. O'Brien was so moved by "My Old Man" that he accepted it without hesitation, even though it wasn't his usual practice to print previously unpublished work.

While the Hemingways were staying at **Hotel Splendide** in Rapallo, they met a pair of writers—Robert McAlmon and his English wife, Annie Ellerman (who wrote under the name of Bryher)—while dining with the Straters. Though McAlmon wasn't initially sold on Hemingway's personality, he would use his small press, Contact Editions, to produce Hemingway's first book—a three hundred-print run of *Three Stories & Ten Poems*—later that year. The collection includes the stories "Up in Michigan," "My Old Man," and "Out of Season." Hotel Splendide would become the setting for one of my favorite Hemingway stories, "Cat in the Rain," inspired by two cats on top of a table in the garden of the hotel.

Toward the end of winter, Hadley and Ernest joined the Pounds on a walking tour of the **Emilia-Romagna** region. Pound, who was working on his *Malatesta Cantos* in Rapallo, had planned the tour around places associated with Sigismondo Malatesta. Known as the "Wolf of Rimini," Malatesta was a fifteenth-century Brescian nobleman and poet who commanded the Venetian forces against the Ottoman Empire. The Pounds and the Hemingways stopped every day at noon to have lunch "al fresco with native cheeses, figs, and wine, spreading the simple fare in the shade of hillside trees in sight of vineyards and olive groves."[5] At Sirmione, the two couples parted ways, and the Hemingways headed for **Cortina d'Ampezzo** in the Dolomites.

In Cortina, Hadley and Ernest stayed at **Hotel Bellevue**, frequenting the bar at **Hotel Posta** (today **Hotel de la Poste**), where the alchemy of the mountains had a positive effect on Ernest's creativity. Bolstering this was an invitation for him to contribute to the "Exiles" volume of *The Little Review*, a Chicago literary magazine published from 1914 to 1929. For the review, scheduled to come out that April, Ernest produced six sketches, mostly based on second-hand events. In April and May, Hemingway spent six weeks covering the occupation by France and Belgium of Germany's Ruhr district. *Star Weekly* published ten of Hemingway's pieces on the occupation, six of them on the front page. Following these, Hemingway wrote his first short story since Hadley had lost his manuscripts at Gare de Lyon.

Hemingway's short story, "Out of Season"—based on a drunk fishing guide who had failed to inform Hadley and Ernest that trout were not in season—was his first attempt at leaving out details in a story in order to increase its emotional impact. James Joyce may have introduced Hemingway to the premise of this covert literary device, though this is unsubstantiated. In *Death in the Afternoon*, Hemingway describes what would come to be known as the "Iceberg Theory": "If a writer of prose knows enough about what he is writing about he may omit things that he knows and the reader, if the writer is writing truly enough, will have a feeling of those things as strongly as though the writer had stated them. The dignity of movement of an ice-berg is due to only one-eighth of it being above water."[6]

1927

By the middle of March, 1927, Hemingway's first marriage was over. Hadley and Ernest divorced in the wake of Ernest's affair with Pauline Pfeiffer, whom he had met at the Paris flat of F. Scott and Zelda Fitzgerald. Beset with guilt and regret, Ernest agreed to an automobile tour of Italy with friend and fellow journalist, Guy Hickok. Hemingway knew Hickok, a foreign correspondent for the *Brooklyn Daily Eagle*, from the weekly meetings of the Anglo-American Press Club on Paris's Right Bank, and Hadley and Hickok's wife, Mary, had become good friends.

The two writers crossed the border at **Ventimiglia** in Hickok's Ford on March 18, hugging the northwest coast through Genoa and Rapallo. Despite his personal troubles, Hemingway's literary career was booming. *The Sun Also Rises* had sold out of its first printing in 1926, and was warmly received by many fellow authors and literary critics, including Thornton Wilder, Malcolm Cowley, and Edmund Wilson. Wilson "had remarked to [John Peale] Bishop that [it] was the best novel by anyone of Hemingway's generation."[7] One of the most venerable literary magazines, *Atlantic Monthly*, had bought Hemingway's story "Fifty Grand" for $350, making it his highest-earning story to date. *Scribner's Magazine* would soon publish "The Killers"—written in May of 1926—as well as two other stories by Hemingway, and Max Perkins suggested he put together a new collection. Hemingway proposed the title *Men Without Women*, and sent back a list of possible stories. He would eventually include "Now I Lay Me," a Nick Adams story set in war-torn Italy, and "Hills Like White Elephants," which he finished and mailed from his and Pauline's honeymoon at **Grau-du-Roi** in May.

In Rapallo, Hemingway and Hickok had supper with the Pounds. Hemingway also met with Don Giuseppe Bianchi, the priest who anointed him after he was wounded at Fossalta. Ernest needed to prove that he'd been baptized a Catholic in order to marry Pauline—a devout member of the church—and hoped that the "extreme unction" he'd received during the war would suffice. From Rapallo, Hemingway and Hickok headed inland to **Carrodano**, where a young autocrat hitched a ride on their running board to **La Spezia**. The incident would inspire the story "Che ti dice la

Patria?," a sharp attack on Fascism that was first published in the May 18, 1927, issue of *The New Republic* under the title, "Italy, 1927." "Che ti dice la Patria?" would also be included in *Men Without Women*. In La Spezia, Hemingway and Hickok stopped for lunch at a restaurant that was both trattoria and brothel, as the latter was officially illegal under Benito Mussolini's rule. Hemingway had broken the promise to himself not to return to Italy as long as the Fascist dictator, whom he had interviewed when he was in Milan in 1922, was in power. Hemingway's books were banned in Italy until the end of Mussolini's regime in 1943. The censorship began because of Hemingway's depiction of Italy's defeat at the Battle of Caporetto in *A Farewell to Arms*, as well as the novel's general anti-military bent. All of Hemingway's books were subsequently banned for twenty years, until Mussolini fell from power. *The Sun Also Rises* came out in Italy in the summer of 1944, with editions of *A Farewell to Arms*, *For Whom the Bell Tolls*, and *To Have and Have Not* following soon after, as more of Italy was liberated. Outside La Spezia, Hemingway was overcome with feelings of remorse and grief over his divorce from Hadley, and asked Hickok to pull over at an altar so that he could pray. Hemingway prayed frequently throughout the trip with Hickok, and sometimes it was clear afterward that he'd been crying.

After stopping in **Pisa** for the night, Hemingway and Hickok drove east to Florence and **San Marino**. San Marino, an enclaved microstate established in 301 A.D., is the oldest surviving constitutional republic in the world and retains its cobblestone streets and medieval walls. In San Marino, Hemingway paid a visit to an Italian officer he'd known in the war, Giuliano Gozi. He also went to see Don Giuseppe Guidi, the chaplain from the Villa Toso field hospital where Hemingway had initially been taken after his wounding on the Piave. From San Marino, Hemingway and Hickok drove northeast to the resort town of **Rimini** on the Adriatic Sea. Rimini was founded by the Romans in 268 B.C. and is home to the **Arch of Augustus**, the oldest surviving Roman arch. In Rimini, Hemingway collected his mail at the **Grand Hotel Aquila D'Oro**. His letters included several from Pauline imploring him to return to Paris.

From Rimini, the two Americans headed in a northwest line through **Forlì, Imola, Bologna, Parma, Piacenza**, Genoa, and down the coast to the fishing village of **Sestri Levante**. Set on a promontory that was once part of a small island, Sestri has two bays, one of which, **Baia delle Favole** ("Bay of Fairy Tales"), was named for Danish writer, Hans Christian Andersen. Sestri is mentioned in Canto 19 of the *Divine Comedy* by Dante Alighieri. In Sestri, Hemingway and Hickok stopped for a lunch of steak, fried potatoes, wine, and pasta *asciutta* (basil and meat sauce), the same dish that Frederic Henry is eating when he's wounded at the front in *A Farewell to Arms*. When Hickock and Hemingway crossed the border into **Menton**, Hemingway was still wistful, but relieved to be out of Mussolini country. Hemingway wouldn't set foot in Italy again for twenty-one years. When he did come back he would be a forty-nine-year-old father of three and married to his fourth wife, Mary Welsh.

1948–49

Thirty years after the ambitious eighteen-year-old Hemingway had entered the theater of war, he returned to Italy having accomplished many of his goals—"action," writing, travel, and love—but by then felt as though life had lost much of its luster. In late September, 1948, Mary and Ernest Hemingway boarded the Polish steamship *Jagiello*, intending to go on a tour of "Cézanne country" in Ernest's royal blue Buick Roadmaster, which they'd brought aboard as cargo. When the ship reached **Cannes**, they discovered that the wharf had been pummeled by a recent storm and the car wouldn't be able to be unloaded. The Hemingways remained on the ship until it reached Genoa.

Hemingway had become a celebrity in his time away, and the dock at Genoa was jammed with reporters. "The massive bulk of Ernest Hemingway has landed in Genoa,"[8] wrote a reporter from *Secolo XIX*, a local newspaper. Hemingway's arrival at the **Columbia Palace Hotel** (now **Hotel Bristol Palace**) inspired an improvised press conference, during which he said that Italy was the country he loved most after America. Mary hired a local chauffeur, Riccardo Girardengo, to drive the Buick north to Stresa. When she and Ernest arrived at the Grand Hôtel des Iles Borromées—the same hotel where Hemingway had come as a nineteen-year-old ambulance driver on convalescent leave—the concierge came out to greet them, calling Hemingway by name. The hotel looked much the same, but the emotions that its glittering views evoked had become muted in the intervening years. That night Mary wrote in her diary, "Thirty years ago Papa had dreamed of taking his girl here but never managed."[9]

After breakfast the following day, the Hemingways rode to the village of **Pallanza**, across the western arm of Lake Maggiore. Hemingway joined his Italian publisher, Alberto Mondadori, for lunch at his villa in the nearby town of **Meina**, forty-eight miles northwest of Milan. Mondadori informed Hemingway that his books had been enjoying popularity in Italy since they'd become available toward the end of the Second World War. Hemingway hadn't seen any of his Italian royalties, however, since postwar currency laws had prevented them from being transferred to the United States. Mondadori gave Hemingway 400,000 lire in cash from his royalty account, the equivalent of about $650 in 1948.

Ernest and Mary were guests of the **Grand Hotel Alassio**, a resort on the Italian Riviera frequented by the jet set. At **Caffè Roma**, a piano bar near **Alassio**, Ernest found his favorite whiskey—The Antiquary—after a long search. He returned to Caffè Roma several times, eventually drinking the entire case of whiskey that owner Berrino had on hand. The Hemingways rode through **Como** to **Bergamo**, the site of the ancient town of Bergomum, a Roman municipality since 49 B.C. They spent the night at **Hotel Moderno**, where Ernest socialized with the owner while Mary went to see Donizetti's *La Favorita*. The Hemingways settled in for a longer stay at Cortina d'Ampezzo, the enchanting alpine village with the clear air where Ernest and Hadley had spent their last winter before Bumby was born. Normally closed for the autumn season, the owners of **Hotel Concordia** opened especially for Mary and Ernest. While in Cortina, Hemingway would rise early, have a breakfast of *caffè latte* with bread and butter, then go to either the bar at Hotel Posta or to **La Genzianella** caffè to write.

Hemingway met with his Italian translator, Fernanda Pivano, who'd been arrested during the Second World War for translating *A Farewell to Arms*. She and her fiancé, designer Ettore Sottsass, took the Hemingways on a car tour of the Austrian-Italian border to **Dobbiaco**, the mountain town where Gustav Mahler composed his ninth and last symphony in a cabin in the nearby pine forests during the summers of 1908–1910. They stopped for lunch in **Brunnico**, returning to Cortina through **Campolungo Pass** and the **Arabba** ski resort.

Count Federico and Countess Maria Luisa Kechler were in Cortina on holiday, and the Count invited Hemingway to go trout fishing on a preserve in the **Anterselva Valley of South Tyrol**, high in the Dolomites. Hemingway and Count Kechler, who spoke perfect English, would enjoy many afternoons of rabbit and pheasant shooting on Kechler's brother's estates at **San Martino di Codroipo** and **Fraforeano**, across the Tagliamento River in **Friuli**. The Hemingways' inscriptions are preserved in the Fraforeano guestbook.

In October, Girardengo drove Mary and Ernest through **Belluno** and Treviso to La Serenissima (Venice). The Venetians treated them like royalty, bestowing upon Hemingway membership in the Knights of Malta, which made him a Cavaliere di Gran Croce al Merito. Ernest and Mary indulged in the elegance of **The Gritti Palace** and installed themselves at **Harry's Bar**, the chic hominess of which seemed tailor-made for Hemingway.

The Gritti Palace
Campo Santa Maria del Giglio, Venice, 30124. Tel. (+39) 041 794611.

In *Across the River and into the Trees*, Hemingway describes The Gritti Palace as a "three story, rose colored, small, pleasant palace abutting on the Canal."[10] Hemingway's home in Venice, The Gritti Palace overlooks the Grand Canal with its ancient ocher buildings and lazuli water. It has captivating views of the island of **San Giorgio Maggiore**, the **Santa Maria della Salute Basilica**, and the **Peggy Guggenheim Collection**. The Gothic-style palace was commissioned in 1475 and was originally three stories (an additional story was added in the late nineteenth century). The canal façade once had frescoes by Giorgione, a fifteenth-century painter of the Venetian school, but a second Campo façade was designed in the sixteenth century. The palace became the private residence of Andrea Gritti, the Doge of Venice, in 1525, and was converted into a luxury hotel in 1895. The Gritti Palace underwent a sweeping remodel and restoration in 2012 and is filled with sumptuous art and antiques at every turn. Hemingway loved looking out across the Grand Canal from the balcony of rooms 115 and 116, which now comprise the **Hemingway Presidential Suite**.

In April of 1954, the Hemingways returned to Venice after a dispiriting trip to Africa involving two consecutive plane crashes. While recuperating at The Gritti Palace, Hemingway came up with his own medicine: scampi and Valpolicella wine, which Giuseppe Cipriani—owner of **Locanda Cipriani** and Harry's Bar—had introduced him to. Today, the "Hemingway Menu" at The Gritti Palace includes scampi risotto and duck with ginger accompanied by Soave and, Ernest's favorite, Valpolicella. The hotel's **Bar Longhi** was a favorite of Hemingway, as was the **Club del Doge**, a restaurant offering terrace dining from April to October. For maximum relaxation there's **The Gritti Spa**, **Riva Lounge**, and **The Gritti Terrace**—an al fresco dining experience with dazzling views of the **Punta della Dogana** art museum and the Santa Maria della Salute Basilica.

Harry's Bar

Calle Vallaresso, 1323, Venice, 30124. Tel. (+39) 041 528 5777.
Open every day 10:30 A.M.–11 P.M.

> *"The Martinis were icy cold and true Montgomerys."*
> —Ernest Hemingway, *Across the River and into the Trees*

Hemingway filled bars around the world with his rare enthusiasm, but his three favorite hideaways were **Sloppy Joe's** in **Key West**, **El Floridita** in **Havana**, and Harry's Bar in Venice. Harry's Bar, with its simple yet elegant layout and mustard-colored wood, has the feel of your best friend's study. Hemingway, like most people, liked things he could count on, and he could count on the martinis at Harry's Bar to be ice-cold and very dry. "According to Arrigo Cipriani, the son of the founder, the secret lay not only in keeping the bottles in the freezer but also in the 15–1 proportion of gin to vermouth, a cocktail Hemingway took to calling 'Montgomerys', an allusion to his assertion that during the Second World War the British field marshal [of the same name] . . . had only taken on the enemy if he could be sure of a 15–1 advantage in troop numbers."[11]

Giuseppe Cipriani—a former barman at Hotel Europa on the Grand Canal—opened Harry's Bar in 1931 with payback capital from a loan he'd made to a young Bostonian named Harry Pickering. Ever since, Harry's Bar has flourished, becoming a home away from home for locals and celebrities. In addition to what Hemingway felt were the best martinis in the world, Harry's is the original home of the Prosecco-peach cocktail, the Bellini, invented by Cipriani. Cipriani named the Bellini after a color used in a painting by fifteenth-century Venetian artist, Giovanni Bellini. Cipriani also invented the raw meat dish carpaccio, named for the red and white tones used in the works of another Venetian painter, Vittore Carpaccio.

Hemingway had his own corner table at Harry's, where he enjoyed a helping of risotto along with his Montgomerys. In *Across the River and into the Trees*, Colonel Cantwell meets his young lover, Renata, at Harry's for martinis with garlic olives. Hemingway may have been instrumental in establishing the cachet of Harry's Bar, but many other luminaries have helped to cement its prestige, including Barbara Hutton, Peggy Guggenheim, Truman Capote, Jimmy Stewart, Orson Welles, Arturo Toscanini, and Alfred Hitchcock. Evelyn Waugh makes mention of Harry's Bar in his 1945 novel, *Brideshead Revisited*.

On his 1948 trip to Italy with Mary, Ernest returned, once again, to the place where he'd been wounded at Fossalta di Piave, still hoping to rediscover the unsettling yet verdant feeling of a life nearly missed. Once again he was sorely disappointed with the atmosphere and appearance of the place, though perhaps more reconciled to it by then. He cut a divot in the slight depression representing the foxhole where the shell had struck and dropped in 1,000 lire. It was a symbol, he said, of his having given blood and money to the war.

Locanda Cipriani Inn & Restaurant
Piazza Santa Fosca, 29, Island of Torcello, 30142. Tel. (+39) 041 730150.

In 1934, the founder of Harry's Bar, Giuseppe Cipriani, turned a small wine and olive oil business into an inn surrounded by a flower and vegetable garden, with a view of the cathedrals of **Torcello**. In the fall of

1948, Mary and Ernest took the tourist boat from **Fondamente Nuove** across the Venetian Lagoon to the island of Torcello, where they had lunch at the inn. The sparsely populated island had a calming effect on Hemingway. He and Mary were so pleased with the peacefulness of their surroundings that they stayed most of November in a beautiful suite with a fireplace, facing the gardens. Ernest settled into a routine of writing in the mornings and hunting on Baron Raimondo Nanyuki Franchetti's **San Gaetano** estate in the afternoons. Franchetti would become the model for Baron Alvarito in *Across the River and into the Trees*. Torcello is home to a medieval palazzo with a church, cathedral, and basilica, as well as the seventh-century **Cathedral of Santa Maria Assunta**.

The Hemingways returned to Venice in November of 1949, once again staying at Locanda Cipriani on Torcello. They entertained friends and Hemingway continued work on his new book. Arrigo Cipriani recalled that Hemingway would often stay up all night writing and sleep late, the opposite of his usual early morning routine. "Cipriani's aunt Gabriella, who ran the restaurant, told the waiters to keep their voices down so as not to wake Hemingway, especially if there were more than three empty bottles of Amarone di Valpolicella outside his room. His favorite food at lunch or dinner was risotto and fried fish followed by crepes."[12] Ernest and Mary returned to Locanda Cipriani for caviar and vodka during their last trip to Italy in the spring of 1954.

In September of 1948, a month before Hemingway visited Locanda Cipriani for the first time, the early modernist painter, Marc Chagall, was a guest at the inn. Chagall returned to Torcello in September of 1960, this time leaving behind a picture he drew with lipstick. A cavalcade of other celebrities have dined at Locanda Cipriani in the years before and after Hemingway, including Ernest's old friend, John Dos Passos, Peggy Guggenheim, Maria Callas, Cole Porter, Winston Churchill, Vittorio De Sica, Igor Stravinsky, Jean Cocteau, Tyrone Power, Billy Wilder, Greta Garbo, Ingrid Bergman, William Holden, Kirk Douglas, Kim Novak, Audrey Hepburn and Mel Ferrer, Bette Davis, Paul Newman and Joanne Woodward, Sidney Poitier, Jack Lemmon, Jane Campion, Jack Nicholson, Al Pacino, Mick Jagger, David Gilmour, Elton John, and many others.

Giuseppe Cipriani was assisted in the running of Locanda Cipriani for over thirty years by his sister, Gabriella. In the early 1980s, Giuseppe's daughter, Carla, took over for him. She was joined a few years later by his son, Bonifacio Brass, who is the current owner and director of Locanda Cipriani on Torcello.

Basilica di Santa Maria Assunta

Fondamenta dei Borgognoni, 24, Island of Torcello, 30142.
Tel. (+39) 041 730084.

Hemingway was a great fan of mosaics, and those at the Basilica di Santa Maria Assunta—also known as **Torcello Cathedral**—contain the earliest surviving examples in Venice. Hemingway especially appreciated the fifth-century throne of Attila in front of the cathedral. Mary and Ernest also went to view the mosaics at the **Doge's Palace**, as well as those at **Saint Mark's Basilica** in **Piazza San Marco**.

An example of Venetian-Byzantine architecture, Torcello Cathedral is a basilica church founded in 639 by the exarch Isaac of Ravenna. At the time, Torcello—which was first settled in 452—was a rival of the nearby settlement of Venice. The most striking exterior features of the cathedral are the decoration of the façade and the frontal portico, which was enlarged in the fourteenth century. The interior of Torcello Cathedral has a nave and two marble aisles, with the throne of the bishops of Altino and the sepulchre of St. Heliodorus, first bishop of Altino. The mosaics in the main apse include one from the eleventh century of the *Virgin Hodegetria*. Depicted against a gold background, she seemingly floats above a row of twelve saints. The main figure of the virgin was reworked a century later after an earthquake, while the saints remain from the first period. Two major renovations of the cathedral occurred in 864 under the direction of Bishop Adeodatus I, with a final renovation in 1008. The west wall was done in the second phase and contains, from the top: a *Crucifixion* in the gable; a *Harrowing of Hell* with a large figure of Christ; and a *Last Judgement* filling the four lowermost tiers. The counter-façade has a mosaic of the *Universal Judgement*, and there is a mosaic depicting a *Madonna with Child* (of the Hodegetria type) in the middle apse. The cathedral's bell tower dates from the eleventh century.

One rainy Saturday afternoon after duck hunting on the Franchetti estate on the lower Tagliamento near **Caorle**, Hemingway was chasing out the chill with some whiskey. Drying her hair by the fire was Adriana Ivancich, an eighteen-year-old artist whose family lived in a palazzo near **St. Mark's Square** in Venice. Curiously, Hemingway had met Adriana's mother, Dora Ivancich, while wintering in Cortina d'Ampezzo with Hadley in 1923, years before Adriana was born. Seeing Adriana fussing over her wet hair, Hemingway took the comb from his pocket, broke it in two, and handed half of it to her. It would be the beginning of Hemingway's fascination with the young aristocrat.

In December, the Hemingways returned to Cortina d'Ampezzo, where they rented **Villa Aprili** on the outskirts of the village for the winter, paid for by Mondadori. Mary and Ernest spent Christmas in the Dolomites, and Ernest sold his story, "My Old Man," to Hollywood for $45,000. Malcolm Cowley wrote a biographical piece on Hemingway for the January 10, 1949, issue of *Life* magazine, and though Hemingway had authorized the article, he rejected Cowley's follow-up idea for a full-length biography, not wanting one to be written during his lifetime.

In early 1949, Ernest took a trip to Verona to see the Roman amphitheater. He stopped for supper at **Ristorante 12 Apostoli**, where he dined on steak, risotto, and a bottle of Amarone that he selected himself from the wine cellar. That winter in Cortina, Mary broke her ankle skiing and Ernest was in bed with a chest cold for two weeks of February. In March, he ended up in the hospital in **Padua** after an infection in his eye spread across his face. After he'd recovered under large doses of penicillin, one of his first orders of business was to take Adriana and her brother, Gianfranco—who had served at the battle of El Alamein in Egypt in 1942 and in the American OSS—to lunch at The Gritti Palace.

When it came time for the Hemingways to board the *Jagiello* for the return trip to Havana on April 30, Ernest had begun a new story about duck hunting at dawn. The story would soon broaden in scope to become his fifth novel, about a middle-aged colonel in love with a much younger woman. Back home at **Finca Vigía** in Cuba, Hemingway would spend the next six months working on *Across the River and into the Trees*, the title of which is a paraphrase of General Thomas "Stonewall" Jackson's last words.

1950

In November of 1949, Mary and Ernest set off once again from Havana for Europe, this time crossing the Atlantic on the *Île de France* to dock in **Le Havre**. In their month in Paris, Ernest finished the first draft of *Across the River and into the Trees* while staying at **Hôtel Ritz**. Afternoons were frequently spent at the **Auteuil** horse races with writer A. E. Hotchner. On Christmas Eve, the Hemingways headed south through misty pink Provence in a rented Packard. After admiring the parchment-colored walls of **Avignon**, they holed up in **Nice** to wait for better weather before heading to Venice. New Year's Eve was spent at **Hotel Savoia Beeler** in the seaside village of **Nervi**, near Genoa. The Hemingways stayed at Hotel Savoia Beeler several times, and Mary's thank-you notes to the hotel management can be viewed at the local historical society. The last time Hemingway saw Adriana Ivancich was at the Savoia Beeler in June of 1954. Today the former inn houses apartments.

The year 1950 began at Cipriani's inn on Torcello. The Hemingways, Baron Franchetti, and Count Kechler spent two days of shooting on the Kechler estate in Codroipo. Kechler had recently bought paintings by Goya and El Greco, and Ernest had them brought to his bedroom so that they would be the first things he saw in the morning. Evenings in Venice that winter were a flurry of drink and song, and extravagant luncheons were given by the Hemingways on Torcello. One for Basque priest Don Andrés included Princess Aspasia, the mother of King Peter of Yugoslavia, who had something of a crush on Ernest.

Mary and Ernest spent two weeks in Cortina in February at Hotel Posta, where Ernest wrote in bed and Mary spent her days skiing. After Ernest broke out in another skin infection that the doctors decided was an allergy to gunpowder, he returned to The Gritti Palace to continue the rewriting and editing of *Across the River and into the Trees*. On March 5, Mary returned from a ski trip in Cortina, during which she'd fractured her other ankle. She and Ernest gave a dinner party for Alberto Mondadori and his wife on Torcello, where Mondadori told Ernest he believed he was the next in line for the Nobel Prize. Later that March, the Hemingways returned to Paris, where in the cold, damp weather Ernest contracted bronchitis. Charles and Vera Scribner came over from New York for a visit, as did Adriana and her friend, Monique de Beaumont. On March 22, the Hemingways boarded the *Île de France* for an anticlimactic return trip to America.

1954

Africa

On January 23, 1954, Mary and Ernest were on their third day of a journey by air to the **Belgian Congo** from **Nairobi**. Mary had been taking photographs of **Murchison Falls** on the **Victoria Nile** in **Uganda** from her window in the Cessna 180. Their pilot, Roy Marsh, was circling the falls so that Mary could take more photographs when the plane ran into a flock of ibis. In trying to avoid the birds, Marsh diverted the plane into an old cable wire. The wire caught the propeller, and Marsh brought the plane down as gently as possible into the thick brush near the river. Mary was in shock and Ernest had sprained his right shoulder, but otherwise the party was unhurt. If only the luck of that first plane crash had held.

Once they were all clear of the crash, Marsh went back to the plane to radio for help. As the light weakened, Ernest made a fire and the party rested beside it until dawn. At first light, Hemingway spotted a white boat coming down the river. It was the *Murchison*, a craft that had been rented to John Huston during the filming of *The African Queen*. The *Murchison* took them to **Lake Albert**, dropping them at **Butiaba**, on the eastern shore. At Butiaba they were met by pilot Reggie Cartwright, who was scheduled to fly the stranded party in a de Havilland Rapide to **Entebbe**, on a peninsula in Lake Victoria. Some apprehension pervaded the ragged airstrip as Mary, Ernest, and Roy Marsh climbed into the Rapide in the fading light. The plane skidded over the lumps of the derelict runway, barely lifted off, and came crashing down again, igniting on impact. The port-side door was jammed, and Marsh kicked out one of the front windows. He, Mary, and Cartwright made it out through the open window, but Ernest used his head and injured shoulder to butt open the stuck door. In doing so, Ernest smashed his head so hard that his skull was bleeding and leaking fluid. In addition to another case of shock, Mary had injured her knee and was limping.

After riding fifty miles to spend the night at the **Railway Hotel** in **Masindi**, Mary and Ernest rode another hundred miles in a rented car to the **Lake Victoria Hotel** in Entebbe. The press were there when they arrived, as all over the world the worst had been speculated. Ernest put on a spirited front for reporters, but his considerable injuries—first-degree burns, a concussion, a ruptured liver, kidney, and spleen, crushed vertebrae, sprained limbs, and the loss of hearing in his left ear—signaled the end of his prime.

In an attempt to go through with a fishing trip that had been planned before the crash, Marsh flew the Hemingways to **Shimoni** on February 17. Among the group already there were Ernest's son, Patrick, and the English safari guide, Philip Percival. Despite his customary enthusiasm, Ernest was hardly able to participate due to his injuries. To add to his anguish, in an attempt to assist in putting out a brushfire near the camp, Ernest stumbled and fell into the flames, burning his legs, chest, lips, left hand, and right arm. After this cap to his suffering, he stayed onboard the fishing boat in **Mombasa** until he and Mary left for Venice aboard the *Africa*.

By the time the Hemingways arrived in Venice in late March, Ernest had lost twenty pounds. He took to bed at The Gritti Palace, receiving visitors between trips to the doctor. In April, Ernest rode to **Udine** with Federico Kechler, where local writers and artists had a party for him at **Hotel Friuli**. On April 15, they dined at **Ristorante Bella Venezia** in **Garda**, a restaurant Ernest loved. Hemingway and Kechler visited the beach town of **Lignano Sabbiadoro**, where Kechler opened a resort that Hemingway referred to as the Italian Florida. Lignano Sabbiadoro has a public park named for Hemingway, and holds an annual **Hemingway Prize for Literature** in June.

On May 5, a farewell party was held in the Hemingways' suite at The Gritti Palace. The following day, Ernest suffered the drive to Milan, still plagued by nausea and an aching back. In Milan, Ingrid Bergman was playing Joan of Arc at Teatro alla Scala, and Mary and Ernest met her at **Hotel Principe**. Hemingway and Bergman had become acquainted during a *Life* magazine photo shoot at Jack's Restaurant in San Francisco in 1941. Hemingway had been taken by Bergman's performance in the remake of *Intermezzo* two years earlier, and persuaded her to play the role of Maria in the film version of *For Whom the Bell Tolls*.

After Milan, the Hemingways continued their drive through **Torino** and **Cuneo**, where Ernest was spotted by admirers while buying a bottle of Scotch. So intense was the throng, he had to be helped back to the car by a military escort. When he and Mary arrived at **Hotel Ruhl** in Nice, Ernest had his beard shaved off, hoping it would make him less recognizable. After the San Isidro festival in **Madrid**—where Hemingway spoke with George Plimpton and rode out to a bull-breeding ranch near **El Escorial** to watch bullfighter, Luis Miguel Dominguín—the Hemingways rode back to Genoa. On June 6, they boarded the *Francesco Morosini* for the long voyage to Havana. It would be Hemingway's last time in *il bel paese*.

ADDITIONAL PLACES OF INTEREST

VENICE

Mercato di Rialto & Pescaria (Rialto Fish Market)
Sestiere San Polo, 122, 30125.
Open Tues.–Sat. 7:30 A.M.–*12* P.M.

> *"He liked the market best. It was the part of any town he always went to first."*
> —Ernest Hemingway, *Across the River and into the Trees*

Located on the sestiere San Polo side of the **Rialto Bridge**, Hemingway enjoyed losing himself in the smells and shapes of the Pescaria of the Mercato di Rialto, often walking through its stalls of fresh eel, lobster, squid, crabs, and tiger prawns. The main market, established in 1097, extends across the Grand Canal between **Campo San Giacomo** and **Campo della Pescaria** and offers a wide variety of fruits, vegetables, herbs, meats, and cheeses. Settled in the ninth century, the district has been the financial and commercial heart of Venice for centuries. A pontoon bridge was built to provide greater access across the canal, but was replaced by a wooden bridge in 1255. Similar in design to the wooden bridge, the iconic stone **Ponte di Rialto** ("Rialto Bridge") was designed by Antonio da Ponte and completed in 1591. The Rialto Market is referred to in "Sonnet 19" of Elizabeth Barrett Browning's *Sonnets from the Portuguese*, as well as in Shakespeare's *The Merchant of Venice*. Another fish market is located nearby at **Calle de la Pescaria**.

Caffè Florian
Piazza San Marco, 57, 30124. Tel. (+39) 041 520 5641.
Open every day 9–12 A.M.

Leave it to Hemingway to choose the chicest café in Venice as his coffee spot. Caffè Florian in St. Mark's Square opened on December 29, 1720, and is considered the oldest café in Europe. First called **Alla Venezia Trionfante** ("Triumphant Venice"), it was subsequently rechristened Caffè Florian by its clientele in honor of owner Floriano Francesconi. Other writers who have enjoyed the comfort of the great halls of Caffè Florian—decked out as they are with golden ornamentation, crimson upholstery, and magnificent artwork—are Johann Wolfgang von Goethe, Lord Byron, Marcel Proust, and Charles Dickens.

Since 1893, Caffè Florian has hosted the **Venice Biennale**, originally called the Esposizione Internazionale d'Arte Contemporanea, an ever-changing display of the work of contemporary artists. Every two years, the Florian hosts "Temporanea, the art of the possible at the Caffè Florian," an invitation to artists to reinterpret its great halls with contemporary installations. In addition to its dedication to art, in the early 1900s Caffè Florian began the traditional European "café-concert" with a permanent orchestra to accompany its exquisite pastries, sandwiches, and desserts.

Chiesa di Santa Maria del Giglio ("Saint Mary of the Lily")
Campo Santa Maria del Giglio San Marco, 30125.

Located west of Piazza San Marco, the church of Santa Maria del Giglio is more commonly known as **Santa Maria Zobenigo**, after the

Jubanico family who founded it in the ninth century. In *Across the River and into the Trees*, Colonel Cantwell compares this "fine, compact and, yet, ready to be air-borne building"[13] near The Gritti Palace to a P-47—a stalwart American fighter aircraft used in World War II. The spectacular Venetian Baroque façade of Santa Maria Zobenigo is the work of Swiss-Italian architect, Giuseppe Sardi (not to be confused with the Roman architect of the same name). Sardi rebuilt the church for Admiral Antonio Barbaro between 1678 and 1681. Santa Maria del Giglio, or "Saint Mary of the Lily," refers to the classic depiction of the flower presented by the Angel Gabriel during the Annunciation. The marble reliefs on the exterior of the church depict the various places where Admiral Barbaro served, including Candia, Zadar, Padua, Rome, Corfu, and Split. There is a statue of Barbaro sculpted by Josse de Corte in the center, flanked by others representing Honor, Virtue, Fame, and Wisdom. Other statues are of Barbaro's brothers, and at the top of the façade the Barbaro family arms is carved in relief.

Inside the church, a large canvas by Antonio Zanchi adorns the ceiling of the nave. Depictions of the *Via Crucis* (*Stations of the Cross*, 1755–1756) by various artists—including Francesco Zugno, Gianbattista Crosato, Gaspare Diziani, and Jacopo Marieschi—grace the nave's interior. To the right of the entrance, the chapel contains a *Madonna and Child with the Young Saint John*, the only painting in Venice by Flemish painter Sir Peter Paul Rubens. The chapel also has a painting of *Saint Vincent Ferrer* (1750) by Giovanni Battista Piazzetta and Giuseppe Angeli. The altar is flanked by statues depicting the *Annunciation* by Heinrich Meyring, and in the sanctuary behind the high altar are paintings of the *Evangelists* by Jacopo Tintoretto. There is a sculpture by Giovanni Maria Morlaiter in the second chapel, and the organ shutters include works by Alessandro Vittoria. Paintings by Sebastiano Ricci and Palma the Younger round out the ornate interior of this magnificent church.

Attilio Codognato (Codognato Jewelry House)
San Marco 1295, 30124. Tel. (+39) 041 522 5042.

Hemingway was a frequent customer of Attilio Codognato, buying pieces from the famous boutique for his wife Mary, as well as for Adriana Ivancich.

In *Across the River and into the Trees*, Colonel Cantwell buys a piece of jewelry for Renata at the shop and has it delivered to Harry's Bar. Attilio Codognato, near Piazza San Marco, has occupied the same space since it was founded by Simeone Codognato in 1866. Before opening his jewelry house, Simeone Codognato had been a dealer of *objets d'art* and ancient paintings. Many of the pieces at Attilio Codognato were inspired by the fifteenth-century Venetian artist Carpaccio and the eighteenth-century painter Pietro Longhi. In 1897 Simeone left the store to his son Attilio I, who was born in 1867 and trained as a jeweler. Attilio's early designs were elaborate pieces inspired by treasures from Etruscan archaeological digs of the time. He created exclusive *memento mori* pieces featuring striking stones, skulls, and snakes. The jewels of Attilio Codognato have been worn and cherished by such symbols of good taste as Maria Callas, Elizabeth Taylor, and Coco Chanel. Today the shop is still in the family, run by Attilio Codognato III, the great-grandson of the founder.

3

TORONTO

1920

I f being a "real writer" means being paid to have your work published and having confidence in what you write, then Ernest Hemingway became a real writer in Toronto. The thrill of his first byline came after he got a job writing for *Star Weekly* in 1920, and it was in Toronto that he began to develop the poetically succinct style that became his signature. While living in Toronto, Hemingway had time to reflect upon his memories of camping and fishing in the Michigan woods, as well as on his experiences in Italy during the war. It would be these events, as well as the adventures he would begin to have in Paris the following year, that would become the subjects of his mature fiction.

In December of 1919, Hemingway met Harriet Gridly Connable of Toronto while giving a presentation on his World War I experiences to the Ladies' Aid Society at the Petoskey Public Library. She was so impressed by his wounding and heroism in Italy that she invited him to spend the remainder of the winter serving as a paid live-in companion to her son. Mrs. Connable and her husband Ralph—who was the head of the Canadian branch of F. W. Woolworth's department stores—offered Hemingway $50 a month plus free accommodations to act as an intellectual and athletic mentor to Ralph Jr. while they vacationed in Palm Beach for the winter. Hemingway accepted and moved into the Connable mansion on January 8, 1920.

The Connable Home
153-169 Lyndhurst Avenue.

The expansive Connable mansion sits on a hill at the northern edge of what in 1920 were the Toronto city limits. Among the home's cultural and recreational features was a music room reminiscent of Grace Hemingway's in Oak Park that contained an array of instruments, including a pipe organ. Other enjoyments included an exercise room, a recreation room with a billiards table, stables, a tennis court that the Connables flooded in winter to serve as a skating rink, and an outdoor fireplace. During his residence at the Connable mansion, Hemingway not only found time to work on his fiction but enjoyed plenty of time to read. In the Connables' extensive library, he discovered Joseph Conrad, who would have a great influence on his later work. Hemingway also came across *Erotic Symbolism*, a book that fascinated him. Through it he was introduced to the idea of gender-swapping hairstyles, a concept he explored in his posthumously published novel, *The Garden of Eden*.

Arena Gardens (Mutual Street Arena)
88 Mutual Street, just south of Dundas Street.

In order to fulfill his duties as mentor, Ernest looked for ways to keep Ralph Jr. occupied that he himself might enjoy. To that end, he took his charge to see the Toronto St. Patricks—later to become the Toronto Maple Leafs—at Arena Gardens. From 1912 to 1931, Arena Gardens was the premier site for ice hockey in Toronto, and was home to the first ever radio broadcast of an ice hockey game. When the Toronto Maple Leafs moved to their own arena in 1931, Arena Gardens was renamed Mutual Street Arena, becoming a community ice and roller skating rink. The venue also hosted concerts—Frank Sinatra and Glenn Miller performed there during the 1940s. Mutual Street Arena was demolished in 1989 and is now home to a residential complex and Arena Gardens municipal park. A plaque commemorates the site.

Massey Hall
178 Victoria Street.

Always a fan of a good sparring match, while in Toronto Hemingway got his boxing fix at Massey Hall. Throughout his life, Hemingway was known to challenge friends—or even people he'd just met—to an impromptu spar, and often shadowboxed to release some of his abundant nervous energy. Sometimes Ernest brought Ralph Jr. along to the bouts at Massey Hall, but Ralph was repulsed by the violence. In a March 13, 1920, *Star Weekly* satire, "Sporting Mayor at Boxing Bouts," Hemingway skewered Toronto Mayor Tommy Church for angling for votes during a boxing match at Massey Hall: "Any sporting event that attracts voters as spectators numbers His Worship as one of the patrons. . . . The other night the mayor and I attended the boxing bouts at Massey Hall. No; we didn't go together, but we were both there."[1] In addition to sporting events, Massey Hall hosted classical music performances, which Hemingway occasionally covered for the *Star*. In 1922, Hemingway reviewed a performance of the Toronto Symphony at Massey Hall for C.F.C.A., the *Star*'s radio station.

Massey Hall was conceived of by Hart Massey, a Canadian businessman and philanthropist, with the idea of building a meeting place where Toronto's citizens could attend secular music performances at a price affordable to both rich and poor. Completed in 1894, the building housing Massey Hall has a stately neoclassical façade with an interior inspired by Spain's Alhambra Palace and the Chicago Auditorium. Since its debut concert on June 14, 1894, Massey Hall has hosted many dignitaries and acclaimed performers, including Maria Callas, George Gershwin, Winston Churchill, Thomas Mann, Max Roach, Luciano Pavarotti, Bob Marley and the Wailers, and Neil Young.

As Ralph Jr.'s companion and mentor, Ernest was asked to share the same room with his charge, despite there being ample bedrooms in the Connable home. Although Ernest and the reclusive, unathletic Ralph didn't exactly bond, Ernest found pleasure in the conversation and companionship of Ralph's sister, Dorothy, who had spent time working for the Red Cross in France. Dorothy and Ernest exchanged stories about what they'd seen overseas, discussed literature and politics, and enjoyed winter sports with her friends—particularly Bonnie Bonnell, a relative of the Massey Hall Masseys, with whom Ernest sometimes went horseback riding. According to a recent article in the *Toronto Star* by Bill Schiller, "On winter evenings, Hemingway tried skating on the Connables' rink and played pickup hockey with a small group of friends that included the Connables' daughter Dorothy, the chauffeur's son, college student Ernest Smith and others. In warm weather, he played tennis and rode the Connables' horses along Bathurst."[2] During the day, Ralph Jr. attended classes and worked in one of his father's department stores, giving Ernest plenty of time to write. Ernest got along well with Ralph Sr., who'd grown up poor in Chicago and enjoyed a good practical joke. Not long after Ernest arrived in Toronto, the elder Connable exercised his influence to land him his first writing job with a byline.

Toronto Star Offices
18–20 King Street West, near the corner of King and Yonge.

After an interview with editor J. Herbert Cranston, during which Hemingway told tales of his travels and his work for the *Kansas City Star*, Hemingway was offered a job writing features for *Star Weekly*, the newspaper's weekend magazine that featured fiction, humorous vignettes, and other leisure pieces. The *Toronto Star*—originally known as the *Evening Star* and the *Toronto Daily Star*—was founded in 1892 by striking printers and writers of the *Toronto News*. Their leader, Horatio Clarence Hocken, became the *Star*'s founder, along with Jimmy Simpson. Both men would go on to become mayors of Toronto. The *Star* was one of a cluster of daily newspapers—which included *The Globe*, *The Mail and Empire*, *The Toronto World*, and *The Toronto Telegram*—vying for Toronto's largest circulation. *Star Weekly* was launched in 1910 and would continue until 1973. When Hemingway became a feature writer for the *Weekly* in January of 1920, it had a circulation of more than seventy thousand. In an attempt to surpass the circulation of *The Sunday World*, the same year Hemingway joined the staff of *Star Weekly*, its editors made the decision to trade more traditional, stuffy essays and religious discourse for human interest stories and fiction by writers like H. G. Wells and Hemingway's early hero, Ring Lardner.

The four-story building that houses the *Toronto Star* offices is located a few doors down from what in 1920 was referred to as "Skyscraper Corner"—a cluster of buildings that were said to be the tallest in Canada. The main newsroom was located on the third floor, but Hemingway spent most of his time in the *Weekly* offices one floor below.

The first article Hemingway wrote for *Star Weekly* concerned Toronto Mayor Tommy Church who, to Hemingway's disgust, had not volunteered in the war. The story was rejected for being too critical of the mayor, but it showed Hemingway's natural tendency to disregard decorum in favor of honesty. He gave the rejected story to Dorothy Connable, wanting it out of his sight. From the start, Hemingway was sensitive to criticism about his writing. Dorothy recalled that when Ernest showed her one of the *Star Weekly* pieces he was working on and she offered suggestions on ways to improve it, he became angry and depressed.

Hemingway's first story to sport a byline was "Taking a Chance for a Free Shave," published in *Star Weekly* on March 6, 1920. Hemingway was so excited by his "Free Shave" byline that he carried the clipping around in his wallet. In Hemingway's eight-month stint at the *Kansas City Star*, he'd never received a byline, and had been kept to a strict factual reporting formula that didn't allow much, if any, creativity. Stories by cub reporters like Hemingway were rewritten by more seasoned journalists. By contrast, *Star Weekly* reporters came up with their own story ideas—the more flair and humor the better—which were not rewritten, and only lightly edited.

When he began working for the *Star*, Hemingway had not yet discovered the art of editing, and if something he wrote wasn't right the first time, he chucked it. The owner and editor of the *Toronto Daily Star* during Hemingway's time there was Joseph "Holy Joe" Atkinson. He shared the young Hemingway's minimalist editing philosophy, and Hemingway appreciated Atkinson's snappy, jocular style. Hemingway regularly sent clippings of his stories home to his parents, who were glad to have evidence of their son's potential to make a living as a writer. In response to his "Free Shave" story, his father wrote: "The Free Shave story etc. was very good indeed. I am sure you will succeed."[3]

Hemingway loved telling a good adventure tale to his chums at the *Star*, and when he was starting out as a reporter his war stories and early Michigan adventures were all he had. While his time in Toronto wouldn't become the setting for any of his fiction, the features he wrote for the *Star* became the basis for several of his short stories, including one of his most famous, "Big Two-Hearted River." Hemingway's article, "Trout-Fishing Hints," which appeared in *Star Weekly* on April 24, 1920, contains the rough prototype for one of the scenes in the story: "The big difficulty about fishing with grasshoppers has always been the difficulty in catching them. The classic way is to get up early in the morning before the sun has dried the dew and catch the hoppers while they are still stiff and cold and unable to hop more than a feeble foot or two."[4] The passage provides an early glimpse of the clarity and crispness that would give Hemingway's prose its magic.

In May of 1920, the Connable family returned from their winter holiday and relieved Ernest of his duties as Ralph's companion. Ernest stayed on with them until trout season opened in mid-May, when he returned to Northern Michigan for the summer. Though he'd left Toronto, he continued sending feature stories to *Star Weekly*.

It was at the *Toronto Star* that my great-grandfather began to pull away from traditional journalism and release his innate storyteller. From a young age he'd allowed himself to embellish and invent facts, and he employed creative license in his *Star* articles to the point where one might view some of them as his first published fiction. Ernest started inventing the details of his foreign correspondence pieces before he'd even arrived in France in

December of 1921. On the boat trip over, he and Hadley had stopped briefly in the town of Vigo, Spain, where Ernest spotted some tuna fishing boats in the harbor. From the scene, he came up with the piece, "At Vigo, in Spain, Is Where You Catch the Silver and Blue Tuna, the King of All Fish," published by *Star Weekly* on February 18, 1922: "A big tuna is silver and slate-blue and when he shoots up into the air from close beside the boat it is like a blinding flash of quicksilver. He may weigh 300 pounds and he jumps with the eagerness and ferocity of a rainbow trout. . . . The Spanish boatmen will take you out to fish for them for a dollar a day."[5] While the article shows that Ernest had not yet shaken off his tendency toward overwriting, the Vigo piece is an early example of two of his favorite subjects: fishing and locals—tales of which he would soon hone in early short stories like "Big Two-Hearted River" and "Indian Camp."

1923

On August 26, 1923, Hadley and Ernest boarded Cunard's *Andania* at Cherbourg, bound for Montréal. Hemingway wasn't thrilled about leaving Paris, but he'd been offered a job as a staff reporter for the *Toronto Daily Star*, and, considering Hadley wanted to have their baby in Toronto where she'd heard they had better doctors, it seemed the right thing to do.

Clarion Hotel & Suites (formerly the Selby Hotel)
592 Sherbourne Street.

Upon their arrival in Toronto at the beginning of September, the Hemingways spent three weeks in the four-story downtown Victorian mansion that housed the Selby Hotel. Today, the building houses the remodeled Clarion Hotel & Suites Selby-Toronto, which offers a restaurant, fitness center, jacuzzi, and continental breakfast.

Residence of Hadley and Ernest
Cedarvale Mansions Building, 1599 Bathurst Street.

On September 29, 1923, Hadley and Ernest moved into Unit 19 of the Cedarvale Mansions building at 1599 Bathurst Street. Their apartment was to the left rear of the building. In a letter to Ezra Pound, Hemingway reported that the rent was $125 per month. However, the lease—discovered in the Hemingway Collection at Boston's Kennedy Library—lists the rent as $1,020 per year, or $85 per month. Since the Hemingways had only signed a six-month lease, the monthly rent may have been increased. Though it was small, "Hadley decorated the apartment with paintings Ernest had bought in Paris, including works by André Masson [and] Dorothy Shakespear . . . Ernest's father sent a crate containing china and crystal. There was a white rocking chair, a bathtub standing on claw feet and, dominating the cramped space, a rented grand piano for Hadley. They adopted a cat, which they soon discovered was not house-trained."[6] As Hemingway wrote to Ezra Pound, the cat had selected a "shitting place" behind the bathtub. "Later in the evening," Hemingway wrote, "I will track down the piece of Merde by the smell and will carefully wipe it up with the aid of a copy of the *Toronto Star*."[7]

In 1923, the Cedarvale Mansions building—on the corner of Sinclair and Bathurst Streets—was new. Located on what was then the edge of the undeveloped Ontario countryside, it wasn't far from the Connable home. "Despite its name, the Cedarvale building was no mansion. The apartment was nothing more than a small rectangular room with a Murphy bed and a balcony overlooking a ravine."[8] Today, the building has been renamed "**The Hemingway**," and displays a plaque commemorating Hadley and Ernest's time there.

On September 10, Hemingway once again entered the *Toronto Star* offices. Although he wasn't thrilled to be back, he looked forward to being given special treatment as their triumphantly returning foreign correspondent. When he checked the assignments board, however, he found that City Editor Harry Hindmarsh had given him what then-cub reporter Morley Callaghan called "junk assignments."[9] The demotion to staff writer was too much for Hemingway after the freedom he'd had as a roving reporter and feature writer, and the chip he had on his shoulder would remain there for the rest of his time at the *Star*. The staff writer position called for reporters to start work at seven A.M. and work late into the night, six days a week. Hindmarsh was a tall, gruff man who seemingly had no need to be liked, riding reporters so hard that many of them cracked under the strain. In 1923, the starting salary for staff reporters was $20 per week, but following through on a hot lead could garner a raise. For each news story, there were several reporters scrambling for the scoop, and Hemingway had the least seniority.

While Ernest was chasing down stories, Hadley spent her days reading, playing piano, and visiting Harriet and Dorothy Connable. She'd thought returning to Toronto would give her husband a stable job that would afford them more time together, but the opposite turned out to be true. Ernest was frequently gone until after midnight. Once he did get to bed, he would often receive a call a few hours later to cover a breaking story. The combination of grueling hours, long train rides, and their cramped apartment left him unable to write fiction. In a letter to Ezra Pound, Hemingway said that he could not send him samples of his latest stories because he hadn't written any. Some of the younger reporters on the *Star*, like Callaghan, had read *Three Stories & Ten Poems* and thought they saw glimmers of greatness. Others, like veteran reporter Greg Clark, thought Hemingway should stick to feature writing.

In October, "Hard-driving Hindmarsh" assigned Hemingway to cover the visit of former British Prime Minister David Lloyd George and his daughter Megan to North America. Beginning in New York, they were scheduled to embark on a tour of Canada by train. On Hemingway's first day covering the George story, he worked nineteen hours, and published eight stories in four days. While in New York, Hemingway bought a copy of the American literary magazine *The Little Review*, which featured his poem "They All Made Peace," six vignettes from *in our time*, and a piece by his old friend, Gertrude Stein.

Toronto Western Hospital
399 Bathurst Street, on the corner of Dundas and Bathurst Streets.

On October 9, Ernest was headed back to Toronto on the train from New York, unbeknownst to Hadley, who wasn't expecting him home for two days. Feeling especially lonely, she phoned the Connables, who insisted she come over. While listening to Mrs. Connable play the piano after supper, Hadley began having contractions, which she initially tried to conceal. At midnight, the Connables rushed her to Toronto Western Hospital, and just two hours later John Hadley Nicanor "Bumby" Hemingway (named for Nicanor Villalta, one of Hemingway's favorite bullfighters) was born. John Hadley had been Hemingway's double-dealing pen name for re-selling his *Star* articles to other publications while he was a correspondent in Europe. Ernest rushed to the hospital directly from the train station, ignoring a request to report to the *Star*. Years later, Hadley recalled, "Bumby was quite something. And then Ernest came in, in tears and sobbing because he hadn't been there. That's the kind of guy he was . . . frightfully sensitive. It was a misty, misty occasion."[10]

Toronto Western Hospital was conceived of in 1895 by a group of twelve west-end Toronto doctors dedicated to building a hospital in that part of the city. A fundraising effort led to the purchase of a farmhouse property in 1899, on which the current hospital was built. Before the hospital was opened permanently in 1905, patients were treated in tents on the property. Today, Toronto Western Hospital is a 256-bed major research and teaching hospital.

When Hemingway did finally report to Hindmarsh's office the day after Bumby was born, Hindmarsh bawled him out for not having come to the *Star* directly upon returning from New York. Hindmarsh also reprimanded Hemingway for neglecting to report on a speech by acting New York Mayor George Murray Hulbert, which had become a major story. This lack of respect was the beginning of the end for Hemingway, who had become so stressed by overwork and the tensions with Hindmarsh that he was unable to sleep and had developed a nervous stomach. In a letter to Pound, Hemingway wrote: "Was on train at a smut session with correspondents and titled coal barons in the press car while baby was being born. . . . Heard about it ten miles out of Toronto and came in intending to kill City Editor, Hindmarsh. Compromised by telling him would never forgive him of course and that all work done by me from now on would be with the most utter contempt and hatred for him."[11]

As relations worsened, Hindmarsh decided it was best for Hemingway to go back to writing features for *Star Weekly*. J. H. Cranston, the editor who had given Hemingway his start, welcomed him back. Cranston agreed to pay Hemingway a bonus for extra stories written on top of his regular assignments—money Hemingway would earmark for his family's return to Paris. In his determination to get back to Paris as quickly as possible, Hemingway wrote so many features that several of them had to be published under the pen name "Peter Jackson" to avoid the impression that he was the only author of a particular issue. The subjects Hemingway chose to write about—trout fishing in Spain, avalanches in Switzerland, Parisian landmarks—reflected where he truly wanted to be.

Among the last flurry of articles that Hemingway wrote for the *Star* as a resident of Toronto were his first two pieces on bullfighting. The second of these, "World Series of Bull Fighting a Mad, Whirling Carnival," was published on October 27, 1923, and recalls Pamplona's Fiesta de San Fermín: "That was just three months ago. It seems in a different century now, working in an office. It is a very long way from the sunbaked town of Pamplona where the men race through the streets in the mornings ahead of the bulls."[12]

Toward the end of 1923, when Hemingway had reached the height of his frustration with the time-consuming newspaper work that was making it impossible to write fiction, a string of successes marked the beginning of his breakthrough into the literary world. A review by Gertrude Stein of his first book, *Three Stories & Ten Poems*, appeared on November 27 in the *Paris Tribune*. This was followed by a letter from Edward O'Brien confirming that he would publish "My Old Man" in the *Best Short Stories of 1923*. As a bonus, O'Brien asked if he could dedicate the collection to Hemingway. Hemingway wrote back, "Your letter couldn't have had any greater effect if it had been to inform me that I'd just been given 1 million dollars."[13] O'Brien asked Hemingway if he had enough new stories for a book. Hemingway's reply shows just how dismayed he'd become: "Working so that you're too tired at night to think let alone write and then in the morning a story starts in your head on the street car and have to choke it off because it was coming so perfectly and easily and clear and right and you know that if you let it go on it will be finished and gone and you'd never be able to write it. I'm all constipated up inside with stuff to write, that I've got to write before it goes bad in me."[14] During his last few months in Toronto,

Hemingway had soured completely on both Canada and journalism and expressed this in a letter to Gertrude Stein and Alice B. Toklas: "What bothers me is why with my fine intelligence I ever came out here. . . . I am going to chuck journalism I think."[15]

Although Hemingway may not have given it much credence, by the time his career at the *Toronto Star* came to a close, his feature writing had matured significantly. In "The Blind Man's Christmas Eve," published by *Star Weekly* in December of 1923, several of Hemingway's literary techniques—the use of simple adjectives and sentence structure, the evocation of the symbolism of the natural world, and the repetition of words—are evident:

> He was feeling a strange tight feeling inside himself and he was seeing things. He saw broad fields sloping away and he smelt the odor of bacon being fried early in the morning. He heard the pounding that thoroughbred horses' hoofs make as they sweep down in a pack toward a fence . . . He saw a big square bed with linen sheets and a small boy tucked in the bed listening while someone sat on the bed and stroked his head and talked to him. And he saw a small boy rising early in the morning and going downstairs to start out across the frost-rimmed fields with his dog and his gun.[16]

Childs Restaurant
279 Yonge Street, on the corner of Yonge and Dundas Streets.

Hemingway had few solaces while working for the *Star,* but among them were his friendships with fellow reporters Mary Lowrey and Morley Callaghan. They and other *Star* reporters would meet up at locals' hangout Childs to chew over the day's news and happenings, and no doubt to complain about Hindmarsh. The building that housed the restaurant chain's Yonge Street location was built in 1918 and designed by the company's internal architect, New York-native John Corley Westervelt. First launched in New York City's Financial District in 1889 by William and Samuel S. Childs, there were approximately 125 Childs restaurants in the U.S. and Canada, including four locations in downtown Toronto. One of the first national restaurant chains, Childs was popular with working people for its reasonably priced meals and quick service. The Yonge Street location was in operation until 1963, and was one of the last remaining Childs restaurants to close.

Angelo's Restaurant
144 Chestnut Street, on the corner of Chestnut and Edward Streets.

Hemingway introduced some of the *Star* reporters to another of their hangouts, Angelo's Restaurant. Angelo's served whiskey and red wine in teacups to sidestep liquor laws, and Hemingway showed off his worldliness by dipping his bread in the wine. Angelo's was started in 1921 by Italian immigrants, Clelia Bollo and Angelo Balfanti. They bought the three-story building on the corner of Chestnut and Edward in what was then called "The Ward" district of Toronto. At Angelo's, Bollo and Balfanti served authentic pasta dishes in a homey atmosphere. According to John Lorinc in the May 26, 2016, *Toronto Star* article, "Once Upon a City: Toronto's premier Italian trattoria": "A beaded curtain, said to be the first of its kind in Toronto, separated the two rooms, which were filled with round tables and checkered tablecloths. Bollo and Belfanti decorated the walls with paintings of Italian dishes and aphorisms (e.g., 'Tell me what you eat / I'll tell you who you are'). The extended family lived upstairs."[17] In addition to Hemingway, who was not yet a celebrity when he was a regular at Angelo's, film stars like Lucille Ball, Edward G. Robinson, and Boris Karloff came to enjoy the food and soak up the atmosphere at the popular trattoria. Angelo's closed in 1957 when the city seized the building for development, along with many of the row houses on neighboring streets that contained other immigrant-owned businesses.

Hemingway Stomping Grounds
Bloor and Bay Streets.

During the fall of 1923, Hemingway and cub reporter Morley Callaghan—who was not only versed in the drudgery of the *Star*, but also a fellow fiction writer—met often to exchange stories and talk about writing. One afternoon while taking a long walk from the *Star* offices, Hemingway confided in Callaghan about his deep dissatisfaction over not being able to write fiction in Toronto. In the little bookstore that sat on the corner of Bloor and Bay, Hemingway bought a copy of his first book, *Three Stories & Ten Poems*, and autographed it for Callaghan. After reading some of Callaghan's fiction, Hemingway pronounced him a real writer, as Fitzgerald would later do with Hemingway. While somewhat in awe of Hemingway's persona, talent, and dedication to his calling, Callaghan would go on to become one of Canada's best-known novelists, short-story writers, and playwrights, as well as a TV and radio personality. Today 55 Bloor Street West is home to Indigo Books & Music.

Woodbine Racetrack
Original location (1874–1993): 1151 Eastern Avenue at Queen Street East and Kingston Road. Current location: 555 Rexdale Boulevard.

Hemingway frequently accompanied *Toronto Star* cartoonist Jimmy Frise, an avid gambler, to Woodbine Racetrack, where the two would bet some of their *Star* wages on the horses. Sometimes Hadley too would join Ernest for a day at the races to see how far their luck would take them. Hemingway covered Toronto's underground gambling culture in a December 29, 1923, *Star Weekly* exposé, "Toronto Is the Biggest Betting Place in North America | 10,000 People Bet $100,000 on Horses Every Day," which highlighted the practice of local residents placing cash bets in their homes, offices, and places of business, rather than relying on bookies.

By the time Hemingway made up his mind to go back to Paris after Bumby was born, any semblance of loyalty he'd had to the *Star* was gone. In November, he began double-dealing under a secret pen name for two of the *Star*'s biggest rivals—*The Globe* and *The Mail and Empire*—and on December 26 he formally resigned from the *Star*, effective January 1, 1924. Hemingway waited until the day after Christmas to hand in his notice in order to qualify for his Christmas bonus. "According to newsroom legend, Hemingway typed out a long and scathing letter, taped the sheets of copy paper together, and posted it on the newsroom bulletin board for all to see.

Farcically, Hindmarsh pretended not to notice the letter, which is reputed to have been 16 feet long."[18]

Before leaving for Paris, Ernest took a quick trip to Oak Park to see his family, catching the train from **Toronto Union Station** on December 23. Upon seeing him again, Ernest's mother "wept tears of joy after deciding that her 'thoroughbred,' as she called him, had at last found himself, had finally decided to settle down and make something of himself in life."[19] During this briefest of trips home, Ernest gave Marcelline a copy of his first book, *Three Stories & Ten Poems*. The explicitness of some of it shocked her, and Ernest decided not to share it with his parents. With the publication of *in our time* a short while later, Grace's view of her son was again tarnished. Clarence ordered six copies of the book, but returned them to the publisher after reading the contents. This act would further expand the rift between the modernist author and his Victorian parents. Ernest arrived back in Toronto on Christmas Day to join Hadley for supper with the Connables.

Union Station
61 Front Street West, between Bay and York Streets.

Toronto has had three train stations: the first Toronto Union Station—a wooden structure in operation from 1858 to 1873; the second Toronto Union Station—built in 1873, completely rebuilt in 1896, and in operation until 1927; and today's Union Station—constructed from 1914 to 1920 and in operation since 1927. When Hemingway's train pulled into the second Toronto Union Station on January 8, 1920, he would have seen the newly-completed Union Station—which would not be open to train traffic for seven years—off to the west. The second Toronto Union Station was also the one Hadley and Ernest pulled into when they arrived in 1923, and it was the station Hemingway used when going on out-of-town assignments for the *Star*.

Located in Toronto's downtown business district, today's Union Station is the busiest transportation hub in Canada. Opulently constructed in the nineteenth-century Parisian Beaux-Arts style, it was designed by Montreal's Ross and Macdonald architecture firm, along with Hugh Jones of the Canadian Pacific Railway and John M. Lyle, an architect from Toronto. The station's façade and Roman columns are made of limestone, and its two-story vaulted ceiling is decorated with Spanish Guastavino tiles. The interior Great Hall has several large windows that bathe it in natural light, including two four-story arched windows at either end that were inspired by the Roman baths. Tennessee marble floors round out the classic aesthetic of today's Union Station.

On New Year's Day, 1924, Hemingway reported for his last day of work at the *Star*. He said his goodbyes to Greg Clark in the same office where he'd been given his start four years earlier. It seemed so long ago—before he'd met Hadley, Gertrude Stein, Ezra Pound, or Sylvia Beach; before he'd had Bumby; before he'd had any fiction published. Callaghan stopped by Clark's office to say farewell to his mentor: "Callaghan was nervous as he walked up to shake hands. . . . But to the shock of the older writers, Hemingway took the kid seriously. He told [him] to send any short stories he could produce to him in Paris, care of Guaranty Trust. He promised to spread the word. And then he said, 'I'll see you in Paris.'"[20] In 1928, Callaghan did join Hemingway in Paris, where Hemingway introduced him to his literary circle and the two writers boxed with a besotted Fitzgerald acting (badly) as timekeeper. Callaghan's memoir, *That Summer in Paris*, recalls his friendship with Hemingway.

In order to get out of town, Hadley and Ernest had to break their lease on the Bathurst Street apartment. To fool the landlords, they invited friends to come over and leave with one piece of furniture or luggage each. On their last night in Toronto, the Hemingways attended a party given in their honor at the Connable mansion, and were driven to Union Station the next day in the family's limousine.

Hemingway's final article for *Star Weekly*, "Freiburg Fedora," appeared on January 19, 1924, the same day that he, Hadley, and Bumby sailed for Cherbourg on Cunard's *Antonia*. Although "Freiburg Fedora" was the last article Hemingway wrote for *Star Weekly*, it was by no means the last piece the magazine published having to do with Hemingway. After a wire story reported that Hemingway had been gored by a bull at the San Fermín fiesta in Pamplona that summer, Hemingway sent a letter to Greg Clark describing the adventure. The *Weekly* turned the contents of the letter into an article, "Tackling a Spanish Bull Is 'Just Like Rugby'; Hemingway Tells How He Surprised the Natives."

The article, which was published on September 13, 1924, notes Hemingway's literary accomplishments and mentions his bullfight companions:

> In Paris, where he has lived for four years, except for a brief return to the *Star* last winter, he is engaged in literary work, having published two books of prose and verse, doing newspaper correspondence between times and attending prize fights, bull fights and going fishing during the respective seasons of these three major sports.
>
> In the party with which he went down into Spain for this summer's bull fighting were John Dos Passos, author of "Three Soldiers" and other works; Donald Ogden Stewart, who writes for *Vanity Fair*; Robert McAlmon, author of "Post-Adolescence" and "A Companion Volume"; William Bird, publisher to the younger set of Paris; Mrs. Hemingway and Mrs. Bird.[21]

In a sentimental 1951 letter to *Star Weekly* editor, J. Herbert Cranston, Hemingway wrote: "I never enjoyed myself so much as working under you and with Greg Clark and Jimmy Frise. It was sad to quit newspaper work."[22] In his later years, Harry Hindmarsh, who had become president of the *Star* in 1948 after his father-in-law Joseph Atkinson died, expressed regret for the way he'd treated Hemingway. Hindmarsh died on December 20, 1956, less than a month before his seventieth birthday, while working in his office at the *Star*.

Hemingway's move to Toronto and his subsequent work for the *Toronto Star* and *Star Weekly* was a fateful turning point in his career. The minimalist style he developed as a reporter, feature writer, and foreign correspondent would be the basis for the crisp, declarative sentences he would come to use in his fiction. Additionally, through his work as a journalist, Hemingway saw firsthand how people in tense situations hide their feelings to protect themselves from emotional vulnerability. This knowledge would inform his method of holding back from making the emotional themes of a story too explicit. Without Hemingway's training in writing succinctly about the whimsical and brutal for the *Star*, he may never have developed the sublimely spare style that brought him such literary success.

4

PARIS

"Paris is so very beautiful that it satisfies something in you that is always hungry in America."
—Ernest Hemingway in a letter to his mother,
February 15, 1922

The first time Hemingway set foot in La Ville Lumière was in early June of 1917. He and Ted Brumback were en route to Milan to join the Red Cross Ambulance Corps at the Italian front. German artillery shells fell all around Paris, and the young Americans chased the sounds of them in a taxi until a shell clipped off the front of La

Madeleine, the Roman Catholic Church near the small hotel where they were staying.

1920s

The second time Ernest crossed the Atlantic was with Hadley. The newlyweds arrived in France on December 20, 1921, aboard the Cunard Line SS *Leopoldina*, all expenses paid by the *Toronto Star*. Upon Sherwood Anderson's recommendation, they headed to Hôtel Jacob et d'Angleterre in Paris, where they rang in the new year.

Hôtel Jacob et d'Angleterre
44, rue Jacob. Tel. (+33) 1 42 60 34 72.

Before settling into their flat on rue Cardinal Lemoine, Hadley and Ernest stayed in room 14 of Hôtel Jacob et d'Angleterre in December of 1921. Hemingway wrote an enthusiastic letter to Sherwood Anderson soon after their arrival to let him know that the hotel he'd recommended in the Saint-Germain-des-Prés district was inexpensive and clean, and that the favorable exchange rate was allowing him and Hadley to eat and drink well on relatively little. Hemingway added that he would soon send out Anderson's gracious letters of recommendation to the Parisian literati. Today, this elegant hotel near the oldest church in Paris—the sixth-century **Benedictine Abbey of Saint-Germain-des-Prés**—has a lovely garden and offers beautifully decorated rooms and complimentary breakfast.

Ernest and Hadley's first Paris apartment
74, rue du Cardinal Lemoine.

On January 9, 1922, the Hemingways moved into a cramped three-room apartment on the fourth floor of 74, rue du Cardinal Lemoine, near **Pont de Sully** and **Place de la Contrescarpe**. The *bal musette*—a workers' dance hall—downstairs was dominated by accordion music, and around the corner was the **Café des Amateurs**, where Ernest would often go to write. The animated, all-night **Latin Quarter** would become the setting for his first novel, *The Sun Also Rises*. The main room of their flat was almost entirely taken up by a vast mahogany bed, and they shared a communal toilet—nothing more than a basin—with the rest of the landing's residents. *A Moveable Feast* begins with an evocative description of the autumn wind and rain driving the leaves from the trees of Place de la Contrescarpe, and in the book, Hemingway makes his and Hadley's flat sound pleasant: "When we came back to Paris it was clear and cold and lovely. The city had accommodated itself to winter, there was good wood for sale . . . and there were braziers outside of many of the good cafés so that you could keep warm on the terraces. Our own apartment was warm and cheerful. We burned *boulets* which were molded, egg-shaped lumps of coal dust, on the wood fire, and on the streets the winter light was beautiful."[1] The waste of the Latin Quarter was collected by horse-drawn carts, and in *A Moveable Feast*, Hemingway describes the primitive sewage system: "The squat toilets of the old apartment houses . . . emptied into cesspools which were emptied by pumping into horse-drawn tank wagons at night. In the summer time, with all windows open . . . the odor was very strong. The tank wagons were painted brown and saffron color and in the moonlight when they worked the rue Cardinal Lemoine their wheeled, horse-drawn cylinders looked like Braque paintings."[2] The neighborhood is one of the oldest and liveliest in Paris, and today bustles with restaurants, shops, cafés, and agreeable smells. In *The Sun Also Rises*, Hemingway describes the nearby Café des Amateurs, a notorious drinking establishment at 2, Place de la Contrescarpe. In the novel, Jake Barnes and Bill Gorton are walking after dinner and are put off going into the café after they glance in and see an old drunk eating a plate of stew. Café des Amateurs has been replaced by the lovely **Café Delmas**.

For a short time, James Joyce lived in a mews a couple of doors down from the Hemingways' apartment on Cardinal Lemoine and is said to have finished *Ulysses* there. Joyce and Hemingway enjoyed many nights out together, and Hemingway claimed that the severely nearsighted Joyce would provoke strangers and then tell Hemingway to fight them. Joyce once said, "He's a good writer, Hemingway. He writes as he is. We like him. He's a big, powerful peasant, as strong as a buffalo. A sportsman. And ready to live the life he writes about. He would never have written it if his body had not allowed him to live it. But giants of his sort are truly modest; there is much more behind Hemingway's form than people know."[3]

Midwinter wasn't the ideal time to move to Paris. The same month Hadley and Ernest moved into their unheated flat on rue du Cardinal Lemoine, they took the train to Switzerland, in part to escape a flu epidemic. They settled in **Les Avants**, an Alpine ski village just east of Lausanne, where Ernest recovered from a sore throat and wrote his first pieces as a foreign correspondent for *Star Weekly*. Three human interest stories concerning winter sports and the local Swiss culture were published on February 4, 1922. Since he was getting paid by the article, Ernest churned out as many as he could, seeing his byline forty-six times in the first three months of his new role.

Ernest soon found that the Paris apartment he shared with Hadley was too crowded to write, so he rented a separate room on the sixth floor of an old hotel nearby—the same room where Paul Verlaine had died twenty-five years earlier. As he looked out over the wintry red chimneys and grey zinc rooftops, keeping warm with bundles of twigs purchased from street vendors, Ernest began writing his first successful short stories. A philosophy for writing well also started to take shape—*write honestly about what you know and stop in a place where you know what will come next.*

Jardin du Luxembourg and Musée Luxembourg
19, rue de Vaugirard. Tel. (+33) 1 40 13 62 00.

In the afternoons, Hemingway would walk through the Jardin du Luxembourg and visit the Louvre to see the works of Cézanne, whom he felt painted in the spare, understated style in which he intended to write. Walking among the trees and fountains helped him clear his head after writing, or when he was attempting to save money by skipping meals. In *A Moveable Feast*, Hemingway recalls: "Now you were accustomed to see the bare trees against the sky and you walked on the fresh-washed gravel paths through the Luxembourg gardens in the clear sharp wind. The trees were sculpture without their leaves."[4] In the book, he tells of shooting pigeons to take home to eat, hiding them in Bumby's pram.

Jardin du Luxembourg was created by the widow of King Henry IV, Marie de Medici, in 1612. It is now owned by the French Senate, which meets at **Luxembourg Palace** at 15, rue de Vaugirard.

Hemingway was of two worlds in Paris, divided clearly by the Left and Right Banks of the River Seine. On the Right Bank were many of his fellow journalists, the pricier restaurants, and the cycling and horse races that he loved to bet on and watch. Hemingway felt that these things were a distraction from his "real writing." On the Left Bank were the artists and writers, as well as the cafés where Hemingway wrote and felt at home. The difference between the two worlds came down to the difference between the kind of writing Hemingway did for a living and the kind of writing he wanted to do. He reflected on this dilemma in an unpublished fragment of a draft of *A Moveable Feast*: "As long as I did newspaper work . . . it was necessary to have one presentable suit, go to barbers, and have one pair of respectable shoes. These were a liability when I was trying to write because they made it possible to leave your own side of the river and go over to the right bank and see your friends there, go to the races, and do all the things that were fun and you could not afford or that got you into trouble."[5]

Ezra Pound's studio
70, rue Notre-Dame-des-Champs.

Through an introduction by Sherwood Anderson, the Hemingways went to tea at the home of Dorothy and Ezra Pound. The Pounds lived near the Hemingways in a flat decorated with Chinese paintings. While Hemingway found Ezra Pound's affected bohemianism pretentious, the writers shared a mutual respect for each other's talents and developed a close friendship. In exchange for Pound's *sui generis* literary insights, Hemingway gave the esteemed poet boxing lessons.

Residence of Gertrude Stein and Alice B. Toklas
27, rue de Fleurus.

After meeting Gertrude Stein in the Jardin du Luxembourg, Hemingway was told he could call on her anytime after five in the evening in winter. Along with her brother Leo, Stein was an independently wealthy art collector, and the residence she shared with Alice B. Toklas was furnished with Renaissance-era pieces and filled from top to bottom with renderings by Picasso, Renoir, Cézanne, Delacroix, Matisse, and Toulouse-Lautrec. During the 1920s, the *salon* on rue de Fleurus was, along with Sylvia Beach's **Shakespeare & Company**, one of the centers of the literary and artistic universe. In *A Moveable Feast*, Hemingway describes the *salon* as being "like one of the best rooms in the finest museum except there was a big fireplace and it was warm and comfortable and they gave you good things to eat and tea and natural distilled liqueurs made from purple plums, yellow plums or wild raspberries."[6] Stein advised Hemingway on everything from sex to what books to read, and Hemingway entrusted his poetry and early fiction to her, including part of a novel and his new story, "Up in Michigan." The two formidable Americans seemed to share an instinctual, telepathic wisdom about writing. Stein's use of repetition in her own experimental writing was an early inspiration for Hemingway's evolving cadence and his own ideas about repeating words for emphasis. Hadley and Ernest developed a familial relationship with Gertrude and Alice, so much so that they became godparents to Bumby. Relations between Hemingway and Stein eventually soured, but in *A Moveable Feast* he quotes himself telling Hadley, "You know, Gertrude *is* nice, anyway."[7]

Stein is often credited with a phrase that she heard a garage owner yell to a young automobile mechanic. After Stein expressed dissatisfaction with her car not being repaired quickly enough, the garage owner reprimanded the young man, saying, "You are all a *génération perdue*." Stein borrowed the phrase to describe the generation that had passed through World War I, calling them "a lost generation." Hemingway used the phrase as one of the epigraphs for *The Sun Also Rises*, trying "to balance Miss Stein's quotation from the garage keeper with one from Ecclesiastes."[8]

John Bone was pleased with Ernest's work as a correspondent for the *Star*, and at the beginning of April assigned him to cover the Genoa Economic and Financial Conference. Held at **Palazzo San Giorgio**, the gathering included representatives from thirty-four nations and was attended by hundreds of journalists. The purpose of the conference, put together by British Prime Minister David Lloyd George, was to resolve the major economic and political issues facing Europe after the First World War. The conference began on April 10, 1922, and lasted until May 19, but was largely unsuccessful due to Russia and Germany signing their own agreement at Rapallo. Max Eastman, fellow American and former editor of the Socialist journal *The Masses*, met Hemingway at the conference and was taken by his modesty and manners. After reading some of Hemingway's sketches, Eastman sent them to Harlem Renaissance writer and poet Claude McKay, as well as to the novelist and literary critic Mike Gold. Hemingway also met Lincoln Steffens at the conference, a muckraking New York journalist thirty-three years his senior, who invited him to join the regular meetings of some fellow journalists at a local trattoria. The group included George Seldes, an American investigative journalist, editor, and media critic. Writing articles quickly using the "cablese" shorthand employed by the reporters to reduce wire costs was instrumental in the development of Hemingway's straightforward prose style. In all, he produced fifteen articles for the *Star* on the Genoa Conference, "and accordingly felt justified in returning once more to his experimental work in prose and poetry."[9]

As his writing style developed, Hemingway increasingly used his *Star* articles as springboards for his fiction. In October of 1922, he was sent on assignment to cover the end of the partitioning of the Ottoman Empire during the Greco-Turkish War. The assignment brought with it harsh conditions, and Hemingway contracted malaria. As the Turks overtook Constantinople, thousands of Christian refugees fled, and Hemingway, having read a newspaper account of the desperate scene, cabled a "first person" report of their grueling march:

> In a never-ending, staggering march, the Christian population of Eastern Thrace is jamming the roads toward Macedonia. The main column crossing the Maritza River at Adrianople

is twenty miles long. Twenty miles of carts drawn by cows, bullocks and muddy-flanked water buffalo, with exhausted, staggering men, women and children, blankets over their heads, walking blindly along in the rain beside all their worldly goods. . . . A husband spreads a blanket over a woman in labor in one of the carts to keep off the driving rain. She is the only person making a sound. Her little daughter looks at her in horror and begins to cry. And the procession keeps moving.[10]

Hemingway transformed the account into one of the vignettes included in *In Our Time*:

Minarets stuck up in the rain out of Adrianople across the mud flats. The carts were jammed for thirty miles along the Karagatch road. Water buffalo and cattle were hauling carts through the mud. No end and no beginning. Just carts loaded with everything they owned. The old men and women, soaked through, walked along keeping the cattle moving. The Maritza was running yellow almost up to the bridge. Carts were jammed solid on the bridge with camels bobbing along through them. Greek cavalry herded along the procession. Women and kids were in the carts crouched with mattresses, mirrors, sewing machines, bundles. There was a woman having a kid with a young girl holding a blanket over her and crying.[11]

The assignment to cover the Greco-Turkish War would have a lasting effect on Hemingway, making appearances in several of his works of fiction, including Harry's stream-of-consciousness ruminations on his life in "The Snows of Kilimanjaro," as well as in the retreat from Caporetto in *A Farewell to Arms*.

In November, Ernest took the train to Switzerland to cover the Lausanne Peace Conference, leaving Hadley in Paris with a bad cold. He'd recently given some of his short stories to Steffens, who'd been impressed and had offered to send "My Old Man" to an editor at *Cosmopolitan*. Ernest was elated. When Hadley was well enough to join Ernest in Switzerland, she decided to surprise him and gathered nearly all of his stories, poems, and a partially completed war novel—including the carbon copies—so that he could show them to the other writers at the conference and work on them over the Christmas holiday. She put the manuscripts into a small suitcase and at Gare de Lyon handed the suitcase to a porter to carry to her compartment on the train. That was the last she ever saw of it.

When an anguished Hadley first arrived in Lausanne, she was unable to bring herself to tell Ernest what had happened. In *A Moveable Feast*, he recalled, "I had never seen anyone hurt by a thing other than death or unbearable suffering except Hadley when she told me about the things being gone. She had cried and cried and could not tell me. . . . I was sure that she could not have brought the carbons too . . . It was true all right and I remember what I did in the night after I let myself into the flat and found it was true."[12]

All that remained of Ernest's writing were two stories, "Up in Michigan," which had been put in a drawer in the flat on Cardinal Lemoine, and the copy of "My Old Man" that Steffens had sent to *Cosmopolitan*. After rushing back to Paris to confirm the loss and spending the night in their flat, Ernest went to lunch with Gertrude and Alice before rejoining Hadley in Switzerland. That night on the train he allowed the damage to sink in by writing a poem over a bottle of wine with supper. Later, Scott Fitzgerald told Hadley that he wished someone would have lost his embarrassing early work, but the comment was undoubtedly of no comfort.

After a period of doubt and regeneration, Hemingway's blue notebooks began to again fill with clear and true images, and more of his poems were accepted for publication. First by *The Double Dealer*—a New Orleans-based literary journal that ran from 1921 to 1926—followed by six poems in *Poetry* magazine. In 1923, Robert McAlmon's Contact Publishing printed three hundred copies of Hemingway's first book, *Three Stories & Ten Poems*, a collection that includes "Up in Michigan," "My Old Man," and "Out of Season."

Former Site of Three Mountains Press / *The Transatlantic Review*
29, Quai d'Anjou.

In the spring of 1923, Hemingway was introduced to bullfighting, and wrote five vignettes about what he'd observed in the bullrings, finishing the last two upon his return to Paris in August. He submitted the vignettes to William Bird's Three Mountains Press, later titling them *in our time*, from the English *Book of Common Prayer*: "Give peace in our time, O Lord." In December, Bird, a journalist from New York, printed the thirty-one-page volume of eighteen sketches on a hand-press with handmade paper, with a dust jacket made from a collage of multilingual newspaper articles. Hemingway's second book was part of a series of six edited by Ezra Pound that also included works by William Carlos Williams and Ford Madox Ford. One hundred and thirty of the three hundred copies of *in our time* were damaged when the woodcut on the front bled through, and those copies were given to reviewers and friends. Although less than two hundred intact copies of *in our time* were printed, the book helped to establish Hemingway as a prose writer of importance. Edmund Wilson commented that the bullfight scenes in the book were like paintings by Francisco Goya, that Hemingway "had almost invented a form of his own," and that the book had "more artistic dignity than any written by an American about the period of the war."[13]

The short-lived but influential literary magazine, *The Transatlantic Review*, also had its offices at 29, Quai d'Anjou on the Île Saint-Louis. Upon Pound's recommendation, Ford Madox Ford accepted Hemingway as an editor of the review, which published extracts of Joyce's *Finnegans Wake* and, at Hemingway's request, parts of Stein's *The Making of Americans*.

Ernest and Hadley's second Paris apartment
113, rue Notre-Dame-des-Champs.

Upon their return to Paris after the birth of Bumby, the Hemingway family moved into a larger apartment at 113, rue Notre-Dame-des-Champs. The downside was that it was directly above a noisy sawmill and lumber yard, and most mornings Ernest spent writing downstairs at La Closerie des Lilas. He continued to hone his short fiction, writing "Indian Camp" and "Big Two-Hearted River," as well as eight other stories, over the next six months. He combined the new material with the vignettes from *in our time* and submitted them to New York publisher, Boni & Liveright, at the end of 1924.

In March of 1925 the Hemingways were skiing at Schruns, Austria, when Ernest received a cable from Horace Liveright telling him that Boni & Liveright had accepted his manuscript. They offered a $100 advance with an option on his next two books. Boni & Liveright was also Harold Loeb's publisher, and it had been at Loeb's insistence that Hemingway's manuscript be given serious consideration. The first edition of *In Our Time* contains fourteen stories, with the sketches from the original version woven in between chapters.

The year 1925 proved to be momentous both professionally and romantically for Ernest. Shortly after his and Hadley's return from Austria, Ernest met Pauline Pfeiffer—a writer for Paris *Vogue*—at the Fitzgeralds' flat. Despite thinking Ernest dirty and inarticulate at first, Pauline was soon taken with the rough and ready American. In a shrewd move, the assertive and stylish Pauline befriended Hadley, becoming a third party in their relationship, and Ernest soon found that he was in love with both women.

That summer, Hadley and Ernest returned to the Fiesta San Fermín in Pamplona with the group of American and British expatriates—Hemingway's boyhood friend Bill Smith; American screen-writer Donald Ogden Stewart; the recently divorced Lady Duff Twysden; her lover Pat Guthrie; and American writer Harold Loeb, who'd had a brief affair with Lady Duff and was still in love with her—who would become the prototypes for the characters in *The Sun Also Rises*. Guthrie and Lady Duff lived off the increasingly infrequent checks sent by Guthrie's wealthy mother. When a check arrived, they would indulge themselves at Hôtel Ritz, then go back to living hand-to-mouth once the money ran out. In a typical illustration of their financial nonchalance, they didn't have enough to cover their hotel bill at **Hotel Quintana** in Pamplona, much to Hemingway's annoyance. The situation in Pamplona was complicated by the existence of a developing romantic interest between Twysden and Hemingway. At one point during the trip, the tensions between Hemingway and Loeb nearly led to a fist-fight in a Pamplona backstreet. After San Fermín, Hadley and Ernest followed the bull-fighting festivals from Madrid to **València**. On July 21—Hemingway's birthday and a few days after the fiesta ended—Hemingway began work on his first novel. He completed a rough draft in eight weeks, and, after briefly setting it aside, worked on the revisions that winter.

On October 5, the first 1,335 copies of *In Our Time* were available in America. The book garnered endorsements from Ford Madox Ford and John Dos Passos, but Hemingway was disappointed with Boni & Liveright's lackluster promotion. In April, Hemingway had met F. Scott Fitzgerald—by then considered the voice of the Jazz Age—when Fitzgerald had sought him out in a talent scout capacity for Scribner's and found him one afternoon in the **Dingo Bar**. Upon Fitzgerald's assurance to editor Maxwell Perkins that Hemingway was "the real thing," Scribner's expressed interest in giving him a contract, but by then Hemingway had already signed a three-book deal with Boni & Liveright. A potential loophole in the Boni & Liveright contract was that it was contingent on the acceptance of Hemingway's follow-up to *In Our Time*. Hemingway proceeded to write *The Torrents of Spring*, a parody of *Dark Laughter* by his old pal Sherwood Anderson, who was also under contract with Boni & Liveright. Hemingway submitted the manuscript in early December, but Boni & Liveright was not amused by the satirization of one of their best-selling authors and rejected it. Released from any obligation to Boni & Liveright, Hemingway was free to sign with Scribner's, though he denied having written the satirical novella for that reason.

In January of 1926, Max Perkins agreed to publish *The Torrents of Spring*—which Scribner's did in May—as well as any of Hemingway's future work. Hemingway corrected the final proofs of *The Sun Also Rises* in Paris that summer, and a first edition run of five thousand copies was released on October 22. The book made Hemingway famous and established him as the voice of the Lost Generation. Two months later the book was in a second printing of seven thousand. Scribner's also bought the rights to *In Our Time* from Boni & Liveright, and re-released it on October 24, 1930. The new edition featured an introduction by Edmund Wilson, as well as an "Introduction by the Author," which was renamed "On the Quai at Smyrna" for the 1938 publication of *The Fifth Column and the First Forty-Nine Stories*. In a re-issue of *In Our Time* in 1955, "On the Quai at Smyrna" replaces "Indian Camp" as the first story.

In the spring of 1926, Hadley confronted Ernest about Pauline, who had become a constant presence in their lives. When she asked Ernest if he was in love with Pauline, he said he wished she hadn't said it out loud, for in doing so she'd broken the last tether that might have held them together. That summer, Pauline joined Hadley and Ernest at the beach in **Juan-les-Pins** under the guise of helping with Bumby, who was suffering from whooping cough. Gerald and Sara Murphy accompanied the trio to the fiesta in Pamplona, during which they all stayed at Hotel Quintana. Pauline returned to Paris after the festival, and Hadley and Ernest were guests of **Hotel Suizo** in **San Sebastián**, where Hadley felt freer than she had all summer. Her respite wouldn't last long, however, as Pauline followed them with letters mailed to Madrid's **Hostel Aguilar**. In early August, Hadley and Ernest went down to **Cap d'Antibes** to the Murphys' opulent **Villa America**, where Donald and Beatrice Stewart were also vacationing. When the Murphys and the Stewarts learned that the Hemingways planned to separate, they were desolate. To their friends, Hadley and Ernest's relationship had been bright and strong, a rare precedent of what marriage could be. Always wanting to do the most prudent and helpful thing, Gerald volunteered his Paris painting atelier for Ernest to use as an interim residence. Hadley moved to **Hôtel Beauvoir**.

Gerald Murphy's studio
69, rue Froidevaux.

Although both Gerald and Sara Murphy seemed to prefer Hadley to Ernest, when the Hemingways separated, Gerald offered Ernest the use of his studio in the 14th arrondissement, behind **Montparnasse Cemetery**. Ernest stayed there through the spring of 1927, when he and Pauline married and moved into their flat on rue Férou.

Hôtel Beauvoir
43, Avenue Georges Bernanos. Tel. (+33) 1 43 25 57 10.

Before moving into her apartment at **35, rue de Fleurus**, Hadley was a guest of Hôtel Beauvoir. Located across from La Closerie des Lilas and a two-minute walk from Jardin du Luxembourg, this charming hotel offers garden views from some rooms, and suites have views of the Paris skyline. Breakfast is available, and there is a bar and lounge in the lobby.

In August of 1926, Hadley was leaning toward divorce, but in order to make sure of the seriousness of Ernest and Pauline's affair she wrote out a contract on a slip of paper stating that she would only go through with it if Pauline and Ernest were to separate for one hundred days. If they were still in love after that time, she would give Ernest the divorce even he wasn't sure he wanted. Pauline and Ernest agreed, but in order to make sure that they could keep the arrangement, Pauline sailed to America on September 24 to wait out the separation at her parents' home in Piggott, Arkansas. Hadley moved into her own flat down the street from Gertrude and Alice at 35, rue de Fleurus. When Ernest brought Hadley's things to her in a wheelbarrow, he cried. Hadley took a trip down to **Chartres** to give herself space to think, leaving Bumby with Ernest. While she was gone, Ernest wrote to Scribner's asking that they direct all of the royalties from *The Sun Also Rises* to her. When Hadley returned from Chartres, Ernest told her that he was also going to place all of the income from his books into a trust fund for Bumby. In the face of these gestures of finality and remorse, Hadley told Ernest that she would divorce him without any further separation between him and Pauline.

By February of 1927, *The Sun Also Rises* had sold twelve thousand copies. Hemingway's recognizable characters were causing much discussion and resentment between his friends in Paris. After all the drinking, boxing, and bullfights that he and Hemingway had shared, Harold Loeb was especially wounded by his alter ego, Robert Cohn. Hemingway's parents weren't thrilled with the book either—especially Grace, who said she still had faith Ernest would find his true calling. Others, like Scott Fitzgerald and Edmund Wilson, lauded *The Sun*, finding in it a liberating honesty, and appreciating it as the modern tragedy that Hemingway had intended.

When Pauline returned from Piggott to end their separation, she, Ernest, and her sister Jinny took a reprieve from the emotional minefield of Paris to go on a ski holiday in Switzerland. They were at **Hotel Rossli** in **Gstaad** when Hadley and Ernest's divorce came through on January 27, 1927.

Residence of Pauline Pfeiffer and Ernest Hemingway
6, rue Férou.

My great-grandparents were married in the Catholic **Église Notre-Dame-de-Grâce-de-Passy** on May 10, 1927, and moved into a large apartment on rue Férou, adjacent to the Luxembourg Gardens. The Fitzgeralds, who were infamous for their drunken antics, lived around the corner and came to dinner on one occasion, after Scott promised that they'd be on their best behavior. The newlywed Hemingways honeymooned in the Mediterranean resort town of **Le Grau-du-Roi**, where Ernest contracted anthrax through a cut on his foot. Between sunning and swimming, he did manage to finish "Hills Like White Elephants" and "Ten Indians," bringing *Men Without Women* up to fourteen stories. In July, Pauline and Ernest attended the Fiesta San Fermín in Pamplona, spent a week in San Sebastián, and stayed at **Hotel Inglés** during the Feria València. They spent the latter half of August in **Santiago de Compostela**, and took the train to **Hendaye** via **Palencia**, where they spent an additional two weeks. In Hendaye, Ernest began a new novel, which he was well into by the fall. When they returned to Paris, Pauline discovered that she was pregnant. On October 14, *Men Without Women* came out on the heels of the success of *The Sun Also Rises*—which by then had sold more than twenty thousand copies—and by the end of the year Hemingway's new collection of stories had sold fifteen hundred copies.

In March of 1928, Ernest rose in the middle of the night in his and Pauline's flat on rue Férou to use the bathroom. When he tried to flush the toilet, he accidentally pulled the cord of the damaged skylight instead of the toilet chain, and glass came crashing down onto his head. He suffered a deep gash, was knocked unconscious, and was taken to the American hospital, where they sewed him up with nine stitches. By then he was so well-known that his mishap was widely reported on both sides of the Atlantic. When Ezra Pound heard about the incident, he sent Ernest a cable: "Haow the hellsufferin tomcats did you git drunk enough to fall upwards thru the blithering skylight!!!!!!!."[14] The blow to the head served as a switch in Hemingway's battered brain, and he dropped the novel he'd been working on and started another. The new novel would be an exploration of two subjects that had been dancing around in his head since 1918: his affair with Agnes von Kurowsky and the war.

At the end of March 1928, Pauline and Ernest set off from **La Rochelle** for **Key West**, reaching the island—which had been highly recommended by John Dos Passos—by the beginning of April. Much of 1928 was spent in Key West, Kansas City (where Pauline gave birth to their first son, Patrick Miller Hemingway, on June 28), Arkansas, and Wyoming, where Ernest completed the first draft of *A Farewell to Arms*. The Hemingways returned to Paris in April of 1929, and in May, *Scribner's Magazine* began serializing *A Farewell to Arms*, though Ernest was still revising the ending. The Hemingways spent the summer of 1929 following the bullfights across Spain, from Pamplona to València, with a visit to Joan Miró in **Montroig**. They returned to Paris on September 20, and on September 27 *A Farewell to Arms* was published to sterling reviews. The year 1930 was spent in Key West, and Hemingway spent the summer of 1931 following the Spanish bullfights and working on *Death in the Afternoon*. That summer, Pauline prepared their Paris belongings for the permanent move to Key West, and vacationed at Hendaye with Patrick. Ernest returned to Paris in September, and that fall the Hemingways sailed for America on the *Île-de-France*. Onboard the ship, they were introduced to Jane Mason through Beatrice and Donald Ogden Stewart.

Throughout the 1920s, Hemingway and Paris evolved together. In his top-floor studio on the Left Bank and in the cafés of the Latin Quarter he allowed the simplicity and richness of his expatriate life to integrate the parts of him that were necessary to write good fiction. Paris was the backdrop for his foreign correspondent days of feature writing, for his first refined short stories, and it was the soul of his breakthrough novel, *The Sun Also Rises*. Sherwood Anderson had been right—Paris was the best place to become a writer.

1944

During the Second World War, Hemingway returned to Europe as a correspondent for *Collier's*, an American weekly known for its championing of social reform, investigative journalism, and short fiction. He covered the Normandy landings and participated in the liberation of Hôtel Ritz, where he had installed himself at the bar with Fitzgerald many an evening during the 1920s. Before General Leclerc made it to the scene, Hemingway arrived at the Ritz with his entourage in a convoy of jeeps, sporting a gun. He declared the grand hotel, which he'd once compared to his idea of heaven, liberated. To make it official, Hemingway got behind the bar and began popping bottles of champagne.

Hôtel Ritz
15, Place Vendôme. Tel. (+33) 1 43 16 30 30.

Hemingway loved this 159-room luxury hotel overlooking **Place Vendôme**. Originally a palace built in the classical Louis XIV style beginning in 1705, Hôtel Ritz was founded by Swiss hotelier, Cesar Ritz, and French chef, Auguste Escoffier, in 1898. During World War II, Hemingway, along with a personal bodyguard and a French translator, set up shop in room 31. Among the authors to visit Hemingway during his stay were a young J. D. Salinger (pre–*The Catcher in the Rye*) and Jean-Paul Sartre. At the time, Hemingway's marriage to his third wife, Martha Gellhorn, was breaking down, and Hemingway had begun a relationship with another American journalist, Mary Welsh, while in London. One day, well along in his drinking, Hemingway shot a photograph of Mary's husband—Australian journalist Noel Monks—which he had placed on the cistern in his room. The bullet destroyed the toilet and caused water to leak into the rooms below, but Hemingway's charm and celebrity smoothed things over with the hotel management.

There's no finer place for cocktail hour than the Ritz's butterscotch-and-almond-colored **Bar Hemingway**, where Scott Fitzgerald had a favorite seat and Hemingway and Gary Cooper would sit and talk for hours over cocktails. Guests of Hôtel Ritz may choose to spend the night in the ochre and ivory **Suite Ernest Hemingway**, which features a private terrace overlooking the chestnut trees of the **Grand Jardin**. Or they may prefer the lucent gold of **Suite F. Scott Fitzgerald**. They might lose themselves in a rare book with a cup of tea by the fire in the elegant **Salon Proust**, or have a swim in the crystalline swimming pool reminiscent of *The Great Gatsby*. The grandeur and grace of the Ritz is featured in *The Sun Also Rises*, in Fitzgerald's *Tender Is the Night*, in Sir Noël Coward's play *Semi-Monde*, and in the films *Love in the Afternoon* and *How to Steal a Million*.

Shakespeare & Company (1921–1941)
12, rue de l'Odéon.

After liberating Hôtel Ritz, Hemingway went to check on Sylvia Beach, who had closed her bookshop and lending library during the German occupation of France in 1941 and never reopened it. In her memoir, *Shakespeare and Company*, Beach recalled hearing Hemingway's playful, booming voice calling up to her in the rue de l'Odéon, and how everyone shouted in the streets. When she came down, Hemingway picked her up, spun her around, and kissed her. Hemingway's friendship with Beach was one of the most important and lasting friendships he made in Paris, and she was one of the few with whom he never quarreled.

An expatriate from Baltimore, Beach opened Shakespeare & Company in 1919 and moved it to its location at 12, rue de l'Odéon in 1921. Many expatriate writers living in 1920s Paris used the bookshop as a meeting place, including James Joyce, who nicknamed the shop "Stratford-on-Odéon" and used the dusty sanctuary as his personal office. In 1922, Beach published Joyce's *Ulysses* after it had been roundly rejected by all the publishing houses. For Hemingway, Shakespeare & Company was one of the stops on his daily tour of the Left Bank. He borrowed books, met with the many other writers who stopped in, and even received mail there.

Shakespeare & Company (1951–present)
37, rue de la Bucherie. Tel. (+33) 1 43 25 40 93.
Open every day 10 A.M.–11 P.M.

In 1951, George Whitman, who grew up in Massachusetts, founded **Le Mistral**, a bookshop on the Left Bank modeled after Sylvia Beach's Shakespeare & Company. In 1958, while Whitman was dining with Beach, she symbolically handed the name of her bookshop to him. On the 400th anniversary of William Shakespeare's birth in 1964, Whitman renamed his bookshop Shakespeare & Company. Whitman's Shakespeare & Company became a meeting place for Paris-based writers of a new era—James Baldwin, Anaïs Nin, William Saroyan, Allen Ginsberg, Richard Wright, and Julio Cortázar, among others. Not only did Whitman lend books to those who couldn't afford to buy them, as Sylvia Beach had done, but he also offered free beds to writers, artists, and students staying in Paris. More than thirty thousand people have spent the night in George Whitman's bookshop, and in 1994, I was one of them.

After the French intensive program I'd attended in Avignon ended, I went to Paris, where I'd heard you could stay upstairs at Shakespeare & Company free of charge in exchange for work. I didn't believe it at first, but when I arrived in the steep-staired maze of beautiful wooden shelves, the attitude of the employees was nonchalant. Of course I could stay; why not? I staked out one of the red velvet-covered beds and made myself at home in a corner of floor-to-ceiling books. There was an old typewriter, a piano, and when Whitman went on a buying trip to London—leaving a menagerie of musicians, writers, artists, and students in charge of his bookshop—we jiggled the door to his apartment and had a party. At one point, I was typing on the dusty Royal while a student from Oxford and a photographer from Cape Town drank wine with a young hippy who had just come back from living with a tribe in what was then Zaire. A composer from Manhattan stood observing from a corner while everyone else danced, sang, read aloud, and—I didn't tell you this—slept in George's bed. Not me. I got into the lumpy bunk tucked between bookshelves, covered myself with the red velvet blanket, and fell asleep, surrounded by the dreams of other artists, while the most romantic bedbugs awakened to my skin. I slept soundly, and the next day took a nervous bath in George's bathtub. When he got back from London, George came to me gravely on the upstairs landing and asked me to sweep. His face said "It's the least you can do," as though he knew what had gone on in his absence and was assigning my penance.

Whitman's Shakespeare & Company remains alive with alchemy and enchantment. Now owned by George's daughter, Sylvia, and her partner, David Delannet, it continues to offer free beds to its residents. The shop's motto, written above the entrance to the reading library, is "Be Not

Inhospitable to Strangers Lest They Be Angels in Disguise." If you sit awhile in the airy room with the cat sleeping in the armchair next to the piano, you begin to feel like each of the visitors wafting in and out across the arthritic wood might be one of them.

1950s

In November of 1956, Hemingway returned to Hôtel Ritz, where he discovered two small trunks containing notebooks and manuscripts filled with detailed impressions from his early Paris years—1921 to 1926—that had been held in storage since 1928. Over the next five years, Hemingway would organize and expand these into his only memoir, *A Moveable Feast*. And in 1959, two years before his death, he would return to Paris to be purified by the city's boundless magic one last time.

When Hemingway arrived in Paris in 1921, Europe's cultural capital was standing on the precipice of modernism. Brimming with artists and writers who would become the definers of an age, it was where the young man from Oak Park found his place in the world. Hemingway would never be the same, literature would never be the same, and Paris would be forever covered in the fairy dust of his genius.

THE CAFÉS

La Closerie des Lilas
171, Boulevard du Montparnasse. Tel. (+33) 1 40 51 34 50.
Brasserie open every day 12 P.M.–12:30 A.M. Restaurant open every day 12–2:30 P.M. & 7–11:30 P.M.

Named for the play *La Closerie des Genêts* by Frederic Soulie, La Closerie des Lilas was built by François Bullier in 1847. The café has a long and illustrious history of artistic patronage—Émile Zola brought Paul Cézanne here, and La Closerie has been frequented by artistic and literary figures such as Pierre-Auguste Renoir, Claude Monet, Camille Pissarro, Paul

Verlaine, Jean-Paul Sartre, Samuel Beckett, Ezra Pound, Pablo Picasso, Oscar Wilde, and Charles Baudelaire. Jake Barnes drinks here with Lady Brett Ashley in *The Sun Also Rises* and Hemingway repeatedly mentions the café in *A Moveable Feast* as a place where he worked and socialized. Hemingway would sometimes invite Joyce or Fitzgerald to meet him at La Closerie, where they would sit on the terrace to discuss their work. It was on this terrace that Hemingway first read *The Great Gatsby*.

The bar of La Closerie des Lilas displays a brass plaque commemorating Hemingway's time there, and patrons may order a *Filet de boeuf Hemingway*, flambéed in bourbon. The piano bar is a fantastic place to enjoy a Cuban Manhattan or a French Martini in the heady atmosphere. The chic café hosts *Le Prix de la Closerie des Lilas*, a literary award for female francophone authors, presented annually by an all-female jury.

Le Pré aux Clercs
30, rue Bonaparte. Tel. (+33) 1 43 54 41 73.
Open Mon.–Sat. 6:30–2 A.M.*; Sun. 8–2* A.M.

This snug bistro on the corner of rue Bonaparte and rue Jacob was a favorite of Hadley and Ernest when they first moved to Paris. A block from their accommodations at Hôtel Jacob et d'Angleterre, Le Pré aux Clercs was where, as Hemingway wrote, they could get a good dinner and wine for twelve francs. Stop in for a selection of Auvergne cheese, try the fillet of bass, or just enjoy *un café avec une crème brûlée* with brown sugar and bourbon vanilla.

Le Dôme Café
108, Boulevard du Montparnasse. Tel. (+33) 1 43 35 25 81.
Open every day 12–3 P.M. *& 7–11* P.M.

This Montparnasse flower of the Belle Epoque opened in 1897 and was referred to by Parisians as the "Anglo-American café" for the expatriates who made it their venue for gossip and lively discussion. It became one of the focal points of the Left Bank community of poets, painters, sculptors, models, art dealers, and writers. Some of its famous clientele have included Paul Gauguin, Wassily Kandinsky, Simone de Beauvoir, W.

Somerset Maugham, Sinclair Lewis, Anaïs Nin, Man Ray, and Robert Capa. Close to Hôtel Jacob et d'Angleterre, Le Dôme was one of the first cafés where Hadley and Ernest felt at home in Paris, patronized as it was by other English speakers. It was also inexpensive; a Saucisse de Toulouse and a plate of mashed potatoes cost the equivalent of one dollar. Le Dôme is now a Michelin-starred restaurant specializing in *poisson*. Enjoy a glass of Alsatian pinot gris with oysters or roasted scallops, risotto, and ceps in the lamplit dining room.

In honor of its artistic tradition, the owners of Le Dôme Café, Maxime and Edouard Bras, with the assistance of Charlotte Dumas Vorzet, created the *Prix Double Dôme*, an award given annually to a selection of emerging francophone musicians, writers, and visual artists.

Café de la Rotonde
105, Boulevard du Montparnasse. Tel. (+33) 1 43 26 48 26.
Open every day 7:15–1 A.M.

Across Boulevard du Montparnasse from Le Dôme Café sits the Parisian institution, Café de la Rotonde. Founded by Victor Libion in 1911, the *brasserie* became a gathering place for the bohemian and intellectual set during the creative period between the First and Second World Wars. Picasso, whose studio was near the café, could frequently be found at La Rotonde and titled his 1901 painting of a waiter and two diners *In the café de la Rotonde*. Many artists, including Amedeo Modigliani and Diego Rivera, frequented the café, as Libion would allow them to sit for hours with a ten-centième cup of coffee. If they couldn't afford to pay, Libion would accept a drawing as collateral until they could; thus the walls of La Rotonde came to be adorned with artwork by its now-renowned clientele.

Le Select
99, Boulevard du Montparnasse. Tel. (+33) 1 45 48 38 24.
Open Sun.–Thurs. 7–2 A.M.*; Fri. & Sat. 7–3* A.M.

Founded in 1923, this late-night *brasserie,* with its well-maintained French Colonial interior and classic brasserie-style menu, looks much the same as it did when it was the favorite café of Jake Barnes in *The Sun Also Rises*. It has been described as the "soul of Montparnasse," and continues to be more of a refuge for artists than tourists. Hemingway's friends Harold Loeb and Lady Duff Twysden, the models for Robert Cohn and Lady Brett Ashley in *The Sun Also Rises*, met at Le Select. Hemingway and Morley Callaghan would come to Le Select for drinks after sparring at the American Club, and it was here that Hemingway introduced Callaghan to Joan Miró. Hemingway purchased his favorite Miró painting, *The Farm*, for Hadley. It now hangs in the National Gallery of Art in Washington, D.C.

Le Select has welcomed many famous personalities over the years—Chagall, Man Ray, Fitzgerald, Beckett, and, more recently, Bill Murray, who is said to favor Le Select's version of the Croque Monsieur.

La Coupole

102, Boulevard du Montparnasse. Tel. (+33) 1 43 20 14 20.
Open Mon. 8 A.M.–11 P.M.; Tues.–Fri. 8–12 A.M.; Sat. 8:30–12 A.M.; Sun. 8:30 A.M.–11 P.M.

Opened on December 20, 1927, by Ernest Fraux and René Lafon, La Coupole is a loving monument to the Art Deco style of the 1920s. The opening party of the *brasserie* had three thousand guests, including Jean Cocteau, and fifteen hundred bottles of Champagne. Hemingway claimed to have danced with Josephine Baker at La Coupole while she was wearing a fur coat with nothing on underneath. He recalled them discussing his fractious romantic life during the period when he was in love with both Hadley and Pauline. The list of celebrity guests of La Coupole is memorable—Georges Braque, Simone de Beauvoir, André Malraux, Ava Gardner, and Ernest's pal Marlene Dietrich were all regulars. Rita Hayworth had dinner here with the Aga Khan. French President François Mitterrand ate his last meal, the house specialty lamb curry, at La Coupole before succumbing to a heart attack in 1996.

La Coupole hosts the *Prix de la Coupole*, a literary award given each June for a novel, story, or collection of French journalism published in the current year that "shows spirit." The prize is 5,000 euros and dinner at La Coupole.

Les Deux Magots
6, Place Saint-Germain des Prés. Tel. (+33) 1 45 48 55 25.
Open every day 7:30–1 A.M.

One of the oldest cafés in Paris, Les Deux Magots—originally a fabric shop at 23, rue de Buci—derives its name from a nineteenth-century play. It moved to its current location in 1873 and became a café in 1884. In 1914, August Boulay bought the business, which is currently managed by his great-great-granddaughter. Les Deux Magots has been host to many famous intellectuals, writers, and artists over the years, including Albert Camus, Pablo Picasso (who was apparently a regular at every café on the Left Bank), James Joyce, Jean-Paul Sartre, Simone de Beauvoir, James Baldwin, Richard Wright, Julia Child, and Hemingway. Vladimir Nabokov references Les Deux Magots in *Lolita*. The café maintains its original look and feel with red banquettes, mahogany tables, and waiters in traditional black and white dress. Among the breakfast choices are *Le Petit Déjeuner Hemingway* and *Le Petit Déjeuner JP Sartre*. The Hemingway includes ham and eggs, while the Sartre offers a "baker's basket" featuring Danish pastries.

Café de Flore
172, Boulevard Saint-Germain. Tel. (+33) 1 45 48 55 26.
Open every day 7:30–1:30 A.M.

Hemingway, Guillaume Apollinaire, Simone de Beauvoir, André Breton, André Malraux, Camus, Sartre, and Picasso were all regular patrons of Café de Flore. First opened around 1887, the café is a Parisian classic with a bustling, cosmopolitan feel and Art Deco features. Café de Flore was named after the sculpture of *Flora*, the Roman goddess of Spring and flowers, that was located on the opposite side of Boulevard Saint-Germain.

In 1994, Frédéric Beigbeder established the *Prix de Flore*, a literary prize awarded each November. In addition to a cash prize, the winner is treated to a glass of Pouilly-Fumé sauvignon blanc at the café every day for a year.

Café de la Paix
5, Place de l'Opéra. Tel. (+33) 1 40 07 36 36.
Open every day 12–3 P.M. & 6–11:30 P.M.

While they were guests of Hôtel Jacob et d'Angleterre in December of 1921, Hadley and Ernest treated themselves to Christmas dinner at nearby Café de la Paix. Designed by architect Alfred Armand, the café opened on June 30, 1862, and is a popular haunt for opera-goers. Café de la Paix has seen a succession of famous clients, from Guy de Maupassant to Marlene Dietrich. The café is splendidly opulent, with mythological figures looking down from high ceilings and marble tables supported by bronze lions' feet.

In 1918 Georges Clémenceau stood on the first floor of Café de la Paix to observe the marching in of the French troops in front of l'Opéra. The café was closed during the Second World War, but reopened and served its first meal to General de Gaulle after the Liberation of Paris.

Harry's New York Bar
5, rue Daunou. Tel. (+33) 1 42 61 71 14.
Open Mon.–Sat. 12 P.M.–2 A.M.; Sun. 4 P.M.–1 A.M.

Harry's New York Bar at "Sank Roo Doe Noo," as a sign outside the bar proclaims, has been a Paris institution since 1911. The bar was acquired in Manhattan by Ted Sloan, a former American jockey, who had the bar dismantled and shipped to Paris. Hemingway was a frequent customer of Harry's Bar, which is the official home of the Bloody Mary—a favorite of both Hemingway and Fitzgerald—as well as the Sidecar. An early version of the French 75 cocktail—which consists of gin, champagne, lemon juice, and sugar—was created here in 1915 by barman Harry MacElhone. In addition to Hemingway, other famous patrons of Harry's New York Bar include Sinclair Lewis, Coco Chanel, Rita Hayworth, Humphrey Bogart, and poet and playwright Brendan Behan, who stated in his memoir *Confessions of an Irish Rebel* that he worked at Harry's Bar during 1948 and 1949. In Ian Fleming's 1960 short story, "From a View to a Kill," James Bond recalls visiting the bar during his first visit to Paris at age sixteen, and it is said that George Gershwin composed *An American in Paris* in the **Ivories** piano bar in the basement of Harry's.

Brasserie Lipp
151, Boulevard Saint-Germain. Tel. (+33) 1 45 48 53 91.
Open every day 8:30–12:45 A.M.

Brasserie Lipp was opened by Léonard Lipp and his wife Pétronille on October 27, 1880. Hemingway often dined here on *cervelas* (sausages), potatoes, and beer, and the *brasserie* is featured in *A Moveable Feast*. Brasserie Lipp is where Hemingway said he could be found when he heard that Harold Loeb was roaming the streets with a gun following his portrayal of him in *The Sun Also Rises*. Frequented by poets Paul Verlaine and Guillaume Apollinaire, this sumptuous classic of La Belle Époque was redesigned in 1920 by Marcellin Cazes, who decorated the *brasserie* with murals by Léon Fargues and ceilings painted by Charly Garrey.

In 1935, Cazes established the *Prix Cazes*, a literary prize awarded each year to an author who has never been recognized for a novel, essay, biography, memoir, or collection of short stories.

Dingo American Bar and Restaurant
10, rue Delambre.

In late April of 1925, two weeks after the publication of *The Great Gatsby*, Hemingway met F. Scott Fitzgerald for the first time at the Dingo Bar. In *A Moveable Feast*, Hemingway describes Fitzgerald approaching him while he is having drinks with Lady Duff Twysden and Pat Guthrie, praising his work, and becoming drunk on a small amount of champagne. Established in 1923, the Dingo Bar was one of the few Parisian drinking establishments that was open all night. The bar was frequented by Pablo Picasso, Nancy Cunard, and Isadora Duncan, who lived across the street. Jimmie Charters, a popular barman at the Dingo, wrote *This Must Be the Place: Memoirs of Montparnasse*, which was published in 1934 and contains an introduction by Hemingway. The premises that was once home to the Dingo Bar is now occupied by Italian restaurant **Auberge de Venise**.

ABOVE: Portrait of Ernest Miller Hemingway at five months by Arnold Studios, Oak Park, Illinois, December 1899. *Courtesy of the Ernest Hemingway Collection, John F. Kennedy Presidential Library and Museum, Boston.* BELOW: Ernest Hemingway as a toddler with a wagon outside his childhood home in Oak Park, Illinois, circa 1903. *Courtesy of the Ernest Hemingway Collection, John F. Kennedy Presidential Library and Museum, Boston.*

ABOVE LEFT: Ernest Hemingway writing while on a fishing trip in Michigan, 1916. *Courtesy of the Ernest Hemingway Collection, John F. Kennedy Presidential Library and Museum, Boston. Public Domain.* ABOVE RIGHT: Grace, Marcelline, Clarence, and Ernest in front of Windemere Cottage, 1901. BELOW: Hemingway family portrait, Oak Park, Illinois, October 1903. L–R: Ursula Hemingway, Clarence Edmonds Hemingway, Ernest Hemingway, Grace Hall Hemingway, and Marcelline Hemingway. *Courtesy of the Ernest Hemingway Collection, John F. Kennedy Presidential Library and Museum, Boston.*

ABOVE LEFT: Ernest, Grace, Clarence, and Marcelline, Walloon Lake, Michigan, 1901. ABOVE RIGHT: Ernest trout fishing in Michigan, 1916. BELOW LEFT: Ernest poses with trout in Horton Bay, Michigan, 1919 or 1920. BELOW RIGHT: Ernest Hemingway wearing a fake mustache and pretending to box. Caption on verso: "Yours for clean sport, John L. Sullivan," circa 1920. *Courtesy of the Ernest Hemingway Collection, John F. Kennedy Presidential Library and Museum, Boston.*

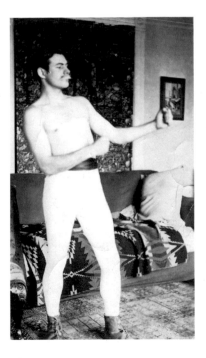

TOP LEFT: Oak Park High School light-weight football team, Oak Park, Illinois, November 1915. Ernest Hemingway is in the front row, second from right. *Courtesy of the Ernest Hemingway Collection, John F. Kennedy Presidential Library and Museum, Boston.* CENTER LEFT: Ernest Hemingway with friends in the Walloon Lake/Petoskey area, Michigan, Summer 1920. L–R: Carl Edgar, Katy Smith, Marcelline Hemingway, Bill Horne, Ernest Hemingway, and Charles Hopkins. *Courtesy of the Ernest Hemingway Collection, John F. Kennedy Presidential Library and Museum,* BOTTOM LEFT: Ernest Hemingway recuperates from wounds on the terrace of the American Red Cross Hospital, Milan, Italy, September 1918. *Courtesy of the Ernest Hemingway Collection, John F. Kennedy Presidential Library and Museum, Boston.* BOTTOM RIGHT: Agnes von Kurowsky and Ernest Hemingway, Milan, Italy, 1918. *Courtesy of the Ernest Hemingway Collection, John F. Kennedy Presidential Library and Museum, Boston.*

ABOVE: Elizabeth Hadley Richardson and Ernest Miller Hemingway on their wedding day, September 3, 1921. BELOW: Wedding of Elizabeth Hadley Richardson and Ernest Hemingway, Horton Bay, Michigan, September 3, 1921. L–R: Carol Hemingway, Ursula Hemingway, Elizabeth Hadley Richardson, Ernest Hemingway, Grace Hall Hemingway, Leicester Hemingway, Clarence Edwards Hemingway. *Courtesy of the Ernest Hemingway Collection, John F. Kennedy Presidential Library and Museum, Boston. Public Domain.*

ABOVE LEFT: Elizabeth Hadley Richardson on her wedding day in Horton Bay, Michigan, September 3, 1921. *Courtesy of the Ernest Hemingway Collection, John F. Kennedy Presidential Library and Museum, Boston.* ABOVE RIGHT: Ernest, Hadley, and Bumby, Schruns, Austria, Spring 1926. *Courtesy of the Ernest Hemingway Collection, John F. Kennedy Presidential Library and Museum, Boston.* BELOW: Portrait of Ernest Hemingway and Pauline Marie Pfeiffer, Paris, 1927. *Courtesy of the Ernest Hemingway Collection, John F. Kennedy Presidential Library and Museum, Boston.*

ABOVE LEFT: Ernest Hemingway and Hadley with the friends who would become the inspiration for the characters in *The Sun Also Rises*, Pamplona, Spain, Summer 1925. L–R: Ernest Hemingway, Harold Loeb (wearing glasses), Lady Duff Twysden (wearing hat), Hadley Richardson, Donald Ogden Stewart, and Pat Guthrie. *Courtesy of the Ernest Hemingway Collection, John F. Kennedy Presidential Library and Museum, Boston.* ABOVE RIGHT: Hemingway participating in the "amateurs" bullfight, Pamplona, Spain, 1925. *Courtesy of the Ernest Hemingway Collection, John F. Kennedy Presidential Library and Museum, Boston.* BELOW LEFT: Ernest Hemingway posing at a bullring in Madrid, Spain, 1923. *Courtesy of the Ernest Hemingway Collection, John F. Kennedy Presidential Library and Museum, Boston.* BELOW RIGHT: Ernest Hemingway with documentary filmmaker and director of *The Spanish Earth*, Joris Ivens, and two soldiers during the Spanish Civil War, circa 1937–38. *Courtesy of the Ernest Hemingway Collection, John F. Kennedy Presidential Library and Museum, Boston.*

TOP: Ernest Hemingway with Ilya Ehrenburg and Gustav Regler during the Spanish Civil War, circa 1937. *Courtesy of the Ernest Hemingway Collection, John F. Kennedy Presidential Library and Museum, Boston.* CENTER: Hemingway, Carlos Gutierrez, Josie "Sloppy Joe" Russell, and Joe Lowe aboard Russell's *Anita*, Havana Harbor, circa 1933. *Courtesy of the Ernest Hemingway Collection, John F. Kennedy Presidential Library and Museum, Boston.* BOTTOM: Hemingway boxing with an unidentified local man on a dock in Bimini, 1935. *Courtesy of the Ernest Hemingway Collection, John F. Kennedy Presidential Library and Museum, Boston.*

Ernest Hemingway during World War II, 1944. *Courtesy of the Ernest Hemingway Collection, John F. Kennedy Presidential Library and Museum, Boston.*

ABOVE: Ernest Hemingway and Pauline Pfeiffer, San Sebastián, Spain, September 1927. *Courtesy of the Ernest Hemingway Collection, John F. Kennedy Presidential Library and Museum, Boston.* BELOW: Hemingway and friends in Schruns, Austria, 1926. L–R: Frau Lent (wife of Herr Walther Lent, ski instructor), Ernest Hemingway, John Dos Passos, and Gerald Murphy. *Courtesy of the Ernest Hemingway Collection, John F. Kennedy Presidential Library and Museum, Boston.*

ABOVE: Josie Russell with Hemingway and an unidentified young man (far left) with a striped marlin, Havana Harbor, 1932. *Courtesy of the Ernest Hemingway Collection, John F. Kennedy Presidential Library and Museum, Boston.* BELOW: Hemingway at the wheel of his boat, *Pilar*, with first mate, Carlos Gutierrez, 1934. *Courtesy of the Ernest Hemingway Collection, John F. Kennedy Presidential Library and Museum, Boston.*

ABOVE: The home of Ernest Hemingway and Pauline Pfeiffer, 907 Whitehead Street, Key West. *Courtesy of the Ernest Hemingway Collection, John F. Kennedy Presidential Library and Museum, Boston.* BELOW: Ernest Hemingway in Key West, 1928. *Courtesy of the Ernest Hemingway Collection, John F. Kennedy Presidential Library and Museum, Boston.*

ABOVE: Ernest Hemingway and Pauline Pfeiffer laughing at their Key West home. *Courtesy of the Ernest Hemingway Collection, John F. Kennedy Presidential Library and Museum, Boston.* BELOW: Patrick, Ernest, and Gregory with kittens at Finca Vigía, San Francisco de Paula, Cuba, circa 1943. *Courtesy of the Ernest Hemingway Collection, John F. Kennedy Presidential Library and Museum, Boston.*

Gregory Hemingway rowing a canoe. On verso: "Giggie gets confused when he tries to row." *Courtesy of the Ernest Hemingway Collection, John F. Kennedy Presidential Library and Museum, Boston.*

ABOVE: The Hemingways with friends at La Floridita, Havana, Cuba, circa 1950s. L–R: Roberto Hererra, unidentified man, Gianfranco Ivancich, Mary Welsh Hemingway, unidentified woman, Ernest Hemingway, and Adriana Ivancich. *Courtesy of the Ernest Hemingway Collection, John F. Kennedy Presidential Library and Museum, Boston.* BELOW: Ernest Hemingway's cats, Friendless's Brother and Willy, watch a monkey outside the window of the Finca Vigía estate, San Francisco de Paula, Cuba. *Courtesy of the Ernest Hemingway Collection, John F. Kennedy Presidential Library and Museum, Boston.*

ABOVE: Patrick Hemingway and Henrietta Broyles Hemingway on the porch of their home in Tanganyika with Ernest Hemingway writing at a table inside and an unidentified man at left, circa 1953. *Courtesy of the Ernest Hemingway Collection, John F. Kennedy Presidential Library and Museum, Boston.* BELOW: Ernest Hemingway at a fishing camp in Shimoni, Kenya, with a blistered hand and other injuries he sustained from two successive plane crashes and a bushfire, 1954. *Courtesy of the Ernest Hemingway Collection, John F. Kennedy Presidential Library and Museum, Boston.*

ABOVE: Hemingway with Mount Kilimanjaro in the distance while on his second African safari, circa 1953–54. *Courtesy of the Ernest Hemingway Collection, John F. Kennedy Presidential Library and Museum, Boston.* BELOW: Ernest Hemingway in London's Dorchester Hotel during the Summer of 1944. *Courtesy of the Ernest Hemingway Collection, John F. Kennedy Presidential Library and Museum, Boston.*

TOP: Ernest Hemingway (waving), Mary Hemingway, and unidentified others in a canal taxi on Venice's Grand Canal. The Campanile di San Marco (bell tower) is in the background. *Courtesy of the Ernest Hemingway Collection, John F. Kennedy Presidential Library and Museum, Boston.* CENTER: Ernest Hemingway, Nanyuki Franchetti, and Bianca Franchetti at Harry's Bar, Venice, Italy. *Courtesy of the Ernest Hemingway Collection, John F. Kennedy Presidential Library and Museum, Boston.* BOTTOM: Ernest Hemingway, Giuseppe Cipriani, and barman Ruggero Caumo at Harry's Bar, Venice. *Courtesy of the Ernest Hemingway Collection, John F. Kennedy Presidential Library and Museum, Boston.*

ABOVE: Ernest Hemingway visits with Spanish matador, Antonio Ordóñez, at Valcargado, the Ordóñez ranch near Cádiz, Spain, 1959. *Courtesy of the Ernest Hemingway Collection, John F. Kennedy Presidential Library and Museum, Boston. Public Domain.* BELOW: Ernest Hemingway and Adamo Simón (funeral director who served as chauffeur) sitting in front of the small stone bridge in San Ildefonso, Spain, that served as the inspiration for the bridge blown up by Robert Jordan in *For Whom The Bell Tolls*, July 1953. *Courtesy of the Ernest Hemingway Collection, John F. Kennedy Presidential Library and Museum, Boston.*

ABOVE: Nancy "Slim" Hawks Hayward, Ernest Hemingway, and Lauren Bacall sitting and laughing outside a Spanish café, Summer 1959. *Courtesy of the Ernest Hemingway Collection, John F. Kennedy Presidential Library and Museum, Boston.* BELOW: Swedish Ambassador to Cuba, Per Gunnar Vilhelm Aurell, presenting the 1954 Nobel Prize in Literature to Ernest Hemingway at his Finca Vigía home, San Francisco de Paula, Cuba. *Courtesy of the Ernest Hemingway Collection, John F. Kennedy Presidential Library and Museum, Boston.*

ABOVE: Ernest Hemingway duck hunting in Idaho, October, 1941. *Courtesy of the Ernest Hemingway Collection, John F. Kennedy Presidential Library and Museum, Boston.* BELOW LEFT: Gary Cooper and Ernest Hemingway in Idaho. BELOW RIGHT: Papa with my Grandfather Gregory in Idaho.

Gregory, Ernest, and Patrick duck hunting in Idaho, October 1941. *Courtesy of the Ernest Hemingway Collection, John F. Kennedy Presidential Library and Museum, Boston.*

Ernest Hemingway and Martha Gellhorn in Sun Valley, Idaho, 1940. The forehead scar from when a skylight fell on Hemingway in Paris in 1928 is clearly visible. *Courtesy of the Ernest Hemingway Collection, John F. Kennedy Presidential Library and Museum, Boston.*

ABOVE: Ernest Hemingway (with hand raised) and Martha Gellhorn with unidentified man on horseback in Sun Valley, Idaho, 1940. *Courtesy of the Ernest Hemingway Collection, John F. Kennedy Presidential Library and Museum, Boston.* BELOW: Ernest Hemingway on a picnic with Lloyd and Tillie Arnold in Idaho, circa 1959. *Ernest Hemingway Collection, John F. Kennedy Presidential Library and Museum, Boston.*

Key West

GULF OF MEXICO

KEY WEST BRIGHT

Greene St.
Flening St.
Caroline Lin.
Margaret St.
Olivia St.
Truman Ave.
Windsor St.
Simonthon St.
Duval St.
Whitehead St.
Thomas St.

1. Casa Antigua
2. La Concha Resort
3. Capt. Tony's Saloon
4. Sloppy Joe's Bar
5. Papa's Pilar
6. Blue Heaven
7. The Ernest Hemingway Home
8. Electric Kitchen
9. Leonte Valladares Book Store
10. Basilica St. Mary Star of the Sea

5

CAYO HUESO

"The Saint-Tropez of the poor."

Imagine being greeted by a tropical breeze in the morning and a spectacular orange-pink sunset in the evening on an island surrounded by bioluminescent water that's the same temperature as the air. Streets lined with mango, coconut, Spanish lime, hibiscus, and sweet-smelling bougainvillea. Imagine waking before dawn, crossing a suspended catwalk from your wraparound porch to your writing studio, doing the thing in the world you love best, and spending the rest of the day fishing in the medicinal waters of the Gulf of Mexico. In the evening, you stroll to the local bookstore, dine on Cuban food, and drink cocktails at your favorite bar before attending a boxing match at the open-air arena a few blocks from your Spanish Colonial-style mansion. This was the life of Ernest Hemingway in Key West.

First Key West Residence of Pauline and Ernest Hemingway
314 Simonton Street.

When Pauline and Ernest first arrived in Cayo Hueso, or "Bone Key," in the spring of 1928, they didn't intend to stay. John Dos Passos had recommended the island, saying it would be a good place for ol' Hem to dry out after the cold, damp Paris winter. The Hemingways arrived on a steamship from Havana in April expecting to find a yellow Model A Ford Runabout waiting for them—a wedding present from Pauline's Uncle Gus—but the car had yet to arrive. They learned that problems with the ferry service from Miami had delayed shipment of the car, and, in order to make up for the inconvenience, the local Ford dealership, Trevor and Morris, gave the Hemingways lodgings above the garage in their own **Trev-Mor Hotel**. Although the rooms were lackluster, the accommodations were in the heart of **Old Town**—near **Duval Street** and **Mallory Square**—and Ernest got back to work immediately on *A Farewell to Arms*.

The building at 314 Simonton was constructed in 1919 and was one of Key West's first hotels. Its thirteen-inch-thick walls were built with bricks from nearby **Fort Zachary Taylor**, and it was marketed as the first fireproof hotel. Remodeled a few decades after Ernest and Pauline's stay, for years it housed **Casa Antigua** and the Pelican Poop Gift Shop. In 2011, I had the honor of attending a party at Casa Antigua as part of the **Hemingway Days Festival**. The event was held inside the atrium entrance and second-floor apartment where Pauline and Ernest were guests in 1928. There's something enchanting about being in a place where your ancestors have been. As I played the piano, I felt as though I were at a soirée when Key West was still the last stop on Henry Flagler's Overseas Railroad, when Duval Street was filled with Cuban cafés, and ripe Key limes dotted its brick streets. From the wraparound balcony I watched party-goers enjoying hors d'oeuvres around the fountain, the brick and limestone walls cooling the evening air. If someone had told me it was 1928, I wouldn't have been surprised.

Ernest Hemingway Home and Museum

907 Whitehead Street. Tel. (305) 294-1136.

Open every day 9:30 A.M.*–4:30* P.M.

Almost as soon as Pauline and Ernest arrived in Key West they met Charles and Lorine Thompson, two of the most prominent members of the community. Charles was a charter boat captain who, along with his two brothers, owned the local marina—Thompson's Docks—as well as several other businesses, including a cigar factory, a fish processing company, a marine hardware and tackle shop, a guava jelly factory, and a turtle fishing and canning business. The day after Hemingway met Charles Thompson they went fishing in the Gulf of Mexico on Thompson's eighteen-foot powerboat. Soon the Hemingways were invited to dine on black beans, yellow rice, conch meat salad, green turtle steak, and Cuban bread at the Thompsons' home. When their car was ready and they were preparing to leave the island, they asked Lorine to find them a house for the following winter, but she didn't think they meant it. But the Hemingways did return—twice over the next two years—and by 1930 were in the market for a conch house of their own. Lorine found them a run-down, nearly eighty-year-old Spanish Colonial on an acre and a half of land.

The Hemingway House—or the "H-House," as my family calls it—was built in 1851 by marine architect and salvage wrecker, Asa Tift. The house was constructed from limestone quarried on-site, which left a hole that was used to create the first basement in Key West; Ernest used it as a wine cellar. White pine for the house was shipped from Tift's land in Tifton, Georgia, a town he'd helped found. In 1931, Pauline's Uncle Gus purchased the mansion at 907 Whitehead Street as a wedding gift for $8,000. Ernest, Pauline, Patrick, and his new brother, Gregory, moved in just before Christmas. Gregory had been born on November 12 by cesarean section, and with Pauline still recovering on their first Christmas in the new home, a tree was erected at the foot of her bed. Ernest loved the new house and wrote to Waldo Peirce that it reminded him of paintings by Utrillo and of his favorite, Miró's *The Farm*.

The Hemingway Home and Museum is located on the southern part of the island, across from the **Key West Lighthouse**. It stands at an elevation of sixteen feet above sea level and is the second-highest site on the island. It was one of the first houses to have indoor plumbing, and the first to have an upstairs bathroom with running water. Pauline's jade toiletry bottles still adorned the sink when I was a kid, and I would sneak upstairs to admire them. The Hemingway House has a built-in fireplace and an outdoor swimming pool, also a first on the island. Pauline paid $20,000 to have the pool installed as a surprise gift for Ernest upon his return from covering the Spanish Civil War in 1938. He disapproved of the exorbitant cost of the pool, and legend has it that he threw a penny on the ground, telling Pauline that she might as well have his last cent. Pauline had the penny cemented into the ground next to the pool and covered it in glass, where it remains. When I was a kid, the face of the penny was still distinguishable, but it has greened with age.

Above the poolhouse is the studio where Ernest wrote two of his most famous short stories, "The Snows of Kilimanjaro" and "The Short Happy Life of Francis Macomber," as well as *To Have and Have Not* and the non-fiction *Green Hills of Africa*. Cabinetmaker and handyman, Toby Bruce, came from Pauline's hometown of Piggott, Arkansas, to build the studio's bookshelves, repair cracks in the plaster, and paint the room a seafoam green. Bruce found a cigar maker's chair with a leather seat and back to serve as Hemingway's writing chair. An old Royal typewriter, which may have been Hemingway's, sits atop his writing desk, but in truth he usually wrote in pencil standing up. He began work as early as five in the morning, a habit carried over from his time in Paris.

When Pauline and Ernest lived in the house, there was a catwalk installed to provide easy access from the second-floor veranda to Ernest's studio. He could wake up, have his coffee, and walk barefoot to work without having to go downstairs. The walkway was blown down in the hurricane of 1935 and never reconstructed, but the wires that connected it are still visible on the railing, painted over with black paint. I spent time in the studio growing up, and there is an energy there, an air that something important has happened, something true, as Ernest might have said. The room holds several of Ernest's trophies from Africa, as well as some of his many books—there are more in the upstairs hallway of the main house—and they have the feel and smell of a different time. When I was a kid, I loved to look at their muted, many-colored covers and marvel at how much my great-grandfather had read.

On September 2, 1935, the now infamous Labor Day hurricane was charging toward the Florida Keys. Hemingway was busy preparing the house on Whitehead Street and the *Pilar*, which was docked in the harbor of the Key West naval base. Hemingway had moored the boat in what he felt was the safest part of the base, making her fast with heavy rope. He brought his sons' toys in from the garden as well as the outdoor furniture, and nailed the green shutters tight to the window frames. That night, the winds came and the spinning clouds dumped buckets of rain. Anxious to check on the *Pilar*, he went out into the storm, and when his car wouldn't start, he ran to the base. Hemingway watched over the *Pilar* in the harbor until around five A.M. when the eerie winds of the hurricane finally died down. The island was a mass of downed trees and was papered with palm fronds. Hemingway, his boat, and his family had all made it through the monster hurricane. After a hard sleep, Hemingway, Capt. Bra Saunders, and machinist J. B. Sullivan went up the Keys to survey the devastation. What they saw was almost unbelievable. The brunt of the storm had barely missed Key West, but the Upper Keys and Islamorada had been torn apart. Bodies hung from tree limbs and were caught in the mangroves. Hemingway had not seen so many dead since the war.

The Hemingways' former home is decorated with antiques and artifacts acquired by Pauline and Ernest on their many trips, complemented by chandeliers made of hand-blown Venetian glass. Another notable feature of the property is a urinal that Ernest took from Sloppy Joe's Bar that has been converted into a drinking fountain for the dozens of cats who inhabit the grounds. Hemingway said that he'd spent so much money at the bar over the years that he had a right to take the urinal. He was bothered when his home was put on the list of sites for tourists to see, so in 1937 Toby Bruce built a brick wall around the property.

The house on Whitehead Street would serve as Hemingway's main residence until 1940, when he left for Cuba. Pauline and Ernest were divorced on November 4, 1940, but Pauline lived in the house on and off until her passing in 1951, and Ernest retained title to it for the rest of his life. His widow, Mary, sold it to Bernice Dixon, who founded the Ernest Hemingway Home and Museum. When I first came to the Keys with my mom as a kid, we stayed in one of the three cabins that Ms. Dixon, as we called her, owned on Little Torch Key, twenty-eight miles north of Key West. It was so rural back then that we didn't even have mail service and had to get a post office box on another island. Sometimes we would visit Ms. Dixon and her sisters at their Key West jewelry store, Beachcomber Jewelers, in the Searstown Shopping Center in what was then referred to as "New Town." Ms. Dixon always made us feel welcome at Papa's house.

Land's End Marina (formerly Thompson's Docks) and Turtle Kraals
Key West Bight, 201 William Street.

The Thompson family owned a fleet of fishing boats docked at their marina, and it was on one of these that Hemingway first fished the turquoise waters off Key West. In 1934, he acquired his own thirty-eight-foot craft from the Wheeler Shipyard in Brooklyn and called it *Pilar*, his nickname for Pauline ("Pilar" is also the name of a Catholic bullfighting shrine in Zaragoza, Spain). When I was a kid, the marina's turtle kraals held enormous loggerhead turtles, most at least eighty years old. Since 1980 the site has been home to a Caribbean seafood restaurant and bar called Turtle Kraals.

Growing up, I had the good fortune to go fishing in the Gulf Stream, and we always departed from Land's End Marina. I used to fantasize about becoming a first mate on one of the charter boats, getting to the marina at sunrise to prepare the boat and cut up the bait, helping to navigate, putting out the lines and throwing the chum into the water, getting to know the sea as my great-grandfather had. To this day, the memories of a day of fishing with my family are some of the fondest of my life. When I was a teenager, my mom went to Bimini in search of what many consider the greatest billfish, the blue marlin. Hemingway paid tribute to this great fish in *The Old Man and the Sea*. I wasn't there to witness her bring in two of these noble fish in one day—one two hundred and fifty pounds, the other five hundred—but I remember the next time I saw her, her arm was swollen to the size of her thigh and cradled in an ACE bandage sling. I was entranced by a photograph of her in the fighting chair, wet towel on her head, straddling the enormous rod and reel.

La Concha Hotel & Spa (formerly the Colonial Hotel)
430 Duval Street. Tel. (305) 296-2991.

When Pauline and Ernest sailed into Key West in the spring of 1928, the first sign of civilization they spotted was the seven-story La Concha Hotel & Spa, the tallest building in Key West. In *To Have and Have Not*, Hemingway describes the boat masts sticking up from the blue-green water of the harbor, and what was then the Colonial Hotel standing out above the conch houses.

The La Concha Hotel & Spa is a rectangular structure with green duckbill awnings on each of its many windows. The lobby has a straight-forward elegance with potted palms, marble floors, and an antique paddle fan pushing through the tropical air. The top floor of the La Concha has the best views on the island, and the outdoor swimming pool is especially pleasant at dusk. Pauline and Ernest frequently booked rooms for their friends and family at the Colonial Hotel, as it was clean and comfortable and the rates—$1–2 per night—were a steal.

Capt. Tony's Saloon (original location of Sloppy Joe's Bar; formerly the Duval Club and The Blind Pig)
428 Greene Street. Tel. (305) 294-1838.
Open every day 10–2 A.M.

When Hemingway arrived in Key West the year before the Great Depression began, it was far from the tourist destination it is today. A poverty-stricken, backwater town only accessible by railway or boat, every speakeasy and diner was "where the locals hang out," since locals were all there were.

Capt. Tony's Saloon is one of those rare places on the island that has never lost its down-to-earth charm. The wood-frame building, constructed in 1852, was first an ice house that doubled as the city morgue. In the 1890s, the building was used as a wireless telegraph station, most famously in 1898 to report the destruction of the battleship *Maine* in Havana Harbor. The message came from Havana to Key West, and from there went around the world. In 1912, the building became a cigar factory. These days it's painted canary yellow and is the kind of place where you can stop in for a game of pool and feel right at home.

Before the repeal of Prohibition in December of 1933, Hemingway's friend and fishing buddy, Josie Russell, ran a charter boat/rum-running operation and corresponding speakeasy on Front Street. When alcohol once again became legal, Russell opened a legitimate watering hole at 428 Greene Street. The new bar, formerly a speakeasy called The Blind Pig, was three times the size of his Front Street operation and with the added benefit, some would say, of being legal. Though the ability to run a legal saloon made Russel less available to fish with Hemingway, it was the beginning of Sloppy Joe's, the most famous bar in Key West—where Hemingway spent many an evening from 1933 to 1937.

In December of 1936, Hemingway was sitting on a stool at Sloppy Joe's talking with Russell when a young woman, her mother, and her brother walked in. They'd been vacationing in Miami, but had decided to venture further south, and had boarded a bus to come down to the Keys. Hemingway bought them drinks and took them around the island in his car. The young woman was Martha Gellhorn and, like Hemingway, she was a midwestern writer. Gellhorn already had one novel and a collection of short stories to her credit, and was working on a third book. She stayed on in Key West for two weeks after her mother and brother left, getting to know Ernest and the island better, much to Pauline's chagrin.

Sloppy Joe's was a rowdy saloon with no front door because it never closed. Hemingway enjoyed watching the "types" who came in to drink after a day of fishing, and the drinks were affordable—a dollar bought ten beers, gin was ten cents, and whiskey was fifteen cents. A scotch and soda—Ernest's drink of choice and the most expensive drink in the place—was thirty-five cents for the average customer or a quarter for Ernest, who preferred Haig & Haig Pinch whiskey. The uniform for Russel and his bartenders was blue twill pants and a white shirt with a tie; Russel sported a bow tie.

When Russell's landlord, Isaac Wolkowsky, informed Russell that he planned to raise his rent from $3 to $4 per week beginning on May 5, 1937, Russell decided to change the location of his bar. In preparation for the relocation of Sloppy Joe's, Russell purchased the old Victoria Restaurant building on the southeast corner of Greene and Duval Streets for $2,500. Russel's lease with Wolkowsky stated that he would have to leave all the fixtures he'd added in his four years of operating the bar on Greene Street, so as soon as his lease expired at midnight, Russell and his customers moved all of the furniture and appointments—including the bar itself—half a block to **201 Duval Street**, where the bar sits today. Unfortunately, Hemingway was in Spain at the time and had to hear about the excitement after the fact.

In 1958, former shrimper, charter boat captain, and gunrunner Tony Tarracino purchased the building on Greene Street that had first housed Sloppy Joe's, and started Capt. Tony's Saloon. In the years to follow, Capt. Tony's was patronized by many celebrities, and was where Jimmy Buffett got his start. A tradition at Capt. Tony's is that a bar stool is added with the name of any celebrity who visits. There are bar stools for Hemingway, Truman Capote, Shel Silverstein, John Prine, John F. Kennedy, Harry Truman, and Jimmy Buffett, among others. In the early 1970s, Capt. Tony paid Buffett to play in tequila instead of cash, and Buffett immortalized Capt. Tony and his bar in the song, "Last Mango in Paris."

A goliath grouper caught by Capt. Tony himself is perched above the bar's sign, and it is said that if you throw a quarter into its mouth, you'll have good luck while on the island. Capt. Tony sold his saloon in 1989, the year he was elected Mayor of Key West. He continued to greet customers and fans at the bar most Thursdays until his death in 2008 at the age of 91.

Sloppy Joe's Bar
201 Duval Street. Tel. (305) 294-5717.
Open every day 9–4 A.M.

The head bartender at the new incarnation of Sloppy Joe's Bar on Duval Street during Hemingway's time was Big Al Skinner, who also served as bouncer. In a 1933 mural by artist Erik Smith—which is still displayed in the bar—Russell is portrayed with Skinner and Hemingway. There's a back room at Sloppy Joe's that in Hemingway's day was called the Club Room, where Hemingway and his friends gambled.

In June of 1941, shortly before Hemingway was to attend a heavyweight championship fight between Joe Louis and Billy Conn at Madison Square Garden with Toby Bruce, Betty Moreno—Bruce's future wife—and Josie Russell, Russell died suddenly following minor surgery in Havana. Sloppy Joe's was a second home to Hemingway, and when he moved to Cuba he put some of his personal effects in the house next door to the bar for safekeeping. The house was later sold and Hemingway's things put in Sloppy Joe's back storage room until 1962, when Mary donated many of them to the bar.

When my mother and I arrived in Key West in the late 1970s, Sloppy Joe's was one of the first places we went. While she met with friends at the open-air bar, I was set up with a stack of quarters in front of the Phoenix video game. I played it for hours, jamming in quarter after quarter, and soon entered my initials in the list of top-ten score holders. I'm sure they're still there. Sloppy Joe's has always embodied the raucousness and community spirit of Duval Street and Key West. It's a genuine place that smells of beer, sweat, and good memories, especially those created by the king of all celebrity look-alike competitions, the **Hemingway Look-Alike Contest**, which the bar has hosted each July since 1980. Back then there was also a beer drinking contest and an armwrestling competition, which some of my family members won fair and square.

Blue Heaven
729 Thomas Street. Tel. (305) 296-8666.
Open every day 8 A.M.*–10:30* P.M.

Hemingway loved trying to best his friends and new acquaintances with his fists—in 1936 he knocked out the decades-older but stout poet Wallace Stevens for making disparaging remarks about his writing while Stevens was vacationing in Key West with Robert Frost. Though Hemingway may not have had the skills to become a prize fighter, he was knowledgeable about boxing, loved to spar, and refereed locals matches at 729 Thomas Street—lovingly referred to in the 1930s as the **Key West Arena**. Two of the fighters Hemingway sparred with at the Key West Arena—Kermit "Shine" Forbes and "Iron Baby" Roberts—also boxed with him in a backyard ring at his home on Whitehead Street for fifty cents a round. I had the pleasure of meeting both Forbes and Roberts and watching them referee and judge a boxing match in a ring set up on the grounds of the Hemingway House during the Hemingway Days Festival many years ago.

Blue Heaven has been many things over the years—dance hall, bordello, playhouse, restaurant, and hotel. It has hosted cock fighting, gambling, poker tournaments, and Friday night boxing. Though it's now strictly a restaurant, an atmosphere of enchantment pervades the grounds, with roosters roaming among the diners under Spanish lime trees and coconut palms. Made of Dade County Pine wood, Blue Heaven is as authentic Key West as one can find. Offering a traditional Caribbean menu, the restaurant employs slate pool table tops from a time when the downstairs served as a billiards hall. Blue Heaven retains the ambience Hemingway would have felt while refereeing boxing matches in the sultry, cigar-smoke-filled nights nearly a century ago.

Once the Hemingways were established in Key West, Ernest was anxious to introduce some of his old friends to the island he called "The St. Tropez of the poor."[1] The first to be invited were Mike Strater, Waldo "Don Pico" Peirce, Bill Smith, and John Dos Passos. When his friends arrived, Ernest booked them into the **Overseas Hotel** at 917 Fleming Street, where the rooms were only $1 per day. Around town, Ernest and his friends were known as "Hemingway's Mob." They frequented the **Electric Kitchen** for breakfast or lunch, swam at the **Navy Yard**, strolled down to **Valladares Book Store**, and frequently had dinner at **Delmonico's** or **Ramon's** on Duval Street.

Electric Kitchen
830 Fleming Street.

This down-to-earth greasy spoon, owned and operated by Mrs. Rhoda Baker, or "Rutabega,"[2] was a frequent hangout of Hemingway's Mob. "In 1935, the Electric Kitchen offered 'club breakfast,' 20 cents to 45 cents; luncheon and dinner, 30 to 50 cents."[3] Electric Kitchen was a sparse operation with a bare lightbulb hanging from its ceiling. The wooden corner building that once housed the restaurant is still there, though sadly one can no longer get one of their affordable homestyle meals. When I was growing up, the beloved Duval Street Cuban café, **El Cacique**—now located at 3100 Flagler Avenue—offered eggs, grits, and Cuban toast for ninety-nine cents, harkening back to the days when locals could get their first meal of the day for a similarly modest price.

Leonte Valladares Book Store
517 Fleming Street.

Following breakfast at Electric Kitchen and a visit to the Thompsons for lunch, Hemingway and his Mob often strolled five blocks down Fleming Street to Valladares Book Store, located in a small wooden building that was formerly a fishermen's café. The store was full of magazines, paperbacks, and hardcover books. Hemingway persuaded thirty-year-old Cuban owner, Leonte Valladares, to stock more hardcovers, and in turn donated copies of *The Sun Also Rises* and *Men Without Women*, autographing them so that Valladares could charge a dollar extra. Hemingway subscribed to several newspapers through Valladares, which were delivered by Valladares' son, Arthur. The first time Arthur saw Ernest, he thought he was poor because he was "wearing moccasins and a pair of shorts held up with a rope."[4]

Growing up, I worked summers at a bookstore two doors down from the former location of Valladares Book Store, **Key West Island Books**. This lovely bookshop carries a diverse assortment of fiction and nonfiction, including a special section dedicated to books written by the many authors who have called Key West home—Ann Beattie, Shel Silverstein, Tennessee Williams, Annie Dillard, Robert Frost, Ralph Ellison, John Dos Passos, Elizabeth Bishop, and Judy Blume (who currently owns **Books and Books** with her husband at the **Studios of Key West**, 533 Eaton Street). It wasn't unusual for local writers like Silverstein or mystery author John Leslie to pop in to Key West Island Books for a chat, and the store had many festive book signings with authors like James Dickey, John Updike, and Jim Harrison. The island's rich literary history was an inspiration to me growing up, and I wrote some of my first fiction while manning the store's counter (with then-owner John Boisonault occasionally coming out of his office in the Rare Book Room to ask, rhetorically, "You wanna help some customers here?").

The Basilica of Saint Mary, Star of the Sea
1010 Windsor Lane. Tel. (305) 294-1018.

When Ernest married Pauline he converted to Catholicism, and The Basilica of Saint Mary, Star of the Sea is where they attended services while living in Key West. The church was built in 1905 and is one of the oldest Catholic parishes in the state of Florida. Its exterior reflects the American Victorian style, as well as the Early Renaissance Revival style. The sanctuary has beautiful blue and gold accents, as well as a stained glass window depicting the church's patroness. According to Toby Bruce's wife, Betty, Ernest was generous to Saint Mary, Star of the Sea, donating an altar to the church.

Papa's Pilar Rum Distillery, Hemingway Rum Company
201 Simonton Street. Tel. (305) 414-8754.
Open Mon.–Sat. 10 A.M.–6 P.M.; Sun. 11 A.M.–6 P.M.

Today "Papa" Hemingway, as he was affectionately called by Key West locals, has a rum named after him called Papa's Pilar. The distillery is located at 201 Simonton Street, on the corner of Simonton and Greene. The friendly staff offers guided tours each day for $10 per person.

From the time Hemingway was introduced to Key West in 1928 until he left in 1939 was a golden period. He was doing what he loved best—rising early to write and getting plenty of sun, fresh air, and time in and on the sea. He was an integral part of the Key West community—drinking with the locals at Sloppy Joe's, refereeing boxing matches at Blue Heaven, and attending cockfights in Bahama Village. He was at ease in Key West in the days before the chain hotels, tours, or even a road connecting it to the mainland. It was a world all its own—the Conch Republic—where Hemingway came to feel at home in his own country.

North Bimini

East Bimini

South Bimini

ATLANTIC OCEAN

Bimini

1. The Compleat Angler Hotel ruins
2. Cat Cay Island, Bahamas
3. Lerner Anchorage
4. Bimini Big Game Club
5. Alice Town
6. End of the World Saloon
7. The Fountain of Youth
8. The Healing Hole
9. Snorkeling to the SS Sapona shipwrek
10. Martin Luther King, Jr. Memorial
11. The Bimini Museum & Heritage Center
12. The Dolphin House Museum

6

BIMINI

"This summer they had experienced happiness for a month now and, already, in the nights, he was lonely for it before it had ever gone away."

—Ernest Hemingway, *Islands in the Stream*

There's nothing like standing on the edge of the tide at two A.M. in your bare feet—air barely cooler than your skin, the dark Gulf Stream as warm as bathwater. If you're looking to alter your perspective, the three islands in this book—Key West, Bimini, and Cuba—should top your list. Of these three, there's no question that Bimini, a place

Hemingway described as "the End of the World,"[1] provides the purest environment for a sea change.

I first came to know the alchemy of the western Atlantic Ocean, made temperate by the Gulf Stream, when I was eight years old. Living on a small island in the Florida Keys, my only friends were a horseshoe crab, a blue heron, and two wild dolphins named Dahl and Sewa who came twice a day to **Dolphin Marina** to be hand-fed buckets of fish. We spent days on the water catching snapper and grouper for supper, throwing back the slick *mahi-mahi* after watching the sun accordion back and forth over their rainbow scales. The biggest fish I ever caught was a three-and-a-half-foot barracuda who flew out of the water several times while I was bringing her in to be measured and released. I watched as a stingray we'd accidentally hooked slid back into the blue-green water and glided away with the floating strokes of an elastic bird.

I grew up fishing for trout that my mother would wrap in bacon and fry in the kitchenettes of various motels on the banks of rivers from Washington State to Florida. When we reached the Keys, I spent most of my time outside our three-room cabin, less than two hundred yards from the water. At night I could hear it splashing against the sea wall and rolling in and out of the tiny lagoon that housed an adolescent barracuda who hung pencil-straight in the clear water. When the variation in temperature from dawn to midnight is only ten degrees, the night becomes friendlier and there's extra energy to be found at first light.

The Bahamas, an archipelago scattered to the east-southeast of Florida's mainland, is made up of more than two thousand rocks and cays and seven hundred islands, of which Bimini is the westernmost. The first known native peoples to call Bimini home were the Ciboney, who were enslaved by the Lucayans when they invaded the islands ("Bimini" comes from the Lucayan word meaning "two islands"). Christopher Columbus landed in the Bahamas in 1492, opening the island chain to the raw grip of global trade, as well as to the enslaving of the Lucayans by the Spanish. The Fountain of Youth legend originated with the Lucayans, who had discovered a freshwater spring in Bimini that they believed had healing powers. The first official—albeit temporary—English settlement of Bimini was by William Sayle in 1646. Two decades later, plantations were introduced, along with the slave labor that would dominate the islands for more than 150 years. At the time, piracy was *de rigueur* in the Bahamas, with Blackbeard living there until 1717. In 1718, the Bahamas became a British colony, and thanks to the first Royal Governor of the Bahamas, Woodes Rogers, who discouraged the area's pirates, swashbuckling activities were banished to legend by 1730. Slavery was abolished in the British Empire in 1834, causing economic collapse in the Bahamas. In the mid-1800s, **Alice Town** on **North Bimini** was established by a group of Bahamian shipwreck salvagers, and the island became a hub for salvaging. A fabled shipwreck tower was constructed where salvagers would lie in wait for the ill-fated ships that ran aground in the shallow waters surrounding the island.

In 1919, Albert Burns "Pappy" Chalk began his infamous single-engine charter plane service from Miami to Bimini. In 1920, Prohibition began in the United States, and the era of rum-running followed—a profitable and somewhat glamorous venture that offset Bimini's depressed economy. Rumrunner Bruce Bethel bought the World War I ship SS *Sapona* in 1924 to store liquor, and, after it ran aground, attempted to turn it into a nightclub. The ship was abandoned after being seriously damaged in the hurricane of 1926. During the mid-1930s, Hemingway would have seen the ghostly silhouette of its rusting hull just offshore, haunting the horizon.

Hemingway heard about the phenomenally big fish to be found just off the coast of Bimini through murmurings from wealthy and adventurous sporting people who'd begun going there to fish in the 1920s. Of these, Zane Grey—a writer and record-setting sports fisherman—was arguably the most influential. Grey had been invited to Bimini by Van Campen Heilner, the first nonnative sports fisherman to devote himself to fishing the area's deep waters brimming with giant gamefish. Heilner had first arrived in Bimini on a yacht in 1920 and had pitched a tent at **Paradise Point**. So taken had he been with the pristine island and waters that he built the first concrete house on Bimini in 1924. In the second edition (1953) of his classic work, *Salt Water Fishing*—for which Hemingway wrote a preface—Heilner writes that he'd been seeking peace and solitude when he found Bimini, and wanted to preserve the unspoiled nature of the island. Once he'd discovered the big marlin that ran in the Gulf Stream just offshore, he'd been torn between a desire to tell his friends and wanting to preserve the anonymity of the island and its bounty.

In mid-April of 1935, Hemingway made his first trip to Bimini aboard the *Pilar*. It had been the fishing, warm nights, and slow pace of island living that had first drawn him to Key West in 1928, and Bimini looked like the new frontier with even bigger fish. Accompanying Hemingway on his first successful trip to the anglers' paradise were Charles Thompson, John Dos Passos, and his wife Katy. They were stunned by the empty white sand beaches, spectacular fishing, tepid water, and relaxed atmosphere.

From 1935 to 1937, Hemingway crossed the Gulf from Key West to Bimini numerous times in the *Pilar*. He took Pauline and the boys out fishing, boxed with locals on the docks, and worked on *To Have and Have Not*. During his extended stays, he often slept on the deck of the *Pilar*, but sometimes lived in the brand new **Compleat Angler Hotel** on Bimini's narrow, four-mile-long North Island.

Compleat Angler Hotel ruins
Queens Highway, Alice Town, North Bimini.

The twelve-room Compleat Angler Hotel was built in 1935 by Helen Duncombe and her husband Henry, a former Bimini British colonial administrator. Helen Duncombe had been inspired to build the hotel by Mike Lerner, who was convinced that sport fishing would bring clientele to the island. The design of the Compleat Angler was modeled after the inns of Kent, England, where Duncombe had spent her childhood. The wood used to build the hotel was taken from an old rum-running ship appropriately named *Dreamland*. Located in the center of Alice Town on the long, slender island of North Bimini, the Compleat Angler had live music, food, and a lively bar. Hemingway wrote a good portion of *To Have and Have Not* at the hotel, and described it in *Islands in the Stream*, saying it felt like a ship with a view of the sea on all sides and a good cross-breeze on hot nights.

My uncle, John Hemingway, who stayed at the Compleat Angler many times, had this to say about the historic hotel:

For my father there was never any question about staying at the Compleat Angler so long as Helen Duncombe owned the hotel. She and her husband Henry had built the inn in 1935 and while other places might have had swimming pools, or marinas or fancy restaurants, nothing could compete with my father's childhood memories. Whenever possible he took me to the same room where he and his father had slept. It was up on the second floor and had a view of the Blue Water Marina across the street. It was small by today's standards, with two single beds and an ancient, wood burning stove in the center. The stove was there for heating, as it could get cold in the winter. When I was eight I remember asking my dad about the stove and he said that I should never touch it during a storm. Years back, when he was a year or two younger than I was then he'd been sitting on my bed and my grandfather was on the other side of the room near the door. There was thunder outside and heavy rain and my father had made the mistake of walking to the stove and touching it to see how hot it could get when a lightning bolt connected with the hotel and threw him back against the wall. It knocked him unconscious and he said that Ernest had picked him up and carried him out into the rain to find a doctor.

Henry Duncombe passed away in 1949. Helen continued as proprietor until her retirement in 1973, when she sold the Compleat Angler to the Brown family. Over the years, the walls of the inn became a shrine to Hemingway with photographs and mementoes. Sadly, the Compleat Angler was destroyed by fire in 2006, during which owner Julian Brown lost his life after helping a guest to safety.

Alice Town
North Bimini.

Established in 1848, Alice Town is a fishing and tourist settlement on North Bimini with two parallel main roads: Kings Highway and Queens

Highway. Many of Bimini's residents live in neighboring **Bailey Town**. The colorful Bahamian buildings that house the bars, restaurants, and shops of Alice Town sit cheerfully against the background of blue sky and blue-green water. Although there are no golf courses, there are plenty of golf carts, which are the preferred mode of transportation other than walking. While strolling the streets of Alice Town in flip-flops, picture Hemingway—pre-golf cart traffic—doing the same after a morning of writing. When one is used to living on the mainland, Alice Town does feel like the end of the world.

During his first summer in Bimini, Hemingway wrote some of his impressions in a July 10, 1935, letter to Sara Murphy:

> You would love this place Sara. It's in the middle of the Gulf Stream and every breeze is a cool one. The water is so clear you think you will strike bottom when you have 10 fathoms under your keel. There is every kind of fish . . . There is a pretty good hotel and we have a room there now because there have been rain squalls at night lately and so I cant [*sic*] sleep on the roof of the boat.
>
> You can catch snappers, tarpon, and 25 kinds of small fish right from the dock here. About 400 people live in the town. Mostly turtling boats and spongers.[2]

Hemingway's love for the waters of the Gulf Stream is evident in the three novels he wrote set in Key West, Bimini, and Cuba—*To Have and Have Not*, *Islands in the Stream*, and *The Old Man and the Sea*. As he had in Key West, Hemingway rose early and generally finished his work by midday with the happy prospect of boundless fishing in the afternoon. Bimini's spectacular fishing is due to the Gulf Stream running just offshore, and its beaches provided hours of effortless entertainment for Bumby, Patrick, and Gregory. In Ernest's letter to Sara Murphy he describes the "perfectly safe seven mile long surf bathing clear sand beach at the back door. Have built a cabaña on the beach out of thatched palms. No insects there and the water is absolutely clear Gulf Stream and always cool but never cold."[3]

Hemingway was a correspondent for *Esquire* while in Bimini, writing articles about his exploits on the island. His July 1935 article, "The President Vanquishes: A Bimini Letter," indicates that, while the climate may have been good for his writing, Bimini's natural distractions sometimes made him nocturnal: "The article opens with a lovely image of Hemingway writing the piece from atop the *Pilar* under a huge moon in the middle of the night as his guests slept below."[4]

Bimini is known as the birthplace of big-game fishing, and it was during the mid-1930s that the ascertaining and keeping of records of the weights of fish began. While Hemingway maintained—possibly out of a premeditated humility in case he didn't catch the biggest fish—that he fished for fun and not to break records, he did like to be a pioneer. On May 21, 1935, he succeeded in landing the first unmutilated giant bluefin tuna on rod and reel, and the following day brought in an even bigger specimen. Hemingway sent fellow sport fisherman Baron Bror von Blixen-Finecke a telegram letting him know that it had taken him seventy minutes to boat the colossal 381-pound bluefin—the world record for which has since climbed to nearly fifteen hundred pounds. The report of Hemingway's feat was big news to anglers all over the world. Hemingway had first observed giant bluefin tuna on his honeymoon with Hadley off the coast of Spain in 1921, and subsequently read about them in the 1927 book, *Tales of Swordfish and Tuna,* by Zane Grey. To bring the goliaths up to the transom's wooden rollers unscathed, Hemingway would gun the engine of the *Pilar* in reverse to outrun opportunistic sharks. He also pioneered the technique of pumping his rod while reeling in the slack to minimize line breakage, one of the earliest tricks I learned as a kid.

Although Hemingway loved catching the biggest fish, he did believe in making it a fair fight, and felt that the type of rod and tackle should be matched to the size and type of fish the angler intended to catch. In "The Great Blue River," an article for *Holiday* magazine, Hemingway wrote: "There is tackle made now, and there are fishing guides expert in ways of cheating with it, by which anybody who can walk up three flights of stairs, carrying a quart bottle of milk in each hand, can catch gamefish over 500 pounds without even having to sweat much."[5]

In May of 1935, Hemingway and Mike Strater were fishing off Bimini when Strater hooked a marlin in the neighborhood of a thousand pounds.

Hemingway took out the Thompson submachine gun he'd convinced fisherman William B. Leeds to part with earlier that month, and started shooting the sharks that were making a feeding frenzy of Strater's catch. After Strater's half-ton marlin was brought in apple-cored—though still weighing five hundred pounds—Strater was convinced that the blood in the water from the dead sharks had led directly to the mutilation of his fish. Frustrating as it was for Strater, the incident may have been an important revelation for the novella that would win Hemingway the Pulitzer Prize for Fiction in 1953.

Lerner Anchorage (now the Blue Water Resort's Anchorage Restaurant & Bar)

Queens Highway, Alice Town, North Bimini. Tel. (242) 347-3166.
Open every day except Tues., 6–10 P.M.

On his first trip to Bimini, Hemingway met Philadelphia native Mike Lerner, a "wildly successful New York businessman and co-founder of the Lerner Shops that eventually became the massive retail chain New York & Company."[6] Lerner and his wife Helen, both skilled anglers, were first invited to Bimini to fish for giant bluefin in 1933 by Heilner. So taken were they with the magic of the island that they built what would become the epicenter of the big game fishing universe, the Lerner Anchorage. Constructed in 1935, the compound became a gathering place for the world's best anglers to meet and swap fishing techniques and stories. Mike Lerner dedicated his life to fishing and to the scientific study of fish, and in 1948 built the Lerner Marine Laboratory—a research station on North Bimini—to assist the scientists of the American Museum of Natural History (AMNH) in their research. Lerner joined the AMNH on expeditions that contributed to the knowledge of several species of saltwater game fish. Lerner and Hemingway shared the goal of developing a universal set of rules for big game fishing, including a system for recording world record catches. From their desire to organize the sport, the International Game Fish Association (IGFA) was born in 1939. Lerner made Hemingway vice president the following year—a position he held for the rest of his life. The Lerner Marine Laboratory closed in 1975.

Located on the original Lerner Anchorage property, the Blue Water Resort's Anchorage Restaurant & Bar offers Bahamian and American cuisine, including sandwiches and seafood specials like curry-stuffed lobster tail. The Anchorage Restaurant has been family-owned by Biminites Betty Sherman and her children for more than forty years. Enjoy the beautiful sunset from a table overlooking **Radio Beach** on a historic site from the pioneering days of big-game fishing.

Cat Cay Island
The Bahamas.

When Hemingway wasn't sleeping on the *Pilar*, at the Lerner Anchorage, or at the Compleat Angler, he could likely be found on Cat Cay, a private island where several of his wealthy friends owned homes. Nicknamed "Tuna Fish Alley" for its reputation of being a hotbed of giant bluefin tuna, Cat Cay is owned by members of the Cat Cay Yacht Club. Admittance for non-members is restricted to the 108-slip marina, which is home to the **Nauticat Restaurant and Lounge**. The island sits fifty nautical miles from Miami and is accessible by water via Gun Cay Cut from the Florida Straits. Island Air Charters offers flights from Ft. Lauderdale: 750 SW 34th Street, unit 106/108; tel. (800) 444-9904 or (954) 359-9942; www. islandaircharters.com. Other options are Hughes Air from Tamiami and Opa Locka airports in Miami: tel. (305) 253-7248; or Tropic Air Express: tel. (786) 231-1039; chris@tropicairexpress.com. A landing strip is available for private aircraft use on Cat Cay for a $50 landing fee.

In the spring of 1935, a wealthy publisher named Joseph Knapp came to Bimini on his yacht *Storm King* and challenged Hemingway to a round of boxing on the docks. As soon as the bout began, Hemingway came at Knapp with two left hooks, followed by two more blows to the head. Hemingway's last punch sent Knapp hurtling unconscious onto the dock. A local calypso band, fronted by singer Nathaniel "Piccolo Pete" Saunders, immortalized the match in a song called "Big Fat Slob." According to Saunders, Hemingway drew a crowd every Sunday with boxing matches held in a ring made of ropes wrapped around four coconut trees, with a canvas sail as a mat. In a show of community spirit, he also hosted fish roasts on the beach to which all were invited.

On May 31, 1935, Hemingway flew from Cat Cay to Key West to meet Pauline and the boys and catch up on his mail, returning to Bimini on June 5. When the big fish runs dwindled later in the month, he took a break from fishing to have the bottom of the *Pilar* painted and the engine redone. During the lull without his boat, Hemingway offered to pay $250 for an opponent who could last three rounds in the ring with him. Willard Saunders, a local with a rough reputation, sent a message to Hemingway on Lerner's yacht that he wanted to fight him immediately on the dock, without gloves. Willard lasted a minute and a half.

Though Hemingway had been periodically distracted from his regular writing routine during the summer of 1935, he was still penning regular articles for *Esquire*. In fulfillment of a promise he'd made to himself after he was wounded in Italy to do what he could to prevent another war, he wrote a warning letter of sorts called "Notes on the Next War." In the article, he correctly predicted another war would come in two to three years and that it was just then taking shape in the minds of its architects. That summer, Hemingway was going over the proofs of *Green Hills of Africa*, which he felt contained his best writing to date. The book was serialized in *Scribner's Magazine* from May to November, and the first edition run of 10,500 hardcover copies was published on October 25, 1935. The nonfiction account of Pauline and Ernest's December 1933 safari in East Africa garnered poor reviews and sent Hemingway into a deep depression. As was his habit when he felt cornered, he looked for people to blame, and found scapegoats in Pauline and his mistress, Jane Mason, for the corrupting influence of their respective riches. Riches that had, in fact, given him more freedom to write. After marrying into Pauline's wealth, he'd had to come to terms with what he would have to accept in order to have that freedom. That struggle and its resulting resentments are reflected in two of his best short stories, "The Snows of Kilimanjaro" and "The Short Happy Life of Francis Macomber," both first published in 1936. Each is set on safari in Africa and concerns an emasculated man and his stridently confident wife with her murderous wealth. Hemingway was often torn between his natural bohemian tendencies and the temptations that accompanied his fame and the wealth of his friends and associates. In the microcosm of Bimini—where Hemingway generally existed barefoot and bare-chested in shorts reeking of fish guts while entertaining some of the richest gamefishers in the world—that lifelong dichotomy is clear.

It was around this time that Hemingway began to question all the hanging about with the rich he'd been doing. He knew too much hedonism coupled with an inflated ego could have a detrimental effect on a writer's talent. A puffed up ego might make a writer lazy—even delusional—as to the quality of their own output. Hemingway knew this instinctively, but he wasn't always able to steel himself against it. Years earlier in Paris he'd accepted that part of writing honestly meant sacrificing some of the midwestern ideals his parents had tried to instill in him. But when *Green Hills of Africa* wasn't as well-received as he'd expected, he began to reckon with the consequences to his self-worth of living a pampered and dependent existence.

By August, Hemingway had spent 115 days of 1935 in Bimini, but the summer was nearly over and Pauline and Ernest made the twenty-six-hour trip back to Key West aboard the *Pilar*. After spending most of the rest of the year and the first half of 1936 at home in Key West—with trips to New York and Cuba in between—Hemingway took his boat back to Bimini on June 4, 1936. With him were his son Patrick, gaff man Carlos Gutiérrez, and a steersman named Bollo. Before setting out, Hemingway had the *Pilar*'s engine replaced in Miami, and it was a good thing because on the way to Bimini the worst storm since the Labor Day hurricane of 1935 hit. While Patrick slept, the boat slid up and down gigantic waves, and Ernest was more frightened than he wanted to admit.

By 1936, Bimini was a regular destination for wealthy sports fisherpeople and their yachts, and one of the merrymakers was *The Yearling* author Marjorie Kinnan Rawlings, who was also published by Scribner's. Hearing she was in town, Hemingway paid a visit to the yacht of Mrs. Oliver Grinnell, where Rawlings was a guest. Expecting an embarrassing show of virility, Rawlings was pleasantly surprised when Hemingway appeared humble and declared himself a fan of her writing. After spending time with some of the rich "sporting people" in Bimini that summer, Rawlings—who would go on to win the Pulitzer Prize for Fiction in 1939—discovered that she had an internal conflict concerning their lifestyle. "She knew things that they would never know. On the other hand, they wore an armour that she would never wear."[7] They didn't understand her particular kind of passion for the world and human nature, and they ran from the deepest things within themselves—the very things she sought to explore. "Mrs. Rawlings found Ernest a fascinating problem in paradox. . . . The clue to his character must lie, she thought, in some sort of . . . conflict between the sporting life and the literary life."[8] Hemingway explained to Rawlings that he needed the physicality of fishing and hunting just as much as the writing, as it was his antidote to spending so much time within himself.

That summer Hemingway continued work on a trio of stories centered on a boat captain-turned-smuggler named Harry Morgan. *Esquire* editor and co-founder Arnold Gingrich flew to Bimini for an editorial conference. He advised Hemingway on several facets of the book and mapped out a proposed structure in three parts, which Hemingway adopted. In mid-July, Hemingway returned to Key West on the *Pilar* with Bumby, and, although he longed to, would not return to Bimini until the following May.

On May 18, 1937, Hemingway arrived at New York Harbor from Europe aboard the *Normandie* with a plan to spend the summer in Bimini, where he would work on the revisions of *To Have and Have Not*. Hemingway piloted the *Pilar* to Bimini on May 26, followed by Pauline and the boys by seaplane. About a week after they had settled in, Hemingway received a telegram from Joris Ivens, director of *The Spanish Earth*—the pro-democracy film Hemingway had worked on with John Dos Passos—letting him know that Martha Gellhorn had arranged for a screening of the film for Franklin and Eleanor Roosevelt at the White House in early July. Later that month, they were scheduled to fly to Hollywood to show the film at fundraising events for the purchase of more ambulances in aid of the Spanish Civil War.

On June 4, Hemingway flew from Bimini to New York to participate in the Second American Writers' Congress, sponsored by the League of American Writers. The gathering was held at Carnegie Hall, where Hemingway delivered an anti-fascist speech and Ivens screened *The Spanish Earth*. Hemingway received a grand welcome when he appeared onstage, and in his speech said that it was impossible for a writer to exist and work under a fascist regime. On

June 22, Hemingway returned to Cat Cay, where he completed the revisions of *To Have and Have Not*, which would be published that fall.

Having been back in Bimini on and off for little more than a month, Hemingway once again flew to the mainland on July 6 to meet Ivens and Gellhorn in New York. At the airport, Gellhorn bought sandwiches in preparation for one of the "notoriously inedible"[9] White House dinners. Hemingway found FDR's manner too affected for his taste, but the Roosevelts appreciated *The Spanish Earth*, though they felt its political message would benefit by being more heavy-handed.

As difficult as it is for me to imagine my great-grandfather in Hollywood, it's a testament to his dedication to *The Spanish Earth* that he made the trip out there to promote it. After the film was shown to a gathering of Hollywood heavies, Hemingway gave a speech laying out some of the many atrocities of the war. Its message was brutal and honest, and resulted in enough funds for twenty battle-ready ambulances. Hemingway left Hollywood as quickly as he'd come, returning to Bimini on July 21 to celebrate his thirty-eighth birthday with his family.

The last documented letter Hemingway wrote from Bimini was to Waldo Peirce on July 27, 1937. On August 3, he, Pauline, and Bumby left the island for the last time aboard the *Pilar*. Whether Ernest had already admitted it to himself or not, his marriage to Pauline was ending. He returned to Spain and Martha Gellhorn over the objections of Pauline and her mother.

The next several years of Hemingway's life would be overtaken by war. His second marriage would end, and his third would begin. He would return to the waters of the Gulf Stream near Cuba, but never again to Bimini. His years in Key West and Bimini with Pauline and the boys were some of the most stable of his life. He wrote productively, had a comfortable home base, and lived with the rhythm of one who is wedded to and moved by waters. Bimini found Hemingway when he was still a relatively young man, at a time when two of his greatest novels—*For Whom the Bell Tolls* and *The Old Man and the Sea*—had yet to be written. He had not yet been ravaged by the head injuries sustained in the plane crashes in Africa nor by alcohol nor by any other defeat. The freedom the island gave him to devote himself to fishing contributed greatly to his knowledge of the sea as a metaphor for happiness and loss. Bimini affected Hemingway's writing in many ways, infusing it with the purity of a place relatively untouched. The simplicity of island life and the boundlessness of the sea allowed him to welcome a meditative loneliness where he could tap into the marrow of his own unconscious. In *Islands in the Stream*, he writes: "He thought that he would lie down and think about nothing. Sometimes he could do this. Sometimes he could think about the stars without wondering about them and the ocean without problems and the sunrise without what it would bring."[10]

ADDITIONAL PLACES OF INTEREST

"The end of the world . . . that would make a hell of a painting."
—Ernest Hemingway, *Islands in the Stream*

Bimini Big Game Club Resort & Marina

Kings Highway, Alice Town, North Bimini. Tel. (800) 867-4764/(242) 347-3391. Email: info@biggameclubbimini.com.

Nassau entrepreneur Neville Stuart opened the Bimini Big Game Fishing Club—a tuxedo-and-tie formal dining establishment—in 1936, and began organizing fishing tournaments that attracted anglers from around the world. In 1954, the club moved to its current location and added a marina and six guest cottages. In 1963, it opened its main hotel building. The resort was later acquired by the Bacardi family, after which it underwent extensive renovations and added a new marina, reopening in 1972.

Today, the 51-room Bimini Big Game Club Resort & Marina is no longer owned by the Bacardis, but it continues to flourish. Located on a peninsula, it is accessible from the International Airport on South Bimini by van and water taxi for $7 per person. The oceanfront resort offers fishing charters, as well as kayaks, paddleboards, and hammocks for guest use. Other amenities include a seventy-five-slip marina, bicycle and golf cart rentals, a freshwater swimming pool, billiards, ping-pong, life-size chess, and several dining options. The **Bimini Big Game Bar & Grill** features fresh fish and American staples, as well as live entertainment. **Sharkies Bar & Grill** offers a traditional Bahamian Fish Fry and barbeque fare on select nights. My cousin Hilary Hemingway donated dozens of photographs in her late father Leicester Hemingway's name, as well as a hundred copies of his newspaper, *Bimini Out Islands News*, to the **Hemingway Rum Bar and Social Lounge**. The **Gulfstream Conference Center** features Bahamas Out Islands murals and can accommodate up to 60 meeting attendees and 150 banquet guests. Sundries and souvenirs can be found at the **Outfitter Shop & Liquor Store**. The Bimini Big Game Club Resort & Marina is also host to **Neal Watson's Bimini Scuba Center**, which operates a 55-foot glass-bottom boat that takes guests on diving, snorkeling, and sightseeing adventures to nearby reefs, wrecks, and the Atlantis/Bimini Road. The center offers PADI diving certification courses, as well as water safaris to view sharks, dolphins, stingrays, and other marine life.

The Bimini Museum and Heritage Center
Kings Highway, Alice Town, North Bimini. Contact Sir Michael and Lady Barbara Checkley: Tel. (242) 347-3038.

When visiting a place with such a colorful history, a trip to its official museum is a must. The Bimini Museum is located inside a pink, two-story wood-frame house built in the 1920s that was the island's original post office and jail. In operation since 2000, it features an exhibit dedicated to Hemingway's time on the island that includes rare film footage of the author fishing. The museum also houses artifacts such as Martin Luther King Jr.'s 1964 immigration card, Congressman Adam Clayton Powell Jr.'s domino set, Prohibition-era photographs, cannonballs, old rum kegs, and many other treasures.

End of the World Saloon
South End of Kings Highway, Alice Town, North Bimini.

For more than fifty years this waterfront locals' hangout has been a fixture in Alice Town. Though unsubstantiated, it seems likely that the End of the World Saloon is named for the passage in *Islands in the Stream* that made the phrase famous. The bar's sand floor and fish tales of former patrons scrawled on the walls give it the relaxed atmosphere of a friend's beach cookout. Adam Clayton Powell Jr.—who in 1945 was the first African American to be elected to Congress from New York—was a frequent visitor to Bimini, and the End of the World Saloon was his chosen venue for interviews. Powell campaigned against discrimination in the armed forces, to desegregate press galleries in Congress, and to prohibit lynching.

Stop in at the End of the World Saloon to relax with the locals, write a message on the wall, and enjoy a locally brewed bottle of Kalik or a Goombay Smash—with pineapple, orange juice, and an array of rums, it's sure to knock your sandals from here to goombay.

The Fountain of Youth
South Bimini Airport Road, South Bimini.

Ponce de León set out to discover the Fountain of Youth in the early 1500s. His search took him to Florida and to the shallow pools of South Bimini, where he discovered a freshwater well that for centuries has been rumored to be the fabled fountain. Today, a small wooden plaque and a pail with a rope mark the pool. Leicester Hemingway was a firm believer in the Fountain of Youth referenced in the native Biminites' Taíno language, as well as in the lost city of Atlantis. Leicester was a wonderful storyteller and the author of six books, including the 1962 biography, *My Brother, Ernest Hemingway*. For the last few years of his life, Uncle Les edited the monthly newsletter, *Bimini Out Islands News*.

The Healing Hole
North Bimini.

Could Bimini be more idyllic? Not only is the warm saltwater highway of the Gulf Stream home to a stunning array of marine life, North Bimini was discovered to have a natural freshwater pool that contains a high concentration of lithium, a chemical known to have soothing properties. Carved out of the limestone rock by groundwater, the mineral-rich well of Bimini's Healing Hole formed thousands of years ago. Cool freshwater is pumped into the pool during the outgoing tide, creating an oasis amidst four miles of saltwater swamp in the mangroves of Bonefish Creek. The pool is said to have medicinal properties for those who bathe in it, and Leicester Hemingway and his wife Doris both had ailments that were soothed by its waters. Bathing in the natural pool surrounded by mangroves and the Gulf's limpid waters will surely soothe, if not heal, whatever ails you.

Snorkeling to Bimini Road and the SS *Sapona* shipwreck
North Bimini.

Going to Bimini and not snorkeling or diving would be like going to Paris and not visiting Shakespeare and Company. Diving in Bimini is among the best in the world. Its crystal waters are filled with colorful coral, dolphins, turtles, and an array of tropical fish. There are shallow reefs and deep chasms for first-time snorkelers and experienced divers to explore. Wonders abound in Bimini's cerulean waters, and two of its nonliving attractions are Bimini Road and the SS *Sapona* shipwreck.

A mile from the North Bimini shoreline and fifteen feet below the water's surface lies what is known as Bimini Road. Discovered in 1969, this collection of large beach rock slabs—which resemble masonry used in structures in Egypt and South America—appears to have been honed into the shape of steps and is said to have once led to the lost continent of Atlantis. The mythical island nation is the subject of Plato's *Critias*, and sailors and explorers—including my great-uncle Leicester Hemingway—have searched for evidence of it for centuries. The idea that the stones of Bimini Road could be the remains of steps that once led to Atlantis makes this an alluring dive and snorkeling site.

The skeletal hull of Bruce Bethel's abandoned rum-running ship, SS *Sapona*, remains intact just off Bimini—partially above water, partially submerged—offering the chance for divers to compare the long-term effects of weather and sea on a shipwreck.

Martin Luther King Jr. Memorial
Bimini Craft Center, Alice Town, North Bimini.

Although it isn't a Hemingway-related site, the Martin Luther King Jr. Memorial at Bimini Craft Center is a must-see for any admirer of great historical figures who have appreciated the uniqueness of Bimini. A visit to the bronze bust of the civil rights leader is a great way to reflect on the contemplative—some might say prophetic—time Dr. King spent in Bimini. King first came to the island in 1964 to meet with Congressman Adam Clayton Powell Jr. in order to solicit his help with the passage of civil rights legislation. It was Powell—who had a vacation home in Bimini—who introduced King to local fisherman Ansil Saunders. During the trip, King wrote his Nobel Prize acceptance speech, which he would deliver in October of that year.

Dr. King loved the natural wonders of Bimini, and in the spring of 1968 he visited the island for a second time, four days before his assassination. Saunders took him out on the water and remembered King telling him that he didn't think he was going to make it to the age of forty. On that trip King wrote his final speech, commonly known as "I've Been to the Mountaintop," in support of striking Memphis sanitation workers. He delivered the speech three days after leaving Bimini—on April 3, 1968—the day before his death. On that last trip to Bimini, King also penned his own eulogy.

The Dolphin House Museum
Saunders Street, Queens Highway, Alice Town, North Bimini. Tel. (242) 347-3201.
Open Mon.–Sat. 10 A.M.–6 P.M.

Nowhere is the history of Bimini, including Hemingway's time on the island, celebrated with such local flair as at the Dolphin House Museum. The Dolphin House—made from one hundred percent recycled materials like shells, tiles, glass, and other found objects—is, as the sign on the door says, "A bridge between dolphin and human consciousness. A work in progress since 1993." This unique homage to Bahamian history was built by Ashley Saunders, whose grandfather, Uncle Natty "Piccolo Pete" Saunders, died in 2017 at the age of 102. Piccolo Pete celebrated Bahamian history through stories recounted with the help of his banjo. Ashley Saunders plans to make sure that the Dolphin House Museum is preserved for generations to come. The Dolphin House is sometimes available for overnight stays to guests, depending on the season and availability.

Note: A parcel of land that Hemingway owned but never built upon lies just past the Dolphin House on Saunders Street, near the Lerner Anchorage.

7

MADRID

There is no doubt that one of the greatest love affairs of Hemingway's life was with Spain. He once called it "the last good country left."[1] What did he love about the land of toreadors and siestas? Simply everything. The title of his short story set in Madrid, "The Capital of the World," says it all.

Plaza de Toros de Las Ventas

Calle de Alcalá, 237. Tel. (+34) 912 76 12 87.
Box office open every day 10 A.M.–5:30 P.M.; closes at 2:30 P.M. on Dec. 24; closed on Christmas and New Year's Day.

"For the bull was absolutely unbelievable. He seemed like some great prehistoric animal, absolutely deadly and absolutely vicious. . . . He charged silently and with a soft, galloping rush."
—Ernest Hemingway, *Star Weekly*, 1923

In 1923, Hemingway attended his first bullfight with Mike Strater in Madrid. "Don Ernesto," as the Spanish called him, watched in awe from a ringside seat bought from a scalper as the struggle between red, gold, and brown unfurled in the tawny ring. In "Bull-Fighting Is Not a Sport—It Is a Tragedy," an October 20 article written for *Star Weekly*, Hemingway observed: "Bullfighting is not a sport. It was never supposed to be. It is a tragedy. A very great tragedy. The tragedy is the death of the bull."[2]

Located in the Salamanca district of Madrid, Las Ventas was inaugurated in June of 1931, and it is where Hemingway went regularly to see good friends Luis Miguel Dominguín and Antonio Ordóñez display their skills as matadors. Hemingway was considered a bullfight aficionado, and two of his books feature bullfighting. In *The Sun Also Rises* much of the action is set during the week-long fiesta of San Fermín in Pamplona, while *Death in the Afternoon* explores bullfighting's history and practices, as well as Hemingway's deeper ruminations on its cultural and philosophical meaning. During the Spanish Civil War, bullfighting at Las Ventas ceased temporarily, resuming in May of 1939. The bullfight season runs from March to October, with bullfights occurring every Saturday or Sunday and on holidays, beginning at six or seven in the evening. During the annual **Fiestas de San Isidro**—May 11 to 15—bullfights are held every day. The prices of the seats at Las Ventas varies, with the most expensive located closer to the ring in the shade. If you're not interested in seeing a live bullfight, Las Ventas has a museum, and tours of the building are also available.

Hostal Aguilar (formerly Pensión Aguilar)
Carrera de San Jerónimo, 32. Tel. (+34) 914 29 59 26.

In July of 1923, Hadley and Ernest attended the Fiesta San Fermín for the first time, where they were introduced to the centuries-old tradition of running with the bulls. They enjoyed it so much that they came back the following year for the fiesta and to go trout fishing in the **Irati**. At various times between 1923 and 1926, Hadley and Ernest stayed in room 7 of the modest and lovely Pensión Aguilar—now Hostal Aguilar—in Madrid. This homey pension features spacious guest rooms and an old-world dining room and lounge filled with artwork. Visit Hostal Aguilar to be reminded of Hemingway's humble first visits to the country that would inspire so much of his writing.

Sobrino de Botín

Calle Cuchilleros, 17. Tel. (+34) 913 66 42 17.
Open every day 1–4 P.M. *& 8* P.M.*–12* A.M.

Founded in 1725, Sobrino de Botín is the oldest continuously operating restaurant in the world, and was Hemingway's favorite in Madrid. Owner Emilio Gonzalez would have a table waiting for him when he came in to eat lunch and write. Hemingway attempted to learn to cook *paella* at Botín (he wasn't very good at it), and would sit down to eat the specialty of roast young suckling pig served with a mushroom tortilla and *vino rojo*. Hemingway loved Sobrino de Botín so much that he ends *The Sun Also Rises* just after a meal there: "We lunched upstairs at Botín's. It is one of the best restaurants in the world. We had roast young suckling pig and drank *rioja alta*. Brett did not eat much. I ate a very big meal and drank three bottles of *rioja alta*."[3]

I had the pleasure of dining at Botín when I first came to Madrid. The owners sat my friends and I upstairs in the same room where Hemingway used to write. Before we ordered our dishes, the restaurant treated us to *Jamón ibérico de bellota*, a special type of ham made from free-range pigs that roam the oak forests along the border of Spain and Portugal. Both my Spanish friends ordered Hemingway's favorite, the house specialty *Cochinillo asado* (roast suckling pig), our friend from Arkansas ordered *Cordero asado* (roast lamb), my friend from Seattle had *Chipirones en su tinta* (cuttlefish in their own blue-black ink), and I had *Lenguado al horno o frita* (fried flounder). Ernest was right, Botín is one of the best restaurants in the world—the food was impeccable and the owners and staff were warm and gracious. When you step back into the busy streets of modern-day

Madrid after having dined at Sobrino de Botín—with its colorfully tiled, wood-fired oven, brick walls, and arched doorways—you know you've not only had one of the best culinary experiences of your life, but you feel as though you've been in another time and another world.

In 1929, Hemingway returned to Spain to research his treatise on bull-fighting, *Death in the Afternoon*, which he referred to as his "bullfight book." Bullfights, Hemingway felt, were the only place he could study violent death—something a writer must understand intimately—without being immersed in war. The book, complete with a glossary of bullfighting terms and photographs of some of the great bullfighters of the day, established Hemingway as an aficionado of what is a form of valuable cultural expression for some, to others bloodsport.

In 1936, Civil War broke out in Spain, and the following year Hemingway signed on as a war correspondent for the now-defunct North American Newspaper Alliance (NANA). He traveled to Madrid in March of 1937 with Dutch filmmaker Joris Ivens—who was filming *The Spanish Earth*—with the goal of keeping the United States from becoming involved in the brewing conflict. Luis Quintanilla, a Spanish artist and friend of Hemingway, said that Hemingway was "profoundly democratic and liberal in his ideals," fearing that "Europe [was] moving toward dictatorships."[4] In a February 14, 1939, article, "On the American Dead in Spain," Hemingway wrote: "The dead do not need to rise. They are part of the earth now and the earth can never be conquered. For the earth endureth forever. It will outlive all systems of tyranny."[5]

When Martha Gellhorn joined Hemingway in Madrid in 1937, she had never written journalism, but she carried a letter from *Collier's* editor Kyle Crichton stating that she was a special correspondent. The letter was "intended to help her smooth over situations with any authorities wondering what a nice girl was doing in the war-torn city. In truth, Hemingway had arranged the whole thing. It meant nothing: Martha did not yet have an official connection with a magazine or newspaper."[6] To give Gellhorn a sense of the terrain surrounding Madrid, Hemingway took her through the mountains on horseback to view the battlefields below. "He suggested that she write about Madrid, about the people's daily life amid the strife of war. Although Martha had never before reported on a war, she took his encouragement and wrote her first piece. She submitted it to *Collier's* with little expectation, and was surprised when [they] published the piece."[7] Gellhorn would become a regular correspondent for *Collier's*, and one of the most highly-regarded foreign correspondents of all time. The following year, Hemingway traveled back and forth between Key West and Spain, where he witnessed the last Republican stand at the Battle of the Ebro, and was one of the last journalists to leave.

Hotel Florida
Plaza de Callao, 2.

> *"You could learn as much at the Hotel Florida in those years as you could learn anywhere in the world."*
> —Ernest Hemingway

During the Spanish Civil War, Martha and Ernest took up residence at Hotel Florida, where Ernest wrote his only play, *The Fifth Column*, amidst the Siege of Madrid. The play concerns American-born Philip Rawlings, a secret agent for the Second Spanish Republic. *The Fifth Column* was poorly received when it was published in 1938 and has been overshadowed by Hemingway's other works.

Built in 1924, the two-hundred-room—each with its own bathroom—Hotel Florida was a hub for foreign correspondents, intellectuals, prostitutes, and military officials, as well as a hotbed for spy plots. Its location next to a battle line meant substantial amounts of alcohol and other supplies were smuggled in and out. After a rebel shell burst the hotel's hot water tank, the residents of Hotel Florida sought shelter in the basement. As guests came streaming from their rooms, Antoine de Saint-Exupéry—the French aviator and author of *Le Petit Prince*—was observed standing at the grand staircase holding a basket of grapefruit. As each female guest passed, he held out one of the juicy, round fruits and asked politely in French if she would like one. Saint-Exupéry was covering the Spanish Civil War for several French newspapers, and on his press pass he listed his address as "Florida."

John Dos Passos immortalized his stay at Hotel Florida for the January 1938 *Esquire* article, "Room and Bath at the Hotel Florida." The hotel's frenetic atmosphere was also reproduced in the HBO biopic *Hemingway & Gellhorn*. In its day, Hotel Florida's marble façade was a sight to behold. Unfortunately, the hotel suffered so much damage during the war that it was demolished and replaced by a department store in 1964.

On June 30, 1953, Ernest and Mary sailed from Havana to Le Havre, where they were met by Adamo DeSimon, Gianfranco Ivancich's driver, who took them to Madrid via the **Loire Valley** in a Lancia Aurelia. They were guests of Hotel Florida and visited **Museo del Prado** and the location in the **Sierra de Guadarrama** mountains where Robert Jordan blew up the bridge in *For Whom the Bell Tolls*.

Telefónica Building
Calle Gran Vía, 28. Tel. (+34) 915 80 87 00.

When it opened in 1930, the Telefónica Building was the tallest building in Europe and employed more than a thousand workers. During the Spanish Civil War, it was the home of the **Office of Foreign Press**, where Hemingway, Gellhorn, Dos Passos, and Saint-Exupéry filed their reports as war correspondents. So close was the Telefónica Building to the front line that its basement was used as an air raid shelter and the building was hit by numerous bombs and shells.

In 1928, before the building was completed, Gran Vía 28 was the location of the first transatlantic phone call in Spain, between King Alfonso XIII and U.S. President Calvin Coolidge. Today, the building houses **Espacio Fundación Telefónica**, which hosts talks and exhibitions on innovations in art and technology that are free to the public, as well as a permanent exhibit on the history of telecommunications.

Hotel Tryp Gran Vía (formerly Hotel Gran Vía)
Calle Gran Vía, 25. Tel. (+34) 912 76 47 47.

Like Hotel Florida, Hotel Gran Vía was a hub for foreign correspondents and intellectuals during the Spanish Civil War. Hemingway was a frequent guest of the hotel and mentions it in *The Fifth Column*, as well as in the story "Night Before Battle," published in the February 1, 1939, issue of *Esquire*.

Hotel Tryp Gran Vía is close to all that central Madrid has to offer, including **Plaza de España, Plaza Mayor, Plaza Santa Ana, Plaza Cibeles**, and Museo del Prado. Most of the rooms have views, and the hotel's pleasant breakfast room—the walls of which are decorated with photos of Hemingway fishing and hunting—is named for the author.

The Westin Palace, Madrid (formerly the Palace Hotel)
Plaza de las Cortes, 7. Tel. (+34) 913 60 80 00.

While in Madrid, Hemingway often chose to stay at the elegant Palace Hotel—now The Westin Palace, Madrid—in part because of its location across the street from Museo del Prado. In the evenings, Hemingway often had a dry martini at the hotel's **1912 Museo Bar**, as Jake and Brett do in *The Sun Also Rises*, and Salvador Dalí sipped cocktails by the fire in one of Museo's leather armchairs.

The Palace's **La Rotonda** restaurant is housed beneath a stained glass cupola where executive chef José Luque interprets the celebrated recipes of Paul Bocuse, creator of *nouvelle cuisine*. The restaurant offers an extensive breakfast buffet, featuring a wide variety of international dishes, as well as the renowned **Sunday Opera & Brunch** from 1:30 to 3:30 P.M. In addition to La Rotonda, the Palace is home to **Asia Gallery**, offering Cantonese cuisine, and the **Green Tea Sushi Bar**, featuring a blend of Japanese sushi and Spanish tapas.

Gaylord's Hotel
Calle de Alfonso XI, 3.

When the Palace Hotel was converted to a military hospital during the Spanish Civil War, most of the Russian advisors stationed in Spain moved to Gaylord's Hotel. Hemingway first went to Gaylord's in 1937, when he accompanied Joris Ivens to the rooms of Soviet journalist Mikhail Koltsov. Hemingway brought two bottles of whiskey to the gathering, adding to the already abundant cache of wine, vodka, and a large ham. Hemingway and

Koltsov took to each other immediately, and Hemingway later immortalized him as Karkov in *For Whom the Bell Tolls*. Koltsov would write his own book of war experiences, *The Spanish Diary*. In *For Whom the Bell Tolls*, Robert Jordan feels guilty about the luxuriousness of his accommodations at Gaylord's and is afraid he will be corrupted by them. Jordan dreams of bringing his love Maria to the hotel, as well as to nearby **Retiro Park**. One of the most important gathering places for journalists and intellectuals during the Spanish Civil War, the building that was once Gaylord's Hotel now houses private residences.

Museo Chicote
Calle Gran Vía, 12. Tel. (+34) 915 32 67 37.
Open Mon.–Fri. 1 P.M.–3 A.M.; Sat. 1 P.M.–3:30 A.M.; Sun. 1 P.M.–1 A.M.

One of the oldest and most famous bars in Madrid, Museo Chicote opened in 1931 and is where Hemingway, his fellow journalists, and film stars like Grace Kelly and Ava Gardner would sip elegantly-crafted cocktails in the bar's curved booths. As difficult as it is to imagine, Madrid tried its best to be a functioning city while under siege. Museo Chicote was near the front, and soldiers would come in for both drinks and shelter. Hemingway describes the bar in *The Fifth Column*, as well as in his short story, "The Denunciation." His story, "The Butterfly and the Tank," is set in Chicote's, and was published in *Esquire* on December 1, 1938.

The appearance of Museo Chicote hasn't changed much since the 1930s. It retains its Art Deco entryway, long bar, dramatic revolving door, and tinted glass. The bar still has the original couches and chrome chairs where Bette Davis and Frank Sinatra sipped cocktails, and the waiters still don white jackets. Stop in at Museo Chicote for an afternoon martini and imagine Hemingway doing the same while he digested the day's events.

Restaurant El Callejón
Calle de la Ternera, 6.

Restaurant El Callejón was one of Mary and Ernest's preferred lunch spots during their visits to Madrid in the 1950s. Located in the historic Asturias part of the city, El Callejón occupied the basement of Calle de la Ternera, 6. In an article for *Life* magazine, Hemingway wrote that the best food in Madrid could be found at El Callejón. He was such a frequent visitor that he had his own corner reserved for him. The building that housed El Callejón is also famous for being where Luis Daoíz y Torres—a Spanish artillery officer who was a leader in the Dos de Mayo Uprising—was killed by the French army in 1808. The Dos de Mayo Uprising signaled the beginning of the Spanish War of Independence.

In February of 1959, Hemingway made plans to spend the summer attending the bullfights of Luis Miguel Dominguín and Antonio Ordóñez. From May of 1959 until his birthday in July, Hemingway attended more than twenty bullfights. The period became known as "The Dangerous Summer," after a series of articles of the same name that Hemingway wrote for *Life* magazine between October of 1959 and May of 1960. "The Dangerous Summer" pieces chart the rivalry between rising bullfighter Antonio Ordóñez and his brother-in-law, the already-famous Luis Miguel Dominguín, who came out of retirement to challenge him. Hemingway fictionalized Antonio's father, Cayetano, as Pedro Romero in *The Sun Also Rises*.

Hemingway's sixtieth birthday on July 21, 1959, was marked by a lavish celebration at Bill Davis's **Málaga** estate, **La Consula**, on the **Costa del Sol**. Mary had gone to great lengths to plan the event, with dinner and cake on the balcony, an orchestra, and flamenco dancing. After a fireworks display, the champagne- and cocktail-fueled revelry carried on until after breakfast the next day. The festivities were marred by the fact that, while participating in the San Fermín festivities in Pamplona earlier that month, Hemingway had developed a kidney disorder and had begun acting overly sensitive and cruel. Despite all of Mary's efforts, Ernest launched cutting remarks at her, and snapped at his old friend Major General Buck Lanham, the model for Colonel Cantwell in *Across the River and into the Trees*. Mary wanted to return to Cuba, but Ernest insisted on staying at La Consula to begin the first of his bullfight articles for *Life*.

In a July 31, 1960, letter written from New York, Hemingway told his eldest son Jack that he wasn't well and no longer wanted to return to Spain. But, convinced that Ordóñez needed him, Hemingway ignored the warning signs of his own body and mind. In August, an unaccompanied Hemingway boarded an overnight flight to Madrid via Lisbon. At La Consula he rested from the trip, but was agitated and showing signs of an imminent break-down. He wrote to Mary of nightmares and said that he feared a complete collapse. Bullfighting had lost its appeal, and Hemingway, feeling lonely and haunted, was distraught about his magazine pieces on the subject, which he felt were in tatters. That summer, photographs of Hemingway were taken to accompany "The Dangerous Summer" articles, one of which appeared on the cover of *Life*.

Hotel Suecia
Calle del Marques de Casa Riera, 4. Tel. (+34) 912 00 05 70.

Hemingway was a guest of Hotel Suecia during his last trip to Madrid in 1960. The chic 123-room hotel is decorated in warm colors with light-filled windows, and is a ten-minute walk from Museo del Prado. The hotel is equally close to the bustling Plaza Mayor with its many restaurants and cafés. Hotel Suecia's restaurant, **Casa Suecia**, offers Mediterranean and international cuisine, and was one of Hemingway's favorite places for cocktails. To commemorate this history, the hotel has a **Hemingway Cocktail Bar**, decorated in soft velvet with mirrored panels and light-grain hardwood floors. It's a pleasant place to relax and have a glass of Spanish wine, or simulate Hemingway's experience with one of his favorite cocktails. You may also want to head up to the eleventh-floor terrace, **Atico Casa Suecia**, to dine with sweeping views of Madrid.

Museo Nacional del Prado
Calle de Ruiz de Alarcon, 23. Tel. (+34) 913 30 28 00.
Open Mon.–Sat. 10 A.M.–8 P.M.; Sun. 10 A.M.–7 P.M.

In *Death in the Afternoon*, Hemingway wrote that Museo del Prado is worth spending a month in each spring. The area where the museum now stands is named for the Prado, meaning "meadow" in Spanish. The grand structure that houses the museum was initially conceived of in 1785 by José

Moñino, First Count of Floridablanca, as a commission for Charles III of Spain. Its architect was Juan de Villanueva, who also designed the nearby **Real Jardín Botánico** and the **City Hall of Madrid**. Museo del Prado is considered to have one of the greatest collections of European art in the world, as well as the world's best collection of Spanish art. It houses works by many masters, including Francisco Goya, Hieronymus Bosch, El Greco, and Diego Velázquez.

The first time I ever entered Museo del Prado was on a sweltering July day. I was looking for one of Goya's Black Paintings, *A Pilgrimage to San Isidro*. I'd gotten a tattoo of the troubadour from the painting on my arm and wanted to see him in person. The grand hall of the Prado opens like a Roman aqueduct filled with magnificent depictions of all the wonders and tragedies of the world: war, salvation, famine, birth, death, torture, and passion. The room that houses the Black Paintings is cool and dark like the paintings themselves, each with a ripple and shimmer of the starvation and destruction depicted in Goya's haunting scenes. Mouths agape with suffering, the subjects of the paintings toil within their own existence, wearing the dumbstruck epiphany of souls frozen in Purgatory. To see these masterpieces in person is to see the truth that Hemingway admired in them, and that he tried to create in his own stories and novels.

My great-grandfather greatly admired Goya, Velázquez, and El Greco, but of the three, he considered Goya to be the greatest of the geniuses. In *Death in the Afternoon*, Hemingway writes: "Goya did not believe in costume but he did believe in blacks and in grays, in dust and in light, in high places rising from plains, in the country around Madrid, in movement, in his own cojones, in painting, in etching, and in what he had seen, felt, touched, handled, smelled, enjoyed, drunk, mounted, suffered, spewed-up, lain-with, suspected, observed, loved, hated, lusted, feared, detested, admired, loathed, and destroyed."[8]

Hemingway, not generally a fan of museums, revered Museo del Prado. He took great pride in the fact that the Republican government had protected the museum's major works from bombings during the Spanish Civil War by transferring them to València. The paintings were housed there from 1936 until the national troops entered Madrid in 1939. A trip to Madrid would be incomplete without a long visit to the Prado, one of the greatest museums in the world.

Hemingway and Spain were intertwined from the time he was a young man until just before his death. He felt compelled to be there during the country's civil war, and he admired the warmth and dignity of the Spanish people, believing they faced death with courage and lived their lives with gusto, as he made a point of doing in his own life. Italy was where Hemingway had his brutal coming of age, and Paris was where he became an artist, but Spain was Hemingway's spiritual home.

ADDITIONAL PLACES OF INTEREST

Real Jardín Botánico de Madrid

Plaza de Murillo, 2. Tel. (+34) 914 20 30 17.
Open Jan., Feb., Nov. & Dec. 10 A.M.–6 P.M.; March & Oct. 10 A.M.–7 P.M.;
April & Sept. 10 A.M.–8 P.M.; May, June, July & Aug. 10 A.M.–9 P.M.

In a moving passage in *For Whom the Bell Tolls*, Pilar likens the smell of wet earth and dead flowers in the Real Jardín Botánico to death and birth. The botanical garden's lush exhibition of flora has been in its current location since King Charles III of Spain had it conveyed from the Orchard of Migas Calientes, near the banks of the Manzanares River, in 1774. Designed by Francesco Sabatini and Juan de Villanueva, the garden has three tiered terraces: **Terraza de los Cuadros**, **Terraza de las Escuelas Botánicas**, and **Terraza de Plano de la Flor**, as well as two greenhouses. Its nearly twenty acres are home to ninety thousand plants and flowers, and fifteen hundred trees. Real Jardín Botánico contains the largest herbarium in Spain, with some herbs dating back to the eighteenth century. Also located within the grounds are the library and archives of the **Royal Botanic Gardens**, which contain works on botany, natural history, and chemistry. The public entrance to the Real Jardín Botánico is near **Murillo Gate**, in front of Museo del Prado.

Buen Retiro Park
Plaza de la Independencia, 7. Tel. (+34) 914 00 87 40.
In winter open every day 7 A.M.–10 P.M.; in summer 7–12 A.M.

A 350-acre green space not far from Museo del Prado, Buen Retiro Park was created between 1630 and 1640, after several tracts of land were given to King Philip IV for recreational use by Gaspar de Guzman, Count-Duke of Olivares. Buen Retiro became a public park in the late nineteenth century. The park is home to more than fifteen thousand trees and a beautiful lake, on which one can take out a rowboat and enjoy a picnic lunch while reading one of Hemingway's classics. In *For Whom the Bell Tolls*, Robert Jordan imagines living happily with Maria within the extensive gardens of Retiro Park.

Buen Retiro Park encompasses several gardens—**Jardines de Cecilio Rodríguez**, **Jardin de Vivaces**, **Jardines del Arquitecto Herrero Palacios**, the **Roselada** ("rose garden"), and the **Parterre Frances**, which is home to a 400-year-old cypress tree, considered to be the oldest in Madrid. Another exceptional feature of Retiro Park is the **Palacio de Cristal**, or "Glass Palace," created in 1887 to house flora from the Philippines, then a colonial possession of Spain. The Palacio de Cristal is a splendid example of Spanish cast-iron architecture, and is now used as an exhibition hall, as is the park's **Velázquez Palace**. Retiro Park has two museums, **Casón del Buen Retiro**, which hosts a collection of nineteenth- and twentieth-century paintings, and **Ejército Museum**, an Army museum that is home to "La Tizona," the sword of the Spanish warrior, El Cid. Included in the displays of armor at Ejército is a cross that was carried by Christopher Columbus during his voyage to the New World.

The building in ruins
Paseo del Pintor Rosales, 14.

On Paseo del Pintor Rosales, just opposite **Casa de Campo**, there is a bombed-out building in ruins. The stairway has been destroyed and the elevator hangs, twisted in its hollow. The doors of the building, however, stand perfectly intact at the fore like sentries. The building was so close to the front during the Spanish Civil War that one could throw a brick from its balcony directly into the trenches. Hemingway saw the ruins as a symbol of war-ravaged Madrid and proposed that Ivens film parts of *The Spanish Earth* there. The setting of Hemingway's short story, "Landscape with Figures," was inspired by the ruins. The story involves a group of people—Edwin Henry and his film crew, an American female journalist, and a British officer—who are living in a house that has been destroyed by bombings. One afternoon, the British officer sits on the balcony in defiance of the others' warnings and the building is attacked.

Cervecería Alemana

Plaza de Santa Ana, 6. Tel. (+34) 914 29 70 33.
Open Sun., Mon., Weds. & Thurs. 11–12:30 A.M.; Fri. & Sat. 11–2 A.M.

Ever wonder if Hemingway drank beer? Cervecería Alemana—a pub dedicated to beer tasting—was another of Hemingway's favorite Madrid watering holes. He visited it so frequently that he had his own table by the window, and today a photo of him hangs above his favorite seat. In *The Dangerous Summer*, Hemingway commemorates the beer and coffee served at Cervecería Alemana. Ava Gardner, who became friends with Hemingway during the filming of *The Sun Also Rises* in 1957, was a regular patron of the bar when she lived in Madrid from 1952 to 1967. After Gardner's divorce from Frank Sinatra, she was often seen sharing a table with her lover, bullfighter Luis Miguel Dominguín, whom she met through Hemingway.

Cervecería Alemana has been a family business since 1924, and much of its decor remains as it was when it opened in 1904. With dark wood, high ceilings, and whole specimens of *Jamón ibérico* in the window, it has lost none of its charm.

La Venencia

Calle de Echegaray, 7. Tel. (+34) 914 29 73 13.
Open Mon.–Thurs. 12:30–3:30 P.M. & 7 P.M.–1 A.M.; Fri. & Sat.
12:30–4 P.M. & 7 P.M.–1:30 A.M.; Sun. 12:30–4 P.M. & 7 P.M.–1 A.M.

A little-known fact about Hemingway is that he liked a spot of sherry. Hemingway was a regular at La Venencia, with its sawdust floor, old-world feel, and wooden barrels full of sherry. The bar was frequented by Republican soldiers, with whom Hemingway would discuss the latest news from the front. Because the Republicans saw themselves as equals, a no-tipping rule was established, which still holds today, as well as a ban on photographs to prevent information-gathering by fascist spies. A wartime-era "Don't spit on the floor" sign still hangs on the wall, and customers' tabs are written in chalk on the bar. With its dark wood accents and shelves stacked with sherry bottles, La Venencia maintains the feel of 1930s Madrid.

Matadero Madrid
Paseo de la Chopera, 14. Tel. (+34) 913 18 46 70.
Open Tues.–Fri. 4 P.M.–9 P.M.; Sat., Sun. & public holidays 11 A.M.–9 P.M.

> "You must go down the hill in Madrid to the Puente de Toledo early in the morning to the matadero and stand there on the wet paving when there is a fog from the Manzanares and wait for the old women who go before daylight to drink the blood of the beasts that are slaughtered."
>
> —Ernest Hemingway,
> For Whom the Bell Tolls

When Hemingway was in Madrid, he didn't only get up early to write. He made a practice of going down to El Matadero slaughterhouse in the wee hours to watch the novice bullfighters, or *novilleros*, practice their killing. Nearby, old women would stand in line to drink the blood of the bulls, which they believed had health benefits. In *Death in the Afternoon*, Hemingway points out that the Spanish do not waste the meat of the bulls that are killed, but give it to the poor and to orphanages. Today, Matadero Madrid is an arts and cultural center comprised of a complex of pavillions incorporating features of Neo-Mudéjar, a type of Moorish Revival architecture. The complex includes event spaces with a center for readings, a documentary film cinema, a theatre, a design center, and a music pavilion with recording studios, rehearsal rooms, and a stage.

General Headquarters of the International Brigades
Calle Velázquez, 63.

Hemingway was committed to the Republican cause during the Spanish Civil War, and made many friendships through the International Brigades, a group of paramilitary units in operation from 1936 to 1938. Hemingway was a member of the organization, made up of volunteers from all over the world who fought in defense of the Republic. The character of Robert Jordan in *For Whom the Bell Tolls* is an international brigadista. Today, the barracks of the International Brigades has been converted into a beautiful civil building in Madrid's **Salamanca** district.

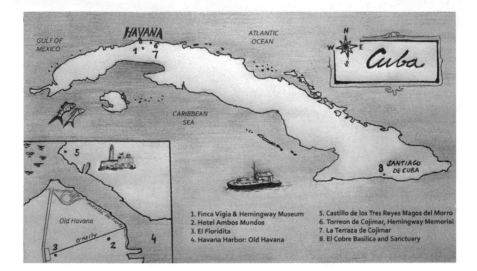

1. Finca Vigía & Hemingway Museum
2. Hotel Ambos Mundos
3. El Floridita
4. Havana Harbor: Old Havana
5. Castillo de los Tres Reyes Magos del Morro
6. Torreon de Cojimar, Hemingway Memorial
7. La Terraza de Cojimar
8. El Cobre Basilica and Sanctuary

8

CUBANO SATO

Surrounded by the blue-green waters of the Northern Caribbean, Cuba is where the Caribbean Sea, Gulf of Mexico, and Atlantic Ocean converge. The island was occupied by the Ciboney Taíno people from 4,000 B.C. until the fifteenth century, when it was colonized by Spain until the American occupation of Cuba during the 1898 Spanish-American War. In 1902, Cuba became semi-independent as a *de facto* protectorate of the United States, and since 1965 has been a sovereign state governed by the Communist Party. Cuba's capital, Havana—Ciudad de las Columnas, or "City of Columns"—was founded in 1515.

The first time Hemingway set foot in Havana was in April of 1928, but it was only in passing. He and Pauline were en route to Key West on a steamship from La Rochelle, France, and transferred to a smaller boat in Havana to take them the last ninety miles. Hemingway returned to Cuba for a longer stay in April of 1932, following the birth of Gregory. He made his way across the Gulf of Mexico that spring aboard Josie Russell's boat *Anita*, a seasoned rum-running vessel that had made more than 150 voyages between Key West and Cuba. Hemingway paid Russell ten dollars per day to charter the boat for fishing. After docking at **San Francisco Wharf** in the afternoon, Hemingway followed Russell to **Donovan's Bar**. As he watched Russell make an illicit liquor deal with the proprietors, the concept for *To Have and Have Not* started to germinate.

Plaza de San Francisco de Asís
Across from Havana Harbor, Old Havana.

The sixteenth-century Plaza de San Francisco Asís is the setting for the opening scene of Hemingway's 1937 novel, *To Have and Have Not*. The novel grew out of the short story, "One Trip Across," first published by *Cosmopolitan* in 1934. In the first scene of the book, a financially desperate boat captain, Harry Morgan, meets the smugglers he will eventually make a deal with at the Pearl of San Francisco Café—based on **Café La Perla**—in the plaza. As Capt. Morgan crosses the square from the dock, a beggar drinks from the **Fuente del Conde de Villanueva**, a white Carrara marble fountain designed by Italian artist Giuseppe Gaggini in 1836. The fountain is referred to by locals as the **Fuente de los Leones** ("Fountain of Lions") for the four lions resting in each corner. Café La Perla was torn down in the 1950s, but Plaza de San Francisco Asís is still home to many shops, restaurants, and art galleries.

The cobblestone Plaza de San Francisco Asís is dominated by the **Basilica Menor de San Francisco de Asís**, a monastery and basilica with a 138-foot bell tower built to house the Franciscans of Havana. The Basilica Menor de San Francisco de Asís was altered in 1730, and from March to August of 1762, the English seized and occupied Havana, taking control of the basilica for their own use. Once Havana was returned to Spain under the 1763 Treaty of Paris, the basilica was no longer used for worship. Today it serves as a concert venue. The cloister of the monastery, built in 1739, is now used to house a collection of sacred art. Next to the basilica is a statue of Saint Junípero Serra (1713–1784), a Roman Catholic Spanish priest and friar of the Franciscan Order who founded missions from Baja California to San Francisco. In the statue, Serra is depicted with a boy of the Acjachemen Nation—the Juaneño Band of Mission Indians—a people indigenous to California. Outside the Basilica Menor de San Francisco de Asís is a life-size statue of José María López Lledín (1899–1985), a well-known street philosopher of 1950s Havana known as El Caballero de París. The newest sculpture in Plaza de San Francisco Asís, *La Conversación* by French artist Étienne, is a compelling modernist bronze of two torso-less people in conversation. It was donated by the French ambassador in 2012. Four blocks from Plaza de San Francisco Asís is **Hotel Ambos Mundos**.

Hotel Ambos Mundos and Room 511 Museum

153 Calle del Obispo, Havana. Tel. (+53) 7 8609529. 24-hour front desk. *Museum open every day 10* A.M.*–5* P.M.

Hotel Ambos Mundos—meaning "both worlds"—was where Hemingway stayed when he first came to Havana in 1932, and it was the regular Havana lodging for himself and visiting friends before he purchased Finca Vigía in 1940. A room at the Ambos Mundos was $1.50 per night—$1.75 when Hemingway had company. He loved the hotel's private simplicity in the heart of Old Havana, as well as its view of **Havana Harbor**, where the *Pilar* was docked. In the warm calm of room 511, Hemingway edited the proofs of *Death in the Afternoon*, worked on the first few chapters of *For Whom the Bell Tolls*, and wrote the wartime Nick Adams story "A Way You'll Never Be."

In 1924, Antolín Blanco Arias commissioned architect Luis Wise Hernandez to design and build Hotel Ambos Mundos, which opened on January 6, 1925. The five-story, coral pink hotel is less than a mile from San Francisco Wharf, on the corner of Mercaderes and Calle del Obispo—a narrow shopping thoroughfare built in 1519 to protect Havana's citizens from the sun. Hotel Ambos Mundos has a restaurant—Papa Hemingway especially enjoyed the oysters—and a rooftop bar with live music offering an "'E. Hemingway' Special" rum cocktail. The bar overlooks the limestone buildings of Old Havana with a spectacular view of the bay, lighthouse, and **El Morro Castle**. Room 511 of Hotel Ambos Mundos has been preserved as a museum dedicated to Hemingway with his bed, dresser, chair, desk with typewriter and spectacles, a pair of loafers, photographs, and other artifacts. The room is open to the public for a nominal fee, payable in the lobby. The airy, old-world lobby of the Ambos Mundos features original metal cage Otis elevators, several photographs of Hemingway, a baby grand piano, an elegant bar, and a marble pool swimming with turtles. Hemingway's favorite Havana lodging offers clean, air-conditioned rooms—some with balconies—laundry and ironing service, satellite TV, room service, and a breakfast buffet.

Castillo de los Tres Reyes Magos del Morro (El Morro Castle)
Havana Harbor. Accessible by taxi and ferry from Old Havana.
Open every day 10 A.M.–*10* P.M.

From room 511 at Hotel Ambos Mundos, Hemingway could clearly see the waves of the Gulf crashing onto the rocks of Castillo de los Tres Reyes Magos del Morro, just beyond Havana Harbor. Named for the three Magis of the Bible, El Morro (*"morro"* in this context meaning a navigational landmark visible from the sea) was built in 1589 from a design by Italian engineer Battista Antonelli. Once El Morro was finished in 1630, a chain was stretched from it to **La Punta Castle** to prevent unwelcome ships from entering the harbor. The British captured the fortress during the Battle of Havana in 1762, destroying its original watchtower. Morro Castle was returned to the Spanish the following year under the Treaty of Paris.

In 1846, **Faro Castillo del Morro** lighthouse—which once housed a school for lighthouse keepers—was added to the fortress. El Morro offers an exhibition on the lighthouses of Cuba, as well as an underwater archeology exhibition. Every night at nine, nineteenth century reenactors hold a ceremony to fire the castle's cannons, which date from 1862—the ceremony was originally done to signal the closing of Havana's walls for the night. During the twentieth century, El Morro was sometimes used as a prison, and Cuban poet and novelist Reinaldo Arenas (1943–1990) was confined there by the Castro regime for criticizing the government. Walk along El Morro's ramparts to take in sweeping views all the way to **Cojímar**.

Havana Harbor
Old Havana.

In 1553, the Spanish governor's Cuban residence was relocated from **Santiago de Cuba** to Havana, making it the country's de facto capital. Havana Harbor was fortified in the sixteenth century to protect the city from attacks by the Dutch, French, and English. On February 15, 1898, the naval battleship USS *Maine*—which had been dispatched to Havana to protect the more than eight thousand U.S. citizens who were then living in Cuba—exploded and sank in Havana Harbor. Hostilities in the wake of the explosion caused the United States to intercede on Cuba's behalf in the Cuban War of Independence against Spain, which led to the start of the Spanish-American War in April of 1898. In 1925, the **Monument to the Victims of the USS *Maine*** was built at the end of Calle Línea on the **Malecón** boardwalk in Havana. The Malecón is a broad esplanade that stretches for five miles from Havana Harbor to the city's **Vedado** neighborhood, where the USS *Maine* monument, the **United States Embassy**, and **José Martí Sports Park** are located. Construction on the Malecón began in 1901 and was completed in 1923. Due to economic reforms that now allow Cubans to own private businesses, many new shops have begun to appear along the Malecón. Locals, fishermen, and tourists of all ages come to stroll along the waterfront, catch a fresh fish supper, and enjoy the sunset. As Hilary Hemingway writes in *Hemingway in Cuba*:

> A ride along the harbor's entrance turns toward the large twin towers of Hotel Nacional, passing faded pastel art-deco apartments, some with old men sitting in doorways with cigars. Across the street, bobbing in the water just beyond the famous Malecón promenade, men drift in large black inner tubes. Using cuban yo-yos, they drift-fish for mutton snapper. Out beyond the fishermen lies a small fleet of fishing smacks. The

men here are long lining; this is a lucky fishing area and they are fortunate to have fish in close to shore.[1]

The first recorded shark attack occurred in Havana Harbor in 1749 when fourteen-year-old British merchant seaman Brook Watson went swimming there alone. The shark attacked twice before Watson—who later became Lord Mayor of London—was rescued; his badly mangled right leg had to be amputated below the knee. The famous shark attack was later the subject of a painting by John Singleton Copley, *Watson and the Shark*, which caused a sensation when it was exhibited at London's Royal Academy in 1778. The painting is now part of the National Gallery of Art collection in Washington, D.C.

Pauline came to Havana for two week-long visits in May of 1932, and she and Ernest went fishing with Ernest's mistress, Jane Mason. In an infamous incident, one afternoon Jane—who was staying in the room next to Ernest on the fifth floor of Hotel Ambos Mundos—displayed her lack of inhibitions by appearing outside his window, having walked the narrow ledge between their balconies. At the time, Ernest was considering taking Arnold Gingrich—who would later marry Jane—up on his offer to write for his new men's magazine, *Esquire*. Ernest kept a ship's log on the *Pilar* to record how and what was caught on each fishing expedition, and would use these notes as inspiration for his *Esquire* pieces. In one of the log entries, an unconfirmed passenger or crew member wrote simply that Ernest loved Jane.

Hemingway returned to Cuba in 1933 for the spring marlin run, once again chartering Russell's *Anita* for April and May. This time, Russell docked his boat at the Casablanca docks near El Morro Castle, where Hemingway bought Carlos Gutiérrez—a billfish expert whom Ernest had met on a previous trip to the Dry Tortugas—a drink and offered him a job as full-time first mate. "Gutiérrez taught Ernest and Russell how to set the lines at varying depths for marlin, how to safely gaff and bring a big marlin on board. With Don Carlos's help Ernest landed a whopping fifty-two marlin that summer, averaging a fish a day for the entire stay. Everything, the skill of the crew and Ernest's knowledge of billfishing, came together the day he brought in the 468-pound blue marlin off El Morro Castle."[2] Jane would become so jealous when Ernest met and fell in love with Martha Gellhorn that she hired Gutiérrez as her boat captain in 1938. Left without someone to man the *Pilar*, Hemingway brought on Gregorio Fuentes, who filled the position admirably.

In May of 1933, Hemingway was joined in Cuba by Pauline, their sons, and nanny Ada Stern. Jane Mason and her husband invited the Hemingways to stay at their estate in **Jaimanitas**, west of Havana. After having observed Ernest's previous interactions with Jane, Pauline felt threatened, though she didn't show it overtly. It must have been painful for my great-grandmother to realize that a similar thing to what she and Ernest had done to Hadley was happening to her. Jane and Ernest had a five-year-long affair that only ended when Jane fell in love with wealthy big game hunter Richard Cooper. The love triangle of Cooper and the Masons inspired "The Short Happy Life of Francis Macomber."

In 1934, Pauline had a boat custom-made for Ernest in an attempt to save their marriage. The thirty-eight-foot Wheeler Playmate fishing boat—cost: $7,500—was Hemingway's beloved *Pilar*, named after the covert pet name Ernest had given Pauline during their 1926 affair in Paris. The boat was outfitted with four seventy-five-gallon fuel tanks, a Chrysler Crown main engine and a forty horsepower trolling engine, an ice chest, and a Model T Ford steering wheel. Bamboo outriggers and a flying bridge were added in 1937, inspired by Bimini fishermen who understood the advantages of being able to observe fish from above. The first time Hemingway took the *Pilar* out in the Gulf Stream, he brought along aspiring writer Arnold Samuelson. Samuelson had hitchhiked to Key West to seek Hemingway's advice on writing, and spent nearly a year transcribing Hemingway's thoughts and observing his daily routines in Key West and Cuba. Samuelson documented the experience in the book, *With Hemingway: A Year in Key West and Cuba*. During the 1934 fishing season, Charles Cadwalader and Henry Fowler of the Philadelphia Academy of Natural History came to Cuba to conduct a study of billfish and to collect specimens, and Hemingway took them out on the *Pilar*. Hemingway had himself been wondering many things about the creatures he so deeply admired, and recorded these thoughts in his seventh article for *Esquire*, "Out in the Stream: A Cuban Letter."

By the spring of 1939, the Spanish Civil War was ending, and so was Ernest's marriage to Pauline. Ernest returned to Cuba to begin work on *For Whom the Bell Tolls*, and in April, Martha joined him at Hotel Ambos Mundos. As the seriousness of their affair increased, Martha decided that Cuba, with its privacy and excellent access to fishing, would be a fine place for them to make a permanent home. She came upon an advertisement for a countryside rental property nine miles outside of Havana that sounded promising. Ernest had always preferred rural to city life, but after driving through the overgrown acacia and royal poinciana trees leading up to Finca Vigía, what they came upon was a decaying alcazar: "The walls, once white, were peeling and stained with black mold. Ernest was unimpressed, though Martha regarded the Finca as a diamond in the rough."[3] Determined to make it their home, while Ernest was away on a fishing trip Martha had the Finca transformed. Ernest was so impressed by her improvements to the sprawling farmhouse that not only did they move in right away, but it inspired him to begin planning their future. As he wrote to Max Perkins, "I don't care about going to war now. Would like to live a while and have fun after this book and write some stories. . . . Also would like to have a daughter. I guess that sounds funny to man with five of them but I would like to have one very much."[4]

Finca Vigía and Hemingway Museum, San Francisco de Paula
From Havana, follow Carretera Central east for nine miles. Tel. (+53) 7 6910809.
Open Mon.–Sat. 10 A.M.–4 P.M.; Sun. 9 A.M.–1 P.M. Cost: $5 CUC.

Finca Vigía ("Lookout Farm") was built by Catalan architect Miguel Pascual y Baguer in 1886. Located on a hillside nine miles east of Havana, Hemingway bought the property—which included a tennis court, swimming pool, and ten acres of mango, Spanish lime, avocado, mamey, sugar-apple, and royal palm (the national tree of Cuba)—with royalties from *For Whom the Bell Tolls*. Hemingway wrote *Islands in the Stream*, *The Garden of Eden*, *Across the River and into the Trees*, *The Old Man and the Sea*, and *A*

Moveable Feast at Finca Vigía. The house contains thousands of Hemingway's letters, papers, books, paintings, and jazz and opera records, as well as his beloved *Pilar*, which is dry docked on the property. Hemingway kept and bred many pets at the Finca, including dogs—Black Dog, whom he'd brought over from Idaho was his favorite—but mostly there were cats. The feline brood had begun with an Angora from Key West named Princessa and two Cuban kittens, Good Will and Boise. Hemingway wrote about Boise's daily adventures and included him in *Islands in the Stream*. Other of Hemingway's "purr factories" included Zane Grey, Feather Puss, Clark Gable, and Furhouse.

In January of 1959, the Cuban Revolution ousted the U.S.-backed Batista regime, and, even though Hemingway was on good terms with Fidel Castro's new government—Castro won Hemingway's billfish tournament and was presented with a trophy by Hemingway himself in 1960—Ernest and Mary made the decision to leave Cuba for Idaho on July 25, 1960. In the fall of 1960, Castro's new government expropriated the Finca, along with a good deal of property owned by other foreigners. In response, the U.S. government ended diplomatic relations with Cuba in October of that year and imposed a partial financial embargo. On April 17, 1961, Cuban exiles invaded the Southern Coast of Cuba in an unsuccessful attempt to overthrow Castro's government at the Bay of Pigs, and in May Cuba declared itself a Communist state. Due to the hostile climate, the Hemingways were never again able to live in Cuba. Because Mary was only permitted to return to the Finca to gather a few easily moveable pieces of property after Ernest's death, the estate has remained a time capsule. "Ernest's personal library of nine thousand books, his furniture, the animal heads, even the artwork—including a Picasso plate of a bull—still hangs on the walls. Ernest's slippers lie beside his bed, his reading glasses rest on the night table."[5] The house was restored by the Cuban government and reopened to the public in 2007, though visitors are generally only permitted to view the interior through the windows, except by special arrangement.

For Whom the Bell Tolls was published on October 21, 1940, and Ernest and Martha were married on November 5, the day after Ernest's divorce from Pauline became final. Ernest asked Otto Bruce to negotiate the purchase of Finca Vigía, which he bought on December 28 for $12,500 from the D'Orn family. After a working honeymoon in China that ended in a bad quarrel, the new Mr. and Mrs. Hemingway returned to the Finca. Ernest's three boys, who were fond of their stepmother, visited frequently. Ernest organized some of the local children into a baseball team that he named the Gigi All-Stars after his nickname for Gregory. As Ernest's parents had done at their homes in Oak Park and Walloon Lake, Ernest employed help in the daily running of his Spanish *palacio*. There was a comforting bustle when the Finca was filled with children, friends, and the household staff. When the boys left at the end of the summer, however, it left Hemingway with a loneliness that is reflected in *Islands in the Stream*. But, as always, distractions were on the horizon.

Though far from Europe, the threat of war had become very real in Cuba by 1942, with as many as "thirty-five Allied ships a week . . . being sunk in the Gulf of Mexico, the Florida straits, and the Cuban and Bahamian waters."[6] As he had during World War I, Hemingway wanted to be a part of the fighting of this new war. He came up with the idea for a counter-intelligence operation and was invited to present his plan to Ambassador Spruille Braden. Braden approved the mission and obtained permission for it from the Cuban Prime Minister. The unofficial code name for the group of men Hemingway assembled to help carry out his operation was the "Crime Shop," but Hemingway nicknamed it the "Crook Factory." At first, the enterprise was limited to monitoring German spies in Havana, but this wasn't enough "action" to satisfy Hemingway. He made up his mind to track down German U-boats in the Gulf, and Braden obtained approval for a variety of guns, radio equipment, and explosives to outfit the *Pilar*.

Hemingway dubbed his U-boat tracking mission "Friendless," after one of his favorite cats. He chose eight crew members—polo champion Winston Guest; Marine Sergeant Donald Saxon; Basque seaman Juan "Sinbad the Sailor/Sinsky" Dunabeitia; frequent Finca visitor Paxtchi; exiled Catalan waiter Fernando Mesa; Spanish Cuban Roberto Herrera; Capt. Gregorio Fuentes; and a local man named Lucas. To prepare for their mission, Hemingway and Fuentes met with local fishermen who'd had close encounters with German submarines boarding their boats to steal water, food, and other supplies. Hemingway had the *Pilar* fortified with steel plates and had larger motors installed to keep pace with the U-boats. Unfortunately, *Pilar*'s first U-boat-hunting mission didn't make it out of the harbor. The special additions had made the boat so heavy and unwieldy that it almost sank, and the steel plating hadn't been properly secured.

Despite *Pilar*'s setbacks, the Crook Factory continued with their mission, patrolling the waters off the Coast of Cuba. At first they attempted to lure German submarines by posing as fishermen whose catch the Germans might be tempted to steal, but after proper radio equipment was installed, they were able to track the U-boats' positions and set out to find them. There were sightings of what looked like submarines a few times, but there was only one incident that could be regarded as a close call. Hemingway's crew sighted a sub and headed toward it—an altercation and possible glory close at hand after months of uneventful searching—but as they did, the U-boat pulled away as calmly as a cat slinking into the bushes. After months of late-night parties following the Crook Factory's fruitless patrols, Martha was frustrated. She felt Ernest was wasting his time and that they should both be covering the war in Europe, which was rapidly descending into chaos. In 1943, she followed through on her convictions and set off for Europe on assignment for *Collier's*. Left to his futile missions, Hemingway soon found the days long and lonely at his Spanish estate. When Martha returned in March of 1944 to try and persuade Ernest to come to Europe with her, he was more than ready to make the trip to London as a war correspondent for *Collier's*. Ever journalistic rivals, the war widened the gulf between Martha and Ernest, and Martha left for Italy immediately after reporting on the Normandy invasion, effectively ending their relationship.

In London, Ernest had met the woman who would become his fourth wife, writer and journalist Mary Welsh. Mary first came to Finca Vigía in May of 1945. She took it upon herself to learn Spanish and expressed enthusiasm for fishing, much to Ernest's delight. Martha and Ernest were divorced on December 21, 1945, and Mary and Ernest were married in Havana on March 14, 1946. The ceremony took place at the home of Ernest's lawyer, with Patrick, Gregory, and Winston Guest as witnesses. On their wedding night, Mary and Ernest got into the first of many rip-roaring arguments, but the next morning agreed never to get married again.

Ernest had always harbored hopes of having a daughter, and by July of 1946, Mary was pregnant. Sadly, her pregnancy ended with the life-threatening rupture of one of her fallopian tubes. After she recovered, Mary took to redecorating the Finca, making additions to its gardens and designing a tower to house a writing studio for Ernest. It was in this "White Tower" that Hemingway began writing *The Garden of Eden* in 1947. He soon realized that he preferred to write in his bedroom within earshot of the Finca's daily activities, however, and the studio was relinquished to their many cats. Hemingway liked company. Feeling lost without it is a major theme in *Islands in the Stream*, and it is Santiago's profound loneliness that leads him to talk to himself, an exhausted warbler, and the marlin he loves but feels he must kill in *The Old Man and the Sea*. The protagonists in Hemingway's works—from Nick Adams to Jake Barnes to Robert Jordan—are guardedly independent, wistful, and forsaken.

Hemingway had been working steadily on *The Garden of Eden* when he decided to take a break and return to Europe with Mary in 1948. In October of 1950, Adriana Ivancich, her mother Dora, and her brother Gianfranco traveled to Cuba as guests of the Hemingways. Feeling threatened by Ernest's infatuation with Adriana, Mary began a frivolous flirtation with Gianfranco. Ernest took the Ivancich family hunting at **Club de Cazadores del Cerro**, fishing on the *Pilar*, and for drinks and supper at El Floridita.

El Floridita (formerly La Piña de Plata)
Located at the end of Calle Obispo, on the corner of Calle Montserrat, Havana. Tel. (+53) 7 8671300.
Open every day 11–12 A.M.

Finca Vigía and Hotel Ambos Mundos aren't the only places where Hemingway's spirit can still be strongly felt in Cuba. A short walk from the Ambos Mundos and across from the **Museo Nacional de Bellas Artes de La Habana** (National Museum of Fine Arts of Havana) is Hemingway's *numero uno* Havana hangout—the bar and seafood restaurant, El Floridita. In an NPR interview, Ernest's niece, Hilary Hemingway, explained how Ernest happened upon El Floridita out of necessity: "In the early 1930s,

Hemingway went into the Floridita to use the restroom one day. People in the bar were bragging about the daiquiris that were being served there. So he ordered one and took a sip. Ernest asked for another one, this time with 'less sugar and more rum.' And that's how the Papa Doble, or the Hemingway Daiquiri, was born."[7]

There was mutual respect between Hemingway and his favorite Cuban bar. Hemingway memorialized El Floridita in *Islands in the Stream*, and the bar enshrined his barstool, which is now permanently occupied by a life-size bronze statue of Hemingway by Cuban artist José Villa Soberón. The bronze rendition of Hemingway looks as though he's waiting for his next daiquiri—which the red-and-white-suited *cantineros* of El Floridita still place in front of him every day. The bar that is now El Floridita opened in 1817 as La Piña de Plata, or "The Silver Pineapple," in the same Habana Vieja location. When Prohibition came about in 1920, many Americans escaped to the Caribbean to let loose and indulge without fear. By 1926, around ninety thousand American tourists were coming to Cuba every year. La Piña de Plata became such a popular destination for Americans during the first quarter of the twentieth century that the owner decided to change its name to the more recognizable "El Floridita."

Twenty-six-year-old Catalan immigrant Constantino "Constante" Ribalaigua Vert—who had been trained as a bartender by his father—began mixing cocktails at the popular Havana hangout in 1914. By 1918, Constante had saved enough money to buy the place. Dubbed El Rey de los Coteleros, or "The Cocktail King of Cuba," by locals, Constante wasn't the inventor of the daiquiri, but he was the first to add chipped ice to the cocktail in the early 1930s, creating what is now known as the frozen daiquiri. The drink came to be associated with El Floridita, now referred to as *la cuna del daiquiri*, or "the cradle of the daiquiri." The word daiquiri comes from the indigenous Taíno word given to the beach and iron mine of the same name near Santiago de Cuba. Constante made four versions of the daiquiri, and for the Papa Doble he added grapefruit, lime juice, and maraschino liqueur. He invented more than two hundred cocktails, many of which are still served in American bars. In a June 5, 1943, letter to Martha Gellhorn, Hemingway wrote, "Oh those daiquiris that nobody makes like old Constantino."[8] Constantino "Constante" Ribalaigua Vert died in 1952, but his spirit keeps Hemingway's company behind the polished wood bar of El Floridita.

Many Cuban intellectuals and artists, as well as Hemingway's Hollywood friends Ava Gardner and Gary Cooper, have enjoyed the world-class cocktails at El Floridita. Hemingway's author pals Ezra Pound and John Dos Passos were regular customers, as were Tennessee Williams and the English author of *Our Man in Havana*, Graham Greene.

After *Across the River and into the Trees* was lambasted by critics following its publication in 1950, Hemingway took claims that he'd lost his touch as a challenge. Before Adriana and her family left the Finca in February of 1951, Hemingway began writing *The Old Man and the Sea*. The idea for the novella began as an essay about an old man fishing alone in a skiff off of **Cabañas** that Hemingway wrote for *Esquire* in 1936. He'd first begun what would become *The Old Man and the Sea* in 1938, but had been sidetracked by the Spanish Civil War and writing *For Whom the Bell Tolls*. *The Old Man and the Sea* was published in 1952 and won the Pulitzer Prize the following May. The book redeemed Hemingway's reputation and is considered by many to be his finest work. Hemingway liked it too: "When Hemingway sent the manuscript to his editor, Wallace Meyer, he said, 'I know that it is the best I can write ever for all of my life, I think, and that it destroys good and able work by being placed alongside of it.' Then he added that he hoped it would 'get rid of the school of criticism that I am through as a writer.'"[9] William Faulkner praised the novel in the literary magazine, *Shenandoah*: "His best. Time may show it to be the best single piece of any of us . . . Praise God that whatever made and loves and pities Hemingway and me kept him from touching it any further."[10]

For years, Hemingway's tendency to guard his true feelings regarding the people and things most important to him led him to hide his yearning for a prize he referred to carelessly as "That Swedish Thing." In a sense, *Across the River and into the Trees* was the luckiest book he ever wrote, since it led him to write the *The Old Man and the Sea*, without which he may never have won the Nobel Prize. Hemingway had been a rumored contender for the Prize several times, but in 1954 the talk was louder than ever. After the accounts of his near-death—and false reports of his actual death—in Africa earlier that year, he was worried that he might be awarded the Nobel Prize, at least in part, out of sympathy. As Hilary Hemingway writes in *Hemingway in Cuba*, "Ernest had done everything to build up the impression that he didn't care one way or another whether he won the prize, when in fact he had hungered for it for years."[11]

When Hemingway accepted the Nobel Prize on October 28, 1954, he was at home at the Finca. "Filled with good cheer, he hurried outside and rounded up the staff—gardeners, chauffeur, everybody—and began plying them with drinks, drawing them fully into the party that was now spilling out onto the grounds with him. There were eleven employees at the Finca, and Hemingway had always regarded them as extended family . . . They were his Cuban family, and living in Cuba had finally won him his Nobel Prize."[12] Hemingway dedicated his Prize to the Cuban people, but rather than place the gold medal in the custody of the Batista government, he entrusted it to the Catholic Church for display at El Cobre sanctuary.

Basílica Santuario Nacional de Nuestra Señora de la Caridad del Cobre (National Basilica Sanctuary of Our Lady of Charity of El Cobre)
Located in El Cobre, twelve miles west of Santiago de Cuba, on the opposite end of the island and 526 miles from Havana.

In *The Old Man and the Sea*, Santiago promises to make a pilgrimage to "the Virgin de Cobre" if he's permitted to bring in his giant marlin intact. Tucked into the foothills of the Sierra Maestra Mountains, Basílica Santuario Nacional de Nuestra Señora de la Caridad del Cobre is Cuba's most famous pilgrimage site. The white stone Roman Catholic Church is seated atop 254 steps on **Cerro de la Cantera**, or "quarry hill." El Cobre has been a copper mining site for centuries, and the current mine is visible from the hill opposite the basilica. The first hermitage at El Cobre was built in 1608, with a larger shrine added a century later. The present-day sanctuary was built in 1926 and features a bell tower flanked by two domed side towers made of red brick. Downstairs, **Capilla de los Milagros** (Chapel of Miracles) houses the altar of Our Lady of Charity, the Patron Saint of Cuba.

Many offerings have been brought to the altar and it is where Hemingway entrusted his Nobel Prize. In the 1980s, the Nobel Prize medal was stolen from the sanctuary, but was quickly restored after Raúl Castro, Fidel's younger brother, issued an ultimatum to return it within seventy-two hours, "or face the consequences."[13]

By the middle of January 1960, Ernest had returned to Cuba following his dangerous summer in Spain. He resumed work on the pieces for *Life* with the assistance of young journalist, Valerie Danby-Smith. The articles, contracted at 10,000 words, had become 120,000 by the end of May. In June, Hotchner arrived at the Finca to help Ernest cull the manuscript. After cutting nearly half, Hotchner presented the trimmed manuscript to the managing editor of *Life*, Ed Thompson, who bought a portion of it, along with the Spanish language rights, for $100,000. *The Dangerous Summer* was published posthumously as a book in 1985. Although work on "The Dangerous Summer" articles had exhausted Ernest and ushered in the first unsettling signs of confusion, he was determined to return to Spain in the summer of 1960.

Hemingway considered himself a *Cubano sato*, or garden-variety Cuban, and enjoyed the privacy and freedom of dress that the island allowed. He wrote some of his best works at Finca Vigía, and spent many of his happiest days roaming Old Havana barefoot in swim trunks and a soiled *guayabera*. Hemingway's spirit lives on throughout the island on the edge of the Gulf Stream, as that of a native son.

ADDITIONAL PLACES OF INTEREST

Cojímar

"He only dreamed of places now and of the lions on the beach. They played like young cats in the dusk and he loved them as he loved the boy."

—Ernest Hemingway, *The Old Man and the Sea*

Cojímar village, Torreón de Cojímar, and Hemingway Memorial
From Havana, follow Carr. Central de Cuba northeast for 7.8 miles.

Less than eight miles from Havana is the fishing village of Cojímar, home of Capt. Gregorio Fuentes (1897–2002), Hemingway's longtime first mate. Fuentes has been speculated to be one of the main inspirations—along with Hemingway's original first mate Carlos Gutiérrez—for Santiago in *The Old Man and the Sea*, though Hemingway disputed his iconic main character being based on anyone in particular. Hemingway kept the *Pilar* docked at Cojímar's pier in the care of Fuentes, who checked on and maintained the boat every day.

Overlooking the lovely harbor at Cojímar is an old Spanish fort, **Torreón de Cojímar**, constructed in 1649 by Juan Bautista Antonelli, the eldest son of the architect of El Morro Castle. Now used by the Coast Guard, the fort at Cojímar was the first to be taken by the British when they attacked Havana in 1762. Next to the fort and encircled by a blue and white stone collonade is the **Hemingway Memorial**, a bronze bust erected in 1962 by Cuban sculptor Fernando Boada Martín and the residents of Cojímar. "The fishermen of Cojímar each contributed a small bronze cleat or old propeller to be used when the artist cast the bust, in memory of their friend."[14] The Hemingway Memorial at Cojímar was the first official monument to be dedicated to Hemingway after his death.

La Terraza de Cojímar (formerly Las Arecas)
Calle Real No. 161 esquina a Candelaria, Cojímar; twenty minutes by taxi from Havana. Tel. (+53) 7 7639486.
Bar open every day 10–12 A.M. Restaurant open every day 12 P.M.–12 A.M.

> *"They sat on the Terrace and many of the fishermen made fun of the old man and he was not angry. Others, of the older fishermen, looked at him and were sad."*
> —Ernest Hemingway, *The Old Man and the Sea*

Overlooking Cojímar Bay, the charming La Terraza de Cojímar is "the Terrace" referred to in *The Old Man and the Sea* where Santiago brings the skeleton of his tragic catch. The restaurant first opened as Las Arecas in 1925, but new ownership changed its name to La Terraza in 1940. The airy, brightly colored dining room memorializes its Hemingway connection with photographs and Ernest's favorite corner dining table, which is permanently set and roped off with a view toward the Northern Coast of Cuba. Offering live music and fresh seafood, La Terraza is a great place to meditate on what Hemingway considered his finest work.

9

LONDON

I n 1944, London was a city of contradictions. The regal capital had
somehow maintained its identity during five years of relentless war—
the cream-colored buildings of Belgravia were still elegant, the cobbled
lanes of Hampstead retained their village-like charm, and Trafalgar Square
held particular meaning and grace. London's stately hotels had managed
to preserve their grandeur, while at the same time becoming hideaways for
war correspondents, Royal Air Force servicemen, and military figures
planning the imminent D-Day invasion. Two of the war correspondents
residing in Mayfair's **Dorchester Hotel** were Martha Gellhorn and
Ernest Hemingway.

Gellhorn had been consulting with Roald Dahl—former fighter pilot for the Royal Air Force, assistant air attaché, and future author of *James and the Giant Peach*—about how to get Hemingway to Europe. Dahl said that it was impossible to obtain air passage for people not engaged in priority war business, but that it would be available to Hemingway if he would agree to report on the activities of the RAF. Hemingway agreed, and was hired as a correspondent for *Collier's*. Gellhorn and Hemingway arrived in New York in May of 1944, but they didn't travel to London together. Gellhorn departed on May 13, 1944, aboard a cargo ship laden with dynamite. Uncomfortable with the mode of transportation, Hemingway got a seat on a Pan American flight four days later, arriving in London weeks before Gellhorn. When Hemingway arrived in London, it was his first visit to the city founded as Londinium by the Romans in 43 A.D. Hemingway's ancestry being English on both sides, he took the visit as a homecoming of sorts. He and Gellhorn both witnessed the invasion of Normandy on June 6, 1944, and reported on it, but Gellhorn's was the more elegant and thorough account. She was the only woman to land at Normandy on D-Day, and made it ashore by stowing away on a hospital ship disguised as a male stretcher-bearer. Gellhorn left for Italy immediately after reporting on the invasion, which was the final knell in her marriage to Hemingway.

Shortly after his arrival in London, Hemingway met Mary Welsh. Originally from Minnesota, Welsh had come to England as a feature writer for the *Daily Express*. Welsh and her husband Noel Monks—an Australian reporter for the *Daily Mail*—lived in a penthouse at 31 Grosvenor Street, near The Dorchester Hotel.

The Dorchester Hotel

53 Park Lane, Mayfair, W1K 1QA. Tel. (+44) 20 7629 8888.

In May of 1944, Hemingway took up residence at The Dorchester. The stately hotel opened its doors on April 18, 1931, and was declared to be able to withstand explosives, earthquakes, and fires. As German bombs rained down during World War II, The Dorchester was a haven where people could still enjoy pre-war occupations like dining and dancing.

General Dwight D. Eisenhower—then the Supreme Commander of the Allied Forces in Europe—planned the D-Day invasion in a suite at The Dorchester, which is now called "**The Eisenhower Suite**." Throughout the 1930s the hotel established a reputation as a haunt for writers and artists, including W. Somerset Maugham and poet Cecil Day-Lewis, and held prestigious literary gatherings like the **Foyles Literary Luncheons**, which continue today.

Weeks prior to D-Day, there were plenty of parties at The Dorchester. Among the people with whom Hemingway celebrated was the society hostess and shipping heiress, Lady Maud "Emerald" Cunard, who was a permanent resident of the hotel. According to an account by Welsh, Cunard left notes and trinkets around Hemingway's room as if marking her territory. On one occasion, Dahl—who became Hemingway's minder while in London—reportedly saw Hemingway apply hair restorer to his thinning pate, then resume partying with Hungarian war photographer Robert Capa and American writer Irwin Shaw. At another party, Hemingway showed up with part of a buzz bomb and convinced some of the guests that it might go off.

In Hemingway's article for *Collier's*, "London Fights the Robots," he expresses his admiration for the RAF pilots, and describes one squadron leader as "a fine man, tall, small-spoken . . . with the light brown circles under his eyes and the purple complexion of a man whose face has been burned away."[1] Hemingway also notes that he wasn't able to understand what the English pilots were saying over the intercom: "Your pilotless-aircraft editor never went to college (here we call it a university), so now he is going to the R.A.F. instead, and the main subject he is studying is trying to understand English on the radio telephone. Face to face with an Englishman, I can understand almost everything he says."[2]

In the early hours of May 25, 1944, Hemingway was returning to The Dorchester from a party at the grand Belgrave Square flat of Robert Capa—the celebrated war photographer who had accompanied him on assignment during the Spanish Civil War. On the way back to the hotel, the car transporting Hemingway collided with a steel water tank at **35 Lowndes Square**. Hemingway was thrown into the windshield, sustaining a deep gash across his scalp, a concussion, and injured knees.

Some newspapers reported that he was killed. It was this injury that would prevent him from going ashore at Normandy.

The Lanesborough (formerly St. George's Hospital)
Hyde Park Corner, Knightsbridge, SW1X 7TA. Tel. (+44) 20 7259 5599.

Following his automobile accident, Hemingway was taken to St. George's Hospital on Hyde Park Corner in Central London. Founded in 1844 and designed by architect William Wilkins, the building that once housed St. George's Hospital is a beautiful example of neoclassical style on a grand scale. Today it is the location of The Lanesborough, which opened in 1991. The rooms of The Lanesborough are decorated in sumptuous pale blue, yellow, and rose. Art Deco fixtures adorn the dining room of **Celeste**, the hotel's Michelin-starred restaurant, which serves modern European cuisine and afternoon tea. During daylight hours, Celeste's dining room is illuminated by a domed glass roof that gives it an ethereal glow.

Once Hemingway was admitted to St. George's, it took fifty-seven stitches to close up the wound on his scalp. Mary and Martha both visited Ernest while he was a patient, though Martha wasn't too sympathetic, laughing at his Tolstoyan beard and bandaged head. Ernest's worn appearance was due in part to too much sun and salt from being out on the *Pilar* many days in a row before coming to London. His skin had become irritated from exposure and he'd let his beard grow to protect it. Ernest's brother Leicester—in London covering the war with a documentary film crew—also came to see his brother at St. George's. Uncle Les, as my mother called him, had a rare nature; inclusive, energetic, and warm. He called everyone "Lady" and "Captain," and was a one-of-a-kind soul for whom every day was "Great!" I will never forget his laugh, nor his truly original voice, which was similar to Ernest's in its precise enunciation and timbre, and equally full of excitement when telling a story.

The Lanesborough is home to the classic **Library Bar**, which serves a special Hemingway Daiquiri. The bar consists of a cozy and sophisticated pair of adjoining rooms decorated like a writer's dream study. Its deep wood glows in the light of chandeliers and the afternoon sun, which has been known, on occasion, to peek through the half-drawn curtains of the back room, decorated with wall-to-wall books. When I visited the Library Bar, the head bartender was kind enough to concoct a Hemingway Daiquiri for me. The cocktail is a perfect balance of sweet and tart, and I was soon a little cockeyed under its spell. In the evenings, live piano wafts through the bar; the perfect atmosphere to enjoy a cocktail among friends, or in the company of one's own thoughts.

The House of Hô (formerly the White Tower restaurant)
1 Percy Street, Fitzrovia, W1T 1DB. Tel. (+44) 20 7323 9130.
Open Mon.–Fri. 12–3 P.M. & 6 P.M.–12 A.M.; Sat. 12 P.M.–12:30 A.M.

Mary Welsh first became acquainted with Hemingway at the White Tower restaurant, which opened in 1938 and is now a lovely Vietnamese eatery called The House of Hô. The afternoon she met Hemingway, Welsh was having lunch with writer Irwin Shaw at a table next to the door on the second floor. "They were ushered upstairs to a room with several tables filled with journalists. Across the room, a group of men stood talking over drinks at a bar. Shaw waved to the bearded one, and Hemingway waved back. He was dressed in his heavy wool R.A.F. uniform, having been granted permission by the Air Ministry to fly with British pilots on a bombing run."[3] Shaw introduced Hemingway to Welsh on Hemingway's insistence.

Mary and Ernest met again for a lunch date at the White Tower and were seated outside. On their second meeting, Ernest described his reporting on the RAF and Mary found his manner shy and serious. Their first meeting had apparently been love at first sight for Ernest, and he proposed to Mary at The Dorchester soon after, despite both of them already being married. Toward the end of the war, Mary made the decision to divorce Monks, and Martha and Ernest also resolved to go their separate ways. Monks wrote of the affair to Welsh on February 8, 1945: "Apparently Mister Hemingway has put it all over Paris that you are the only woman who has ever managed to love him for himself, and that he's nuts about you . . . How charming. . . . I'm sure you must be one of the most envied women in the world. . . . I know I could never compete against Mister Hemingway. I couldn't even match his beard."[4]

I had the pleasure of having lunch at The House of Hô with Tatiana Beca Osborne, the great-granddaughter of celebrated Spanish bullfighter Juan Belmonte, who was a close friend of Hemingway. Before lunch, we enjoyed drinks at a table near the door of the intimate upstairs bar, just as Welsh and Shaw had done. The restaurant's extensive sharing menu features phở, sushi, and dumplings—delicious! The main floor dining room has the gracefulness of a Cape Cod cottage, with large front windows and a covered terrace, where we enjoyed glasses of Pimm's to cap off the afternoon.

Frisco's
40 Sackville Street, Mayfair, W1S 3DE.

After they began meeting regularly, Hemingway and Welsh enjoyed drinking whiskey at bygone club Frisco's. Hemingway knew the owner, Jocelyn "Frisco" Augustus Bingham, from his Paris days. He felt at home in the wistful atmosphere of the club, which played American tunes like "Saint Louis Blues" and "Thanks for the Memory." Frisco had run clubs in Paris and moved in the same circles as Josephine Baker and Louis Armstrong. American journalist A. J. Liebling frequently dropped in at Frisco's, as did American boxer Joe Louis, and French journalist and novelist Joseph Kessel. In *Mollie & Other War Pieces*, Liebling described Frisco's as being "in a bomb-damaged retail shop whose glassless windows were masked with heavy cardboard."[5] Frisco was always able to get large supplies of whiskey, while even the best hotel bars could only offer gin.

The Savoy
2 Savoy Court, Strand, Westminster, WC2R 0EZ. Tel. (+44) 20 7836 4343.

Hemingway could often be found sharing rounds of cocktails with pals like Marlene Dietrich or the Fitzgeralds in the **American Bar** at the opulent Savoy hotel. The Savoy was built by impresario Richard D'Oyly

Carte in 1889 with profits from his Gilbert and Sullivan operas. It boasted hot and cold running water in all of its 268 rooms, with speaking tubes for guests to summon room service at all hours. Its seven stories of glazed brick had a subterranean power plant and an artesian well to provide independent sources of energy and water for its guests. Opened in 1893, the adjoining rooms of the American Bar feature a sparkling Deco-inspired bar with a piano centerpiece and photographs of its many famous patrons. Legendary American bartender Harry Craddock—author of *The Savoy Cocktail Book*—was head barman from 1925 to 1938. Craddock trained as a bartender in America, but fled to London during Prohibition.

The stage of The Savoy's **Beaufort Bar**—originally the **Beaufort Room**—was the setting for George Gershwin's British premiere of *Rhapsody in Blue* in 1925. I had the good fortune of sampling the lounge's Hemingway tribute cocktail, the Neverending Story. The daiquiri has two extra ingredients—crème de cacao and absinthe—which elevate this rich cocktail to the realm of the divine.

The Dove
19 Upper Mall, Hammersmith, W6 9TA. Tel. (+44) 20 8748 9474.
Open Mon.–Sat. 11 A.M.–11 P.M.; Sun. 12–10:30 P.M.

Both Hemingway and Dylan Thomas enjoyed a drink at The Dove. This riverside pub sits in a lovely area adjacent to the River Thames and **Furnivall Gardens**. A public house has stood on the site since the seventeenth century. It's an exceptionally snug place to partake of a pint for several reasons, not the least of which is that the compact space to the right of the bar—accessible through an obscure entrance—once held the Guinness world record for the smallest barroom in the world. The main room has a fireplace and an outdoor patio that looks out onto the river. Poet James Thomson wrote the song "Rule, Britannia!" at The Dove, and a copy of the lyrics hangs on the wall. The Dove has been host to many famous patrons, including King Charles II, who romanced his mistress Nell Gwynne here. Alec Guinness was a regular—his drink of choice being . . . *drum roll* . . . Guinness! Meanwhile, Dylan Thomas was known to enjoy The Dove's mild and bitter.

Farlows

9 Pall Mall, St. James's, SW1Y 5NP. Tel. (+44) 20 7484 1000.
*Open Mon.–Weds. & Fri. 9 A.M.–6 P.M.; Thurs. 9 A.M.–7 P.M.;
Sat. 10 A.M.–6 P.M.; Sun. 11 A.M.–5 P.M.*

Founded in Crooked Lane in 1840 by brothers Charles and John King Farlow, this time-honored outfitter offers an extensive array of fishing and outdoor equipment in a grand, high-ceilinged setting. Ernest fished and hunted game wherever he went, and Farlows is where he and his brother Leicester purchased their fly fishing and shooting equipment while in England.

The Wheatsheaf

25 Rathbone Place, Fitzrovia, W1T 1JB. Tel. (+44) 20 7580 1585.
Open Mon.–Sat. 11 A.M.–11 P.M.

This classic pub that was the haunt of London's bohemian set in the 1930s offers a traditional British menu and a rotating selection of ales and craft beers. With a Tudor façade, ornate stained glass windows, and a cozy pub-mosphere, it's no wonder Anthony Burgess, Dylan Thomas, and George Orwell—who, like Hemingway, was in Spain during the Spanish Civil War—all drank here. Orwell was shot by an enemy sniper while having his morning tea, an incident he recounted in *Homage to Catalonia*.

When I visited The Wheatsheaf on a Monday afternoon, there was a woman sitting alone by the window and a couple having a lively—perhaps heated is more the word—conversation in the back. The bar's appeal to writers was evident—it has the imprint of hidden stories. In addition to its quixotic atmosphere, the staff are friendly and the menu offers delicious thick-cut chips in addition to other pub favorites.

Lincoln's Inn

27 Newman's Row, WC2A, Camden. Tel. (+44) 20 7405 1393.

Named for Henry de Lacy, Third Earl of Lincoln, the Honourable Society of Lincoln's Inn is the largest of London's four Inns of Court. Spanning eleven acres, Lincoln's Inn sits on the border of London and Westminster. While poet John Donne was a preacher at Lincoln's Inn, he wrote *Devotions Upon Emergent Occasions, and severall steps in my Sicknes*, from which Hemingway borrowed the phrase "for whom the bell tolls." *Devotions Upon Emergent Occasions* is a series of meditations upon the symptoms of Donne's recurrent malaria, which he contracted while fighting against the Spanish with Sir Walter Raleigh and the Earl of Essex in Cádiz in 1596. The meditations consist of twenty-three chronologically ordered sections, each describing a stage of Donne's illness. The seventeenth meditation of the *Devotions* contains the famous passage to which the title of Hemingway's fourth novel pays homage: "No man is an island, entire of itself; every man is a piece of the continent, a part of the main . . . any man's death diminishes me, because I am involved in mankind, and therefore never send to know for whom the bell tolls; it tolls for thee."[6]

Donne was one of the preeminent metaphysical poets, and his work is known for its vibrant language and inventive use of metaphor. The text of *Devotions Upon Emergent Occasions* faded into obscurity until the end of the nineteenth century, when it was rediscovered by critic Edmund Gosse. It came to Hemingway's attention through the first critical modern edition of 1923. The chapel bell of Lincoln's Inn tolls every night at 9 P.M.

10
THE WOODS: PART II

KETCHUM AND SUN VALLEY

"Ketchum was perhaps the only place in his world that had not changed radically since the good years. Europe had been completely transformed, Africa was in the process of drastic upheaval, and finally even Cuba blew up around him like a volcano."[1]
—Hunter S. Thompson, *The Great Shark Hunt*

Encouraged by Martha, Ernest began writing *For Whom the Bell Tolls* in March of 1939. In August, Martha went to visit her mother in St. Louis and Ernest left for the **L-Bar-T Ranch** in Wyoming to meet his sons at the end of their summer break. The ranch, owned by Olive and Lawrence Nordquist, was a place of refuge for Ernest, where he could immerse himself fully in the outdoor exertion that cleared his mind. At 76,000 words, he'd reached a good stopping point in *For Whom the Bell Tolls* and planned to treat himself to a dose of rugged downtime.

Pauline, who'd been vacationing in Europe with friends, came to join her husband in Wyoming. When she arrived, she was so sick with a cold that she immediately took to bed. Ernest cooked her meals and tended to her, but despite his show of spousal care, he was restless. Pauline had held out hope that their marriage could be salvaged, but it was clear Ernest's heart was now with Martha. He left Pauline to meet Martha and drive west to the High Country of Central Idaho, where Sun Valley lies tucked in the Sawtooth Range of the Rocky Mountains. Ernest had been invited to Sun Valley by W. Averell Harriman, chairman of the Union Pacific Railroad. Harriman had recently opened the **Sun Valley Resort** and was hoping to attract visitors during the off seasons of summer and fall. He hoped inviting celebrity guests might add to Sun Valley's allure, and offered Hemingway free accommodations for two years at the **Sun Valley Lodge** in exchange for helping to publicize the town.

"THE FAMILY"

The first morning Hemingway woke at the Sun Valley Lodge, two men were eager to speak with him. Sun Valley promoters Gene Van Guilder and Lloyd "Pappy" Arnold—who was also the lodge's photographer—were excited to have such a notable person in their ambitious town and offered their services as guides. Hemingway appreciated the men's knowledge of the area and their shared love of outdoor sports, and accompanied them on hunting expeditions after he'd finished his daily work. Evenings were festive and featured gambling in the makeshift casino of Martha and Ernest's suite. Ernest was making good progress on *For Whom the Bell Tolls*, and in just two months he'd reached the eighteenth chapter.

Sun Valley Lodge and The Ram Bar and Restaurant
1 Sun Valley Road, Sun Valley. Tel. (800) 786-8259.

On September 20, 1939, Ernest and Martha moved into Suite 206 (now Suite 226) of the Sun Valley Lodge, which Ernest nicknamed The Glamour House. Crisscrossed with rivers and streams to fish, and with plenty of duck and pheasant, Idaho reminded Hemingway of his boyhood in Northern Michigan. The brisk air, pine-scented mornings, and outdoor activity cleared his head for work, and he finished *For Whom the Bell Tolls* and worked on *The Garden of Eden* and *A Moveable Feast* while staying at the lodge. Today, guests are welcome to stay in the **Hemingway Suite**, decorated with photographs and a bronze statue of the novelist working. Other suites are named in honor of former guests Marilyn Monroe, Norwegian figure skater Sonja Henie, founder Averell Harriman, and Clint Eastwood. During the Golden Age of Hollywood, the Sun Valley Lodge also welcomed Lucille Ball, Clark Gable, Errol Flynn, and other classic film stars.

The Sun Valley Lodge and surrounding Sun Valley Village offer an outdoor pool and café, yoga studio, spa and fitness center, and several eating and drinking establishments, including **The Ram** restaurant and bar. Dominated by wood walls and decor, the historic Ram restaurant has been serving Sun Valley since 1937. Featuring "Heritage Dinners"—specialty dishes from past menus, including Hungarian Goulash and Pork Tenderloin Schnitzel—The Ram is open every evening from five to nine. **The Ram Bar** was one of Hemingway's favorite Sun Valley haunts and is where he first met Pappy Arnold and his wife Tillie, who, with her bobbed hair, Ernest nearly mistook for Pauline. The Ram Bar offers salads, sandwiches, and snacks with local flavors, such as the Smoked Trout Plate. The creative drinks selection includes the "A Farewell to Hemingway" cocktail, made with Koenig Cherry Brandy, lime, raspberry syrup, and club soda.

On the morning of October 28, 1939, tragedy came to Sun Valley. Ernest's new friend, fellow midwesterner Gene Van Guilder, was accidentally shot while duck hunting with Ernest, Pappy Arnold, and Dave Benner. Van Guilder was only in his mid-thirties. His widow Nin asked Ernest to write and deliver the eulogy in Ketchum. On the first day of November, in sentimental language reminiscent of Robert Frost, Ernest spoke of the "great injustice" of the premature passing of his friend. Gene Van Guilder was buried in the same cemetery where Ernest would be laid to rest a little more than two decades later.

My great-grandfather's graveside is the first I ever remember visiting. I was eight years old, and that year my family drove the 3,500 miles from our home in Seattle to Key West for the first time—what would become an annual pilgrimage once Uncle Les, Aunt Doris, my mom, Hilary, her sister, and others founded the Hemingway Days Festival. Before we'd left Seattle, my mother had sat me on the couch and she and her friend had tried to explain the concept of fame to me and the personage in our family who necessitated the talk. Once we reached Ketchum before going on to visit relatives in Montana, I remember the chilly sunshine, the smell of warming pine needles, and the bright green of the cemetery. I stood looking at the resting place of someone whose blood I shared and whose existence reverberated far beyond our family. Who was this man? I would come to know his legacy first through family photographs in a cracked leather-bound album, then through staying up till midnight when I was twelve reading *The Old Man and the Sea*. The immediacy of the writing and vibrancy of the characters in *The Sun Also Rises* blew me away after I chose it from a table of modern classics in English class in high school, but the stories were what affected me most. After reading "Up in Michigan" I felt close to Ernest, as I'd taken to calling him, instead of Hemingway like everyone else. The story had a bareness and honesty I'd never encountered before, and I admired it. Once I discovered "A Clean, Well-Lighted Place" I knew stories could be art because the things you could say in them could be as subtle and true as music or painting or nature itself. The descriptions of the Italian front and of Lieutenant Henry and Catherine Barkley's clandestine romance in Milan in *A Farewell to Arms* made me realize how profoundly what Ernest had experienced had changed him, and I wanted to be changed that way too. Standing at his graveside in Ketchum, far too young to realize any of these things yet, I was comforted by the majestic evergreen that would watch over and keep my great-grandfather company after we'd gone.

∽

Following Gene Van Guilder's funeral, Martha left Sun Valley on an assignment for *Collier's*. With Christmas approaching, Ernest decided to spend the holiday in Key West with Gregory and Patrick, who were then eight and eleven. Pauline didn't approve; leaving her in Wyoming had been the final straw. She advised Ernest that if he was planning on going back to Cuba with Martha after Christmas, he'd better not come to Key West. By the time he arrived, she'd taken the boys to New York, leaving him on his own in their mansion on Whitehead Street. By the new year, 1940, and for the next twenty years, Hemingway's permanent residence would be Finca Vigía in San Francisco de Paula, Cuba.

By August, Hemingway had made the final cuts to *For Whom the Bell Tolls* at home at the Finca. He received the good news that the book would be published on October 21 and would be a Book of the Month Club selection, which meant a first printing of 100,000 (that number would soon double). *For Whom the Bell Tolls* was unanimously recommended by the Pulitzer committee to be awarded the Prize for Fiction for 1941. The president of Columbia University, Nicholas Murray Butler—whose approval was needed for the prize to be awarded—found the book offensive, however, and the decision of the board was reversed. Hemingway would have to wait more than a decade to receive his Pulitzer Prize for *The Old Man and the Sea*. On September 1, 1940, Hemingway drove cross-country to Sun Valley with Otto Bruce, and was soon back at the Sun Valley Lodge working on the proofs of *For Whom the Bell Tolls*. Martha and Ernest were planning to be married as soon as Pauline and Ernest's divorce was final, and Martha, Jack, Patrick, and Gregory all joined him in Sun Valley.

To add to Sun Valley's growing cachet, Gary Cooper and his wife Veronica ("Rocky") came for a hunting vacation, as did Dorothy Parker and her husband Alan Campbell. Hemingway and Cooper, both zealous outdoorsmen, became fast friends, and Martha needled Ernest to clean up his appearance to be more stylish like Cooper. Hemingway was keen to have Cooper play Robert Jordan if his new book were made into a film. The rights to *For Whom the Bell Tolls* were indeed bought by Paramount Pictures for $100,000—at the time the highest price ever paid for the film rights to a book—and Cooper was eventually cast to play the role. Hemingway and Cooper remained close friends for the rest of their lives, passing away less than two months apart in 1961.

Overall, the reviews of *For Whom the Bell Tolls* were laudatory. *The Atlantic*, *The New Yorker*, *The New York Times*, and *The Nation* all praised Hemingway's novel of the Spanish Civil War. On November 4, 1940, Pauline and Ernest were officially divorced, and the next day Martha and Ernest were married in the Union Pacific Railroad dining room in **Cheyenne**, Wyoming. They drove to New York to honeymoon at the Barclay, but their stay was soon interrupted. Before they'd left Sun Valley, Hemingway had relaxed into the relief of his book being finished, while Martha—who was always aching to be on assignment—had become restless and asked *Collier's* to send her to China to cover the Second Sino-Japanese War. During their honeymoon, *Collier's* contacted Martha to let her know that they were ready to comply. Wanting to accompany his wife in as useful a manner as possible, Ernest met with Ralph Ingersoll of the new tabloid *PM* and obtained an assignment to cover their journey to the Far East. The newlyweds returned home to Finca Vigía to prepare for the trip.

Back in the States after several months away, Martha and Ernest once again sought the wild hush of Sun Valley in September of 1941. By that time, Hemingway had come to think of Idaho as a second home, where he could teach his boys to hunt and dress their own game as his father had done with him and his siblings. Throughout his life, Hemingway immersed himself in nature for the sense of rebirth and release it gave him. In "Big Two-Hearted River," a story set in Northern Michigan and first published in the 1925 edition of *In Our Time*, nature has a regenerative effect on Nick Adams, a young World War I veteran. Hemingway had experienced the same sense of restoration fishing Michigan's Upper Peninsula after returning from Italy in 1919. In Idaho, he was able to access a similar return to purity. Hemingway wrote about Idaho only once for publication, in "The Shot," a piece about proper hunting methods for the April 1951 issue of *True: The Men's Magazine*. The article is an account of an antelope-hunting expedition that Hemingway, his three sons, Pappy Arnold, and Taylor Williams took to the **Pahsimeroi Valley** on September 26, 1941.

During the fall of 1941, Martha and Ernest were once again joined by the Coopers, as well as another Hollywood couple, Barbara Stanwyck and Robert Taylor. The group gambled in Ketchum and spent late nights in the rustic luxury of Sun Valley Resort hangouts like The Ram.

In Idaho, as everywhere he went, Hemingway espoused the local and down-to-earth, while enjoying access to the more refined pastimes and exclusive company his celebrity afforded. These contrasting parts of his personality mirrored those of his parents—Clarence, the hunter and collector of Native American artifacts who was more comfortable in the woods than anywhere else, and Grace, the voice instructor who wore long, white gloves and enjoyed entertaining. Despite his indulgences, Ernest maintained the belief that he was not a member of the upper classes and never trusted his fame. When the Hemingways left Sun Valley for points south on December 3, 1941, *For Whom the Bell Tolls* had already sold over half a million copies. They were driving into Texas on their way to Key West when they heard about Pearl Harbor on the car radio.

By the time Hemingway returned to Sun Valley in September of 1946, many things had changed. From the end of 1942 until December of 1945, the Sun Valley Resort had been closed to guests and used as a convalescent hospital for the Navy. At the beginning of August, Ernest—now divorced from Martha and married to Mary—began the long drive to Sun Valley in his Lincoln, and by the eighteenth he and Mary had checked into a motor court in Casper, Wyoming. The next morning, Mary woke in tremendous pain. Without warning, she had suffered a ruptured fallopian tube due to an ectopic pregnancy. At the nearest hospital, the surgeon had gone fishing. After Mary's veins collapsed, the intern suggested that Ernest say his last goodbyes to his new wife. But after almost having lost Pauline to childbirth and immortalizing that feeling—drawn out to its most feared conclusion—in *A Farewell to Arms*, Ernest refused to accept premature death as Mary's fate. "[H]e made the intern probe for a vein . . . inserted the needle, and stayed at Mary's side until her pulse resumed, her respiration returned to normal, and the surgeon appeared."[2] Ernest said the incident showed "it never paid to quit."[3]

By the beginning of September, Mary and Ernest were back in Sun Valley with Ernest's boys for another lively fall. This time, they stayed in the **MacDonald Cabins** in Ketchum. They hunted and ate their own game, from elk steaks to pheasant and duck. The Coopers were on hand for the first time since before America had entered World War II, as was Nancy "Slim" Keith, the socialite and fashion icon who was then married to Hollywood director Howard Hawks. There was a private showing of *The Killers*, starring Ava Gardner and Burt Lancaster—one of the few films based on Hemingway's work of which he approved. After a day of pheasant hunting on Halloween, Hemingway's life was nearly ended fifteen years early when Slim Keith's gun accidentally went off "so close to [Hemingway's] bent head that it singed the hair on the back of his skull."[4]

On November 10, 1946, the Hemingways packed up and once again descended from the High Country. They spent the end of the year in New York before returning to the Finca, where Hemingway worked on *The Garden of Eden* before a series of hardships began. In April of 1947, Patrick and Gregory were involved in a car accident while visiting their mother. Gregory wasn't seriously injured, and at first it didn't appear that his brother had been either. But by the time Patrick returned to Cuba, the headache he'd had since the accident had gotten worse. Ernest correctly diagnosed his son with a concussion and devoted himself to his recovery, even sleeping on a mattress outside his bedroom door. After convalescing through the spring under the care of Ernest and Pauline, who'd come to be with her son at the Finca, Patrick had fully recovered. On June 17, Hemingway's beloved friend and editor, Maxwell Perkins, died, and later that summer Hemingway received a dire warning about his own health. His blood pressure had reached a dangerous level due to his weight, and he decided that Sun Valley was the place to get back in shape.

In September, Hemingway and Otto Bruce made the drive to Idaho from Key West in Ernest's new Buick Roadmaster. On the way, they stopped to visit Ernest's sister Sunny at the family cabin on Walloon Lake. Hemingway was clearly moved by the visit to his boyhood arcadia, and spent much of the rest of the trip telling Bruce stories of his youthful exploits. On September 29, they arrived "back home" at the Sun Valley Lodge. Hemingway had been unnerved by the recent deaths of several friends—Katy Dos Passos, Ramón, the cook at the Finca, *The Killers* producer Mark Hellinger, two of Hemingway's comrades from his days as a correspondent during the Spanish Civil War, and Max Perkins. A fall of outdoor activity brought down Hemingway's weight, and by the end of 1947 he'd shaved off almost thirty pounds. By December, the calm scene in Sun Valley had become crowded with Mary, Bumby, Patrick, Gregory, and Hemingway's friends, Juan Duñabeitia and Roberto Herrera, who was also Ernest's personal secretary. The crowd of visitors put a stop to Hemingway's work on *The Garden of Eden*, but "Mary cooked duck, pheasant, and venison dinners every night, with pies for the children and endless chocolate cakes, which they finished off at breakfast."[5]

When the fall of 1948 came around, instead of making the usual preparations to go to Sun Valley, Hemingway decided it was time to revisit Europe for the first time since the war. He felt the crowds being drawn to Sun Valley by its prestige were destroying some of its backwoods charm. Hemingway would not return to Idaho for a decade.

By 1958, Hemingway had tired of Cuba's political unrest and recent cool and unsettled weather followed by unrelenting heat, which caused unpredictable fishing. Pappy Arnold found a house for the Hemingways to rent in Ketchum, and in early October, Mary and Ernest met up in Chicago for a pleasant drive out west with Betty and Otto Bruce. "[Ernest] insisted on stopping at grocery stores in the smaller towns to buy apples, cheese, and pickles, which he washed down with Scotch and fresh lime juice. They listened to the World Series on the car radio."[6]

The invigorating air of Idaho, combined with revisiting the relatively simple days of Paris in his work on *A Moveable Feast*, brought about a misplaced vitality in Hemingway. He had mostly recovered—at least physically—from the injuries sustained in the airplane crashes in Africa and was working well. Back in Ketchum, his Idaho family—Pappy and Tillie Arnold, Clara Spiegel, the Atkinsons, Taylor Williams, Don Anderson, and Dr. Saviers—welcomed Ernest, and, as he'd done four decades earlier in Northern Michigan, he found comfort in a homemade chicken dinner prepared by a family friend. Hotchner and Cooper joined Hemingway for bird hunting in the marshes and fields, and he nearly felt like his old self again.

In January of 1959, Fulgencio Batista's dictatorship fell and Fidel Castro's forces moved in to take over Havana. The Finca had been somewhat damaged in the fighting, but was mostly intact. Worried about his future in Havana and not eager to return amidst all the unrest, Hemingway decided to purchase a home in Idaho.

The Ernest and Mary Hemingway House and Preserve
Ketchum.

In March of 1959, Hemingway wrote a $50,000 check for the house that would be his last residence. Built in 1953 by Bob Topping, Mary and Ernest's Ketchum home is a two-story, concrete structure covered in faux wood that sits about a mile outside of Ketchum. Ernest felt that the low humidity and sturdiness of the house would protect the thousands of documents and papers he planned to bring there from moisture and potential fire. Surrounded by 13.9 acres of Sawtooth Wilderness—with the Big Wood River rushing below and the Boulder Mountains in the distance—the house offered Hemingway immediate access to nature, his truest and most reliable ally, at a time when his inner world was starting to betray him.

Hemingway lived in the Ketchum house until his death on July 2, 1961, after which Mary lived mostly in New York City until her death in 1986. In May of 2017, ownership of the Ernest and Mary Hemingway House and Preserve shifted from The Nature Conservancy—to whom Mary had left it—to **The Community Library** in Ketchum. The house was listed on the National Register of Historic Places in 2015. The Ernest and Mary Hemingway House is closed to the public, but The Community Library in Ketchum has plans to use an apartment on the property as the site of a residency program for writers, scholars, and artists. Artifacts from the house will be integrated into The Community Library's Regional History Collection, and will be accessible to the public through periodic displays at both The Community Library and its associated **Regional History Museum**.

Ernest and Mary left Idaho in March 1959 to spend the summer in Spain. The months away had taken a lot out of Hemingway, and on the voyage back from Europe on the SS *Liberté* he was still battling a kidney infection, as well as a cold he'd caught at the Ritz. Before heading out west with Carmen and Antonio Ordóñez, Hemingway delivered the manuscript of what would become *A Moveable Feast* to Charles Scribner in New York on November 3. Almost immediately after arriving in Ketchum, Antonio was called away on a family emergency, spoiling Ernest's plan to take him duck hunting.

Ernest's hopes of getting in shape by way of outdoor activity were further frustrated when, on a November 27 hunting outing with Dr. Saviers, Mary slipped and fractured her elbow. Ernest complained about having to run errands and assist her at the hospital, fearing that he wouldn't be in shape for the revisions to *A Moveable Feast* and further work on "The Dangerous Summer" articles. He asked Hotchner to come to Idaho, and on the way back from picking him up at the train station, Hemingway was convinced the FBI was following him. While it was true that the Feds had a file on Hemingway—not out of the ordinary for a public figure who had conducted U-boat hunting missions during World War II—the scope of his imaginings was extreme. As heartbreaking as his delusions were, more tragic was his hope that he would come out of the breakdown to have another great success, as he had with *The Old Man and the Sea*. Hemingway's breakdown wasn't just mental—his limbs had lost their usual athletic appearance, he was pale, and his blood pressure was alarmingly high. The unanimous consensus was that he needed both physical and psychological treatment. Hospitalization at the Mayo Clinic in Rochester, Minnesota was arranged, and on November 30, Dr. Saviers made the flight east with Hemingway.

After a complete physical examination and numerous tests, the results were generally normal. Hemingway's corporeal troubles included a mild case of diabetes mellitus and an enlarged liver. The symptoms suggested to his doctor, Hugh R. Butt, that he might have hemochromatosis, a disease caused by toxic levels of iron absorption that is sometimes the result of excessive alcohol consumption. At the time, Dr. Butt elected not to perform the biopsy necessary to confirm the theory. Underlying all of Hemingway's delusions and anxiety was a stubborn bleakness that he had been unable to lift himself out of by the usual means: inspiration followed by hard work. Without the former, the latter was impossible. As he hoped for the flash he'd relied upon so many times before, his doctors concluded that his depression might be caused in part by his hypertension medication. They recommended that it be discontinued, and his psychotherapist, Dr. Rome, prescribed a course of shock treatments twice a week through the beginning of January 1961. These caused further problems—headaches, confusion, and memory loss.

On January 11, the fact of Hemingway's presence at the Mayo Clinic was no longer kept under wraps, and old friends from across the expanse of his life reached out to wish him well. The following day, President-elect John Kennedy sent a telegram inviting the Hemingways to his inauguration. Ernest wired the next day offering his and Mary's congratulations, saying they were honored by the invitation, but would be unable to attend. Two days after watching the January 20 inauguration on television, Ernest flew home to Idaho.

In Ketchum, Hemingway set to arranging the vignettes of *A Moveable Feast*, rising early as usual and finishing just after midday. "After lunch and a nap he walked the snowy roads for exercise, sometimes alone, a too-slender figure in checked cap and heavy boots, pausing to wave to the schoolchildren on their way home."[7] Only drinking a little wine with meals, Hemingway was attempting to be kinder to his body, but undoubtedly felt himself slipping away. Most of his vast collection of books was still in Cuba, and, in search of a title for *A Moveable Feast*, he asked Charles Scribner to send him copies of the King James Bible and the *Oxford Book of English Verse*. Though Hemingway was going about the task of finishing his Paris memoir, he was not writing any new material.

The gulf between Hemingway and the outside world was growing all the time, and throughout February he became increasingly withdrawn. He stopped going into town and inviting members of his Ketchum family to visit. A chasmic hush surrounded the man who'd always had so much to say. This involuntary calm would be his protracted last verse. Asked to write a line for a book to be presented to President Kennedy, Hemingway struggled all day. When Dr. Saviers came for his usual visit, Hemingway told him that the words weren't coming anymore, and cried.

One late morning in April, the unfamiliarity with himself became too much and Hemingway sought to escape in the same way his father had. Mary came downstairs to find Ernest in the living room with a shotgun and two shells nearby on the windowsill. She spoke to him in even tones until Dr. Saviers arrived and talked him into handing over the gun. Dr. Saviers brought Hemingway to the Sun Valley Hospital before he was flown back to the Mayo Clinic on April 25. Before his departure, Hemingway made a more fervent and barely thwarted attempt at suicide.

In the middle of May, Hemingway's friend of two decades, Gary Cooper, died of cancer in California. Hemingway received further electroshock treatments at the Mayo Clinic until June, when he was deemed well enough to return home. Before he was discharged, Mary—who had initially stayed behind in Ketchum—arrived in Rochester. She wasn't convinced that Ernest was stable enough to be released and wanted him transferred to another clinic in Hartford, Connecticut. But despite Mary's efforts to keep her husband in treatment, the doctors didn't recommend the move and discharged him.

On June 26, George Brown, Ernest's old sparring partner, flew from New York to Rochester to drive Mary and Ernest home to Idaho in a rented Buick. They arrived in Ketchum on the last day of June. The following day, Ernest paid a visit to Dr. Saviers, and in the evening the Hemingways took George Brown to dinner at the Christiania restaurant, where they sat at Ernest's favorite corner table. While Ernest was brushing his teeth in the upstairs bathroom that night, Mary began to sing a whimsical Italian love song that she and Ernest had learned at Cortina d'Ampezzo. Ernest joined her in song, put on his pajamas, and Mary left him alone to sleep. In the early morning hours of July 2, 1961, Ernest Miller Hemingway rose as usual, crept downstairs in his bathrobe, unlocked the gun cabinet in the basement, and, I would like to believe, rejoined his father in their favorite place—the woods. I can certainly feel them there.

ADDITIONAL PLACES OF INTEREST

"Like many another writer, Hemingway did his best work when he felt he was standing on something solid—like an Idaho mountainside."[8]

—Hunter S. Thompson, *The Great Shark Hunt*

Silver Creek Preserve

165 Kilpatrick Bridge Road, Bellevue. Located 33 miles south of
Sun Valley on Highway 75 South and Gannett Picabo Road.
Tel. (208) 788-2203.
*Open sunrise to sunset year-round. Visitor Center open Memorial Day to
Labor Day. Catch-and-release fishing open Memorial Day to November 30.*

In a 1939 letter to his eldest son, Jack, Ernest wrote: "You'll love it here,
Schatz . . . there's a stream called Silver Creek where we shoot ducks from a
canoe . . . Saw more big trout rising than have ever seen . . . Just like English
chalk streams . . . We'll fish it together next year."[9] Silver Creek is where three
spring-fed creeks converge in a panoramic valley at the base of the Picabo
Hills. When Hemingway first arrived in Sun Valley, the area was owned
by the Union Pacific Railroad and known as the **Sun Valley Ranch**. In the
autumn of 1939, and for many autumns thereafter, Hemingway came to fish
and hunt duck on the Sun Valley Ranch, and, later, on a ranch owned by the
Purdy family. The writer who'd grown up in the Northern Michigan woods
took to the knitted greenery cut through with a slippery blue vein like a
native; the expanse of blue-grey hills dotted with elk reminded him of Spain.

During Jack Hemingway's time as Idaho's Fish and Game Com-
missioner in the 1970s, he assisted the Nature Conservancy in their
purchase of the 2,882 acres that now make up Silver Creek Preserve.
An avid fly fisherman, Jack had first come to the area with his father
and younger brothers as a teenager, and had fallen in love with the
"high, humpbacked, sagebrush-covered hills."[10] The ecstatic diversity
of wildlife surrounding Silver Creek includes bobcats, mountain lions,
moose, elk, deer, coyotes, eagles, hawks, waterfowl, a host of songbirds,
and one of the highest densities of stream insects in North America.
In addition to what many—including Ernest—have come to know as
the best fly fishing in America, the preserve is an excellent place for
canoeing and snowshoeing. Beginning at the **Silver Creek Preserve
Visitor Center** there is a self-guided nature trail where 150 bird species have been identified. More than ten thousand acres surrounding
Silver Creek Preserve have been protected by the Nature Conservancy
through conservation easements.

Silver Creek Preserve is home to a rock bearing one of the epigraphs to Hemingway's first novel, excerpted from Ecclesiastes: "One generation passes away, and another generation comes. But the earth abides forever. The sun also rises, and the sun goes down, and hastens to its place where it arose." It is of great comfort to know that the expanse of unspoiled wilderness surrounding Silver Creek has been preserved as my great-grandfather knew it, and that it will hopefully remain that way.

Hemingway Memorial
Trail Creek Road, Sun Valley. Tel. (208) 622-2135.

Just off Trail Creek Road and about a mile northeast of the Sun Valley Lodge is the Hemingway Memorial. Dedicated on Hemingway's birthday in 1966, the memorial sculpture by Robert Berks is one of my favorites, tucked as it is between the trees on the edge of Trail Creek. The bronze column with a bust of Hemingway looking out across the meadow sits atop a pile of flat stones with the inscription: "Best of all he loved the fall . . . the leaves yellow on the cottonwoods, leaves floating on the trout streams and above the hills the high blue windless skies . . . now he will be a part of them forever," taken from the eulogy Hemingway wrote for Gene Van Guilder. I can think of no better tribute to Ernest than hiking to this restful memorial to read one of his books in view of white-streaked Bald Mountain, with the sound of Trail Creek moving across the valley in the background.

Michel's Christiania and Olympic Bar
303 Walnut Avenue, Ketchum. Tel. (208) 726-3388.
Open every day 5 P.M.–12 A.M.

Hemingway was a regular at Christiania, a cozy and elegant French restaurant established in 1959 and now owned by Lyon native Michel Rudigoz. Known locally as "The Christy," Michel's Christiania offers authentic French fare such as "Escargots steeped in Herbed Garlic Butter with a hint of Pernod" and "Sautèed Filet of Idaho Ruby Trout with Parsley, Lemon, and finished with a touch of Butter," as well as an extensive wine list.

Hemingway felt at home in Christiania's warm and welcoming **Olympic Bar**. With views of Bald Mountain to the west, the ski-themed bar features "Michel's Drink"—a classic French beverage known as Kir, made with Chardonnay and crème de cassis—and the house speciality *pomme frites*, made from Idaho potatoes. Hemingway preferred to sit behind the side of the bar that is now dedicated to the Olympic triumphs of proprietor Rudigoz, a former U.S. Women's Ski Team instructor. Clint Eastwood, a long-time Sun Valley resident, has been known to drink and swap stories with the other patrons of the Olympic.

Sun Valley Inn (formerly the Challenger Inn)
2 Sun Valley Road, Sun Valley. Tel. (800) 786-8259.

First opened in 1937 as part of the Sun Valley Resort, this European-inspired chalet—formerly known as the Challenger Inn—is where Martha, Ernest, and his three sons stayed when they visited Sun Valley in 1941. It is reputed that Hemingway was sometimes distracted during his morning writing routine by the ducks outside his pond-facing window. Located in the heart of Sun Valley Village, the inn's cheerful lodgings feature newly remodeled rooms, a lobby bar, and a fitness center with adjoining outdoor pool.

The Community Library Center for Regional History
415 Spruce Avenue, Ketchum. Tel. (208) 726-3493, ext. 112.
Email: info@comlib.org.
Open Mon.–Sat. 10 A.M.–6 P.M.

The Community Library Center for Regional History is home to a large Hemingway Collection, including books by and about the author, artifacts from Mary and Ernest's Ketchum home, and rare photos and interviews with Hemingway friends and family. In May of 2017, ownership of the Ernest and Mary Hemingway House and Preserve shifted from The Nature Conservancy to The Community Library, so now the house itself is one of the most significant artifacts in the Center for Regional History's Hemingway Collection. Founded in 1955, the library hosts an annual

Ernest Hemingway Seminar the weekend after Labor Day, featuring presentations by Hemingway scholars.

Regional History Museum
180 1st Street East at Washington Avenue, Ketchum. Tel. (208) 726-8118. *Open Weds.–Sat. 1–5 P.M.*

The Community Library Center for Regional History has a permanent exhibit, "Ernest Hemingway: At Home in Idaho," at the Regional History Museum. Located in Ketchum's **Forest Service Park**, the Regional History Museum houses a gallery of framed photographs of Hemingway, the Royal typewriter Hemingway took with him on his and Mary's 1954 trip to Italy, and other memorabilia, including the physician's bag belonging to Hemingway's close friend, Dr. George Saviers. A bronze bust prominently features the scar on Hemingway's forehead, a memento of the 1928 incident in which the young writer was hit by falling glass after yanking on the skylight cord in his Paris bathroom, mistaking it for the toilet chain.

Casino Bar (formerly the Casino Club)
220 North Main Street, Ketchum. Tel. (208) 726-9901. *Open every day 11–2 A.M.*

Built in 1926 with trees taken from Bald Mountain, the Casino Bar was originally a gambling establishment known as the Casino Club. When Hemingway first came to Ketchum in 1939—and until the 1950s when gambling was outlawed in Idaho—the Casino Club was home to craps and blackjack tables, slots, and roulette. When Hemingway wasn't running "Hemingstein's Mixed Vicing and Dicing Establishment" in his suite at the Sun Valley Lodge, he and Mary could often be found having drinks and gambling at the Casino Club on Main Street.

Owned by the Werry family since 1935, this laid-back locals hangout has retained its lack of pretense in the face of Ketchum and Sun Valley's popularity with the rich and famous. In that way the bar is much like Hemingway, whose tendency to wear dirty, worn-out clothes and moccasins endeared him to some who might have otherwise assumed he'd be inaccessible. The Casino Bar—also referred to as the "Casbah" and the "Can't Say No" by locals—makes a point of being a down-to-earth refuge where people can relax, play pool, and be themselves.

Dunchin Lounge

1 Sun Valley Road, Sun Valley. Tel. (208) 622-2145.
Open Mon.–Thurs. 12–11 P.M.; Fri. 12 P.M.–12 A.M.; Sat. 24 hours, until 11 P.M. on Sun.

Located conveniently in the lobby of the Sun Valley Lodge, the Dunchin Lounge was one of Hemingway's favorite local spots for food and drink. Originally designed by Marjorie Dunchin in 1936, this popular *après-ski* hangout was remodeled in 2015 to create a sleek, contemporary feel. The lounge offers late-night snacks such as Tempura Green Beans and Truffle Parmesan Fries made from local potatoes, as well as Hot Buttered Rum made with fresh-cooked batter and lively cocktails like the "Bee Sting," which combines gin, fresh lemon juice, honey, and maraschino liqueur. Once frequented by Marilyn Monroe, the Dunchin Lounge is a good place to unwind, just as it was during Hemingway's time.

Trail Creek Cabin

300 Trail Creek Road, Sun Valley. Tel. (208) 622-2800.
For reservations: trailcreekcabinreservations@sunvalley.com.
Open Weds.–Sun. 5–9 P.M.

Originally built in 1937 as the hunting cabin of Sun Valley founder Averell Harriman, Trail Creek Cabin was one of Hemingway's favorite places to dine and have parties with friends like Ingrid Bergman and Gary Cooper. Following one such occasion on December 27, 1958, Mary described a "dinner-dance" she'd arranged: "Sun Valley's informal log house with its blazing fire-places . . . transformed . . . into a bower of spicy pine with branches protruding from walls and ceilings to embrace us. We dined at tables in a hollow square with Herman Primus playing Austrian mountain songs on his zither in the middle and later wore out our shoes dancing the 'Jelly Roll Blues.'"[11] After Ernest's death, Mary continued to celebrate his birthday each July at Trail Creek Cabin with a party for those he'd considered his Idaho family.

Serving up refined, seasonal mountain fare such as Hagerman Valley Idaho Ruby Trout with succotash and wild rice, Butternut Squash Bisque, and the "1937 Little Gem Salad," Trail Creek Cabin is a great place to honor Hemingway's convivial streak with dinner and drinks in a true hunter's cabin, with a view of sugar-topped Bald Mountain just beyond your table.

Sawtooth Club

231 North Main Street, Ketchum. Tel. (208) 726-5233.
Open every day 4:30–9 P.M. Happy hour 4:30–6 P.M.

In *The Great Shark Hunt*, Hunter S. Thompson attempts to answer the question, "What Lured Hemingway to Ketchum?":

> and in the end he came back to Ketchum, never ceasing to wonder, says [Charlie] Mason, why he hadn't been killed years earlier in the midst of violent action on some other part of the globe. Here, at least he had mountains and a good river below his house; he could live among rugged, non-political people and visit, when he chose to, with a few of his famous friends who still came up to Sun Valley. He could sit in the Tram or the Alpine or the Sawtooth Club and talk with men who felt the same way he did about life . . . In this congenial atmosphere he felt he could get away from the pressures of a world gone mad and "write truly" about life as he had in the past.[12]

Located in a stalwart brick building in downtown Ketchum, the Sawtooth Club has repeatedly been voted "The Valley's Best Overall Restaurant." Many of the Sawtooth's entrées—like the Mesquite Ribeye Steak of Northwest-grown, grass-fed beef—are prepared over a wood flame and can be enjoyed on the outdoor terrace from late May through September. With treats like Butternut Squash Ravioli, Green Bean Fries, and Baked Brie En Croute, as well as craft beers on tap, signature cocktails, and a full wine list, the Sawtooth Club is a cozy and friendly Ketchum mainstay.

Pioneer Saloon (formerly the Commercial Club)
320 North Main Street, Ketchum. Tel. (208) 726-3139.
Open every day 4–10 P.M.

The Pioneer Saloon was one of Hemingway's favorite places to have a cocktail in Ketchum. The bar was first opened by Otis Hobbs as a casino called the Commercial Club in the 1940s. For a time, the space was used as a meeting hall for the American Legion, then as a dry goods store before it reopened as the Pioneer Saloon casino around 1950. In 1953, gambling was outlawed in Idaho and the Pioneer—known to locals as "the Pio"—became a bar and antique store. In 1965, owner Whitey Hirschman turned the Pioneer Saloon into a restaurant, redesigning it in 1972. At the beginning of the ski season each November, "Pio Days" celebrates the establishment's most recent incarnation.

Since 1986, the Pioneer Saloon has been owned and run by the Witmer family. To commemorate Hemingway's Idaho legacy, the restaurant has one of Hemingway's shotguns on display—a 1953 Winchester Model 21 twelve-gauge that he used for duck and pheasant hunting on the nearby Purdy ranch. Specializing in prime rib, steaks, and local rainbow trout, the Pioneer's wood interior, mounted game, and period firearms invoke the feeling of Idaho's frontier days.

Whiskey Jacques' (formerly the Alpine Club)
251 North Main Street, Ketchum. Tel. (208) 726-5297.
Open Mon.–Fri. 4 P.M.*–2* A.M.*; Sat. 1* P.M.*–2* A.M.*; Sun. 11–2* A.M. *Kitchen open every day 4–9* P.M.

When Hemingway was a regular, this sports pub—which burnt down and was rebuilt in 2008—was a quasi-legal casino known as the Alpine Club. Featuring live music and everything from "Philly Cheese Steak" to the wood-fired "Heming's Way" thin and crispy pizza, this brick-and-timber Main Street staple is a locals' hangout extraordinaire.

∽

Hemingway didn't just invent a modern style of writing and he wasn't just an adventurer. He grabbed onto, swallowed whole, and distilled the most dangerous of truths, allowing them to gestate as long as it took. Sometimes it wouldn't be time, and he would wait—often anxiously—making his mark on the landscape and the people around him. Haunted by meaning and so rife with the implications of his realizations, they would frequently take over his personality like a pervasive madness, until that madness manifested itself in the genius of his work. Through Hemingway's writing, we are invited to step into the webbing of pansophy and look around. We feel it and we touch it; it moves through us, and we are changed. My great-grandfather lived inside this tangle—he swam in it, breathed it in, and spat it out. Through his lingering exegesis, he continues to speak for all of us.

ACKNOWLEDGMENTS

I would like to thank Thomas David Evans, Jennifer Moore, Carrie Ellen Moore, Anna Moore Groome, James B. Jaynes Jr., Hilary Hemingway, Jeff Lindsay, John Hemingway, Kristina Efrémova, Patrick Hemingway Adams, Olivia Rosane, Gema Alava, Laura Smith, Kathleen Olp, Tatiana Beca Osborne, Vida Kalcius, Kat Janicka, Erika Howard Dolmans, Maurits Dolmans, Don Smith, Dean Tucker, Dan Frydman, Ben McFall, Cathryn Pitt, Linda Satchwell, Angela Ward, Alexandra Janes, Angela Benvenuti, Lilli Gillmer, Beth Cooke, Jaymes Williams, Rita Troxel, Rae Coates, Toni Tarracino, Carolyn Ferguson, James Plath, Papa John Stubbings, Paul Elwick, Lynne Evans, Sheila Bloomquist Wilmoth, Cristina Raskopf Norcross, Chloe Dee Noble, Constantine Katsiris, Scott Rossi, Óscar Quadrado Mendoza, Richard Crossland, Brian Gordon Sinclair, the Grassnakes, Jane Dystel, and Jessica Case for their support and encouragement.

I would also like to thank Ralph James Mooney, without whose American Legal Biography course I never would have believed I could take on someone else's story.

BIBLIOGRAPHY

Anderson, Fay. *Witness to War: The History of Australian Conflict Reporting.* Carlton, Victoria: Melbourne University Press, 2011.

Baker, Carlos. *Ernest Hemingway: A Life Story.* New York: Penguin Books, 1988.

Baker, Carlos, ed. *Ernest Hemingway: Selected Letters, 1917–1961.* New York: Charles Scribner's Sons, 1981.

Burrill, William. *Hemingway: The Toronto Years.* Toronto: Doubleday Canada, 1995.

Callaghan, Morley. *That Summer in Paris.* New York: Penguin Books, 1963.

Cranston, J. H. *Ink on My Fingers.* Toronto: The Ryerson Press, 1953.

Di Robilant, Andrea. "Retracing Hemingway's Road Trip Through Northern Italy." *Departures,* December 15, 2016. www.departures.com/art-culture/books/andrea-di-robilant-imagines -ernest-hemingway-in-italy.

Donne, John. *Devotions Upon Emergent Occasions,* 1624.

Elder, Robert K., and Mark Cirino. "Hemingway's High School Graduation: 100 Years Later." *Huffington Post,* updated May 15, 2017. www.huffingtonpost.com/entry/hemingways-high -school-graduation-100-years-later_us_59144a0ee4b016248243f1ff.

Fogt, Jan. "Fighting big fish with Ernest Hemingway." *Anglers Journal,* March 25, 2019. www.anglersjournal.com/saltwater/fighting-big-fish-with-ernest-hemingway.

Graden, Dale T. "'The Earth Endureth Forever': Hemingway in Spain." *The Volunteer,* June 10, 2016. www.albavolunteer.org/2016/06/the-earth-endureth-forever-ernest-hemingway-and-the-spanish -civil-war/.

Hemingway's Idaho Geographies. "Mapping Hemingway in Idaho." www.arcgis.com/apps/Map Journal/index.html?appid=8372c1acd90749a489cd937795d788a5.

Hemingway, Ernest. *Across the River and into the Trees.* London: Arrow Books, 2004.

Hemingway, Ernest. "American Bohemians in Paris." *Toronto Star Weekly,* March 25, 1922.

Hemingway, Ernest. "The Art of the Short Story." *Paris Review* (Spring 1981). www.theparis review.org/letters-essays/3267/the-art-of-the-short-story-ernest-hemingway.

Hemingway, Ernest. "The Blind Man's Christmas Eve." *Toronto Star Weekly,* December 22, 1923, quoted in Graeme Bayliss, "In Our Town: Ernest Hemingway in Toronto," *Torontoist,* March 7, 2012. torontoist.com/2012/03/in-our-town-ernest-hemingway-in-toronto/.

Hemingway, Ernest. "Bullfighting is Not a Sport—It is a Tragedy." *Toronto Star Weekly,* October 20, 1923. ehto.thestar.com/marks/bullfighting-is-not-a-sport-it-is-a-tragedy.

Hemingway, Ernest. *The Dangerous Summer.* London: Hamish Hamilton, 1985.

Hemingway, Ernest. *Death in the Afternoon.* New York: Scribner, 2002.

Hemingway, Ernest. *A Farewell to Arms.* London: Arrow, 1994.

Hemingway, Ernest. *Fiesta.* London: Jonathan Cape, 1941.

Hemingway, Ernest. *For Whom the Bell Tolls.* New York: Charles Scribner's Sons, 1968.

Hemingway, Ernest. *The Garden of Eden.* New York: Scribner Paperback Fiction, 1995.

Hemingway, Ernest. *In Our Time.* New York: Scribner, 2003.

Hemingway, Ernest. *Islands in the Stream*. London: Vintage, 2017.

Hemingway, Ernest. "London Fights the Robots." *Collier's*, August 19, 1944. www.billdownscbs .com/2015/08/london-fights-robots-by-ernest-hemingway.html.

Hemingway, Ernest. *Men Without Women*. New York: Scribner Paperback Fiction, 1997.

Hemingway, Ernest. *A Moveable Feast*. London: Vintage Books, 2000.

Hemingway, Ernest. *The Old Man and the Sea*. London: Vintage Books, 2000.

Hemingway, Ernest. "On the American Dead in Spain." *The New Masses*, February 14, 1939.

Hemingway, Ernest. "A Silent, Ghastly Procession." *Toronto Daily Star*, October 20, 1922.

Hemingway, Ernest. "Sporting Mayor at Boxing Bouts." *Toronto Star Weekly*, March 30, 1920. ehto.thestar.com/marks/sporting-mayor-at-boxing-bouts.

Hemingway, Ernest. "Tackling a Spanish Bull Is 'Just Like Rugby'; Hemingway Tells How He Surprised the Natives." *Toronto Star Weekly*, September 13, 1924.

Hemingway, Ernest. *To Have and Have Not*. London: Arrow Books, 2004.

Hemingway, Ernest. "Trout-Fishing Hints." *Toronto Star Weekly*, April 24, 1920.

Hemingway, Ernest. "At Vigo, in Spain, Is Where You Catch the Silver and Blue Tuna, the King of All Fish." *Toronto Star Weekly*, February 18, 1922.

Hemingway, Ernest. "World Series of Bull Fighting a Mad, Whirling Carnival." *Toronto Star Weekly*, October 27, 1923.

Hemingway, Hilary, and Carlene Brennen. *Hemingway in Cuba*. New York: Rugged Land, 2005.

Hemingway, Jack. *Misadventures of a Fly Fisherman: My Life with and without Papa*. New York: McGraw-Hill, 1986.

Jankowski, Nicole. "The Cocktail King of Cuba: The Man Who Invented Hemingway's Favorite Daiquiri." *NPR*, April 25, 2017. www.npr.org/sections/thesalt/2017/04/25/525063025 /the-cocktail-king-of-cuba-the-man-who-invented-hemingways-favorite-daiquiri.

Lanzendorfer, Joy. "11 Facts about Hemingway's The Old Man and the Sea." Mental Floss, last modified May 27, 2015. www.mentalfloss.com/article/64363/11-facts-about-hemingways -old-man-and-sea.

Liebling, A. J. *Mollie & Other War Pieces*. Lincoln: Bison Books, 2004.

Lorinc, John. "Once Upon a City: Toronto's Premier Italian Trattoria." *Toronto Star*, May 26, 2016. www.thestar.com/yourtoronto/once-upon-a-city-archives/2016/05/26/once-upon-a -city-torontos-premier-italian-trattoria.html.

Markham, James M. "Hemingway's Spain." *The New York Times*, November 24, 1985. www.ny times.com/1985/11/24/travel/hemingway-s-spain.html.

McIver, Stuart B. *Hemingway's Key West*. Sarasota: Pineapple Press, Inc., 2012.

Meyers, Jeffrey, ed. *Hemingway: The Critical Heritage*. London: Routledge & Kegan Paul, 1982.

Oliphant, Ashley. *Hemingway and Bimini*. Sarasota: Pineapple Press, Inc., 2017.

Olson, Liesl. "Ernest Hemingway in Chicago." *The Newberry*, June 1, 2012. www.newberry.org /ernest-hemingway-chicago.

Owen, Richard. *Hemingway in Italy*. London: Haus Publishing, 2017.

Reynolds, Michael. *Hemingway: The Paris Years*. New York: Norton, 1989.

Sanford, Marcelline Hemingway. *At the Hemingways: A Family Portrait*. London: Putnam, 1962.

Schiller, Bill. "How Hemingway came of age at the Toronto Star." *The Toronto Star*, last modified 2012. ehto.thestar.com/marks/how-hemingway-came-of-age-at-the-toronto-star.

Sinclair, Brian Gordon. "The Nobel Prize Medal of Ernest Hemingway." *Canadian-Cuban Friendship Association Toronto*, December 6, 2011. www.ccfatoronto.ca/articles-of-interest/178 -the-nobel-prize-medal-of-ernest-hemingway.

Thompson, Hunter S. *The Great Shark Hunt: Strange Tales from a Strange Time*. London: Picador, 2010.

Wagner-Martin, Linda. *Ernest Hemingway: A Literary Life*. London: Palgrave Macmillan, 2007.

ENDNOTES

1: THE WOODS: PART I: OAK PARK, MICHIGAN, AND CHICAGO

1   The Historical Society of Oak Park and River Forest, 2018, oprfmuseum.org/brief-history -oak-park.

2   Carlos Baker, *Ernest Hemingway: A Life Story* (New York: Penguin Books, 1988), 4.

3   Marcelline Hemingway Sanford, *At the Hemingways: A Family Portrait* (London: Putnam, 1963), 11.

4   Sanford, *At the Hemingways*, 11–12.

5   Sanford, *At the Hemingways*, 53.

6   Sanford, *At the Hemingways*, 33.

7   Sanford, *At the Hemingways*, 81.

8   Sanford, *At the Hemingways*, 81.

9   Sanford, *At the Hemingways*, 67.

10 Sanford, *At the Hemingways*, 54.

11 Sanford, *At the Hemingways*, 5.

12 Sanford, *At the Hemingways*, 15.

13 Baker, *Ernest Hemingway: A Life Story*, 7–8.

14 Sanford, *At the Hemingways*, 102.

15 Robert K. Elder and Mark Cirino, "Hemingway's High School Graduation: 100 Years Later," *Huffington Post*, updated on May 15, 2017, www.huffingtonpost.com/entry /hemingways-high-school-graduation-100-years-later_us_59144a0ee4b016248243f1ff.

16 Sanford, *At the Hemingways*, 136.

17 Baker, *Ernest Hemingway: A Life Story*, 36–37.

18 Baker, *Ernest Hemingway: A Life Story*, 38.

19 Elder and Cirino, "Hemingway's High School Graduation."

20 Carlos Baker, ed., *Ernest Hemingway: Selected Letters, 1917–1961* (New York: Charles Scribner's Sons, 1981), 25.

21 Clarence Hemingway to Ernest Hemingway, June 4, 1920, Hemingway Foundation.

22 Liesl Olson, "Ernest Hemingway in Chicago," *The Newberry*, June 1, 2012, www.newberry.org /ernest-hemingway-chicago.

23 Sanford, *At the Hemingways*, 208.

2: MILAN AND VENETO

1   Sanford, *At the Hemingways*, 156.

2   Baker, *Ernest Hemingway: A Life Story*, 66–67.

3   Baker, *Ernest Hemingway: A Life Story*, 71.

4   Sanford, *At the Hemingways*, 172.

5   Baker, *Ernest Hemingway: A Life Story*, 162.

6   Ernest Hemingway, *Death in the Afternoon* (New York: Scribner, 2002), 154.

7   Baker, *Ernest Hemingway: A Life Story*, 274.

8   Andrea di Robilant, "Retracing Hemingway's Road Trip Through Northern Italy," *Departures*, December 15, 2016, www.departures.com/art-culture/books/andrea-di-robilant -imagines-ernest-hemingway-in-italy.

9   Di Robilant, "Retracing Hemingway's Road Trip Through Northern Italy."

10   Ernest Hemingway, *Across the River and into the Trees* (London: Arrow Books, 2004), 37.

11   Richard Owen, *Hemingway in Italy* (London: Haus Publishing, 2017), 124.

12   Owen, *Hemingway in Italy*, 148.

13   Hemingway, *Across the River and into the Trees*, 55.

3: TORONTO

1   Ernest Hemingway, "Sporting Mayor at Boxing Bouts," *Toronto Star Weekly*, March 30, 1920, ehto.thestar.com/marks/sporting-mayor-at-boxing-bouts.

2   Bill Schiller, "How Hemingway came of age at the Toronto Star," *The Toronto Star*, last modified 2012, ehto.thestar.com/marks/how-hemingway-came-of-age-at-the-toronto-star.

3   Clarence Hemingway to Ernest Hemingway, March 18, 1920, The Ernest Hemingway Foundation.

4   Ernest Hemingway, "Trout-Fishing Hints," *Toronto Star Weekly*, April 24, 1920.

5   Ernest Hemingway, "At Vigo, in Spain, Is Where You Catch the Silver and Blue Tuna, the King of All Fish," *Toronto Star Weekly*, February 18, 1922.

6   William Burrill, *Hemingway: The Toronto Years* (Toronto: Doubleday Canada Limited, 1995), 179–180.

7   Hemingway to Ezra Pound, October 13, 1923, Baker, ed., *Selected Letters*, 97.

8   Burrill, *Hemingway: The Toronto Years*, 179.

9   Morley Callaghan, *That Summer in Paris* (New York: Penguin Books, 1963), 25.

10   Schiller, "How Hemingway came of age."

11   Hemingway to Ezra Pound, October 13, 1923, Baker, ed., *Selected Letters*, 96.

12   Ernest Hemingway, "World Series of Bull Fighting a Mad, Whirling Carnival," *Toronto Star Weekly*, October 27, 1923.

13   Hemingway to Edward O'Brien, November 20, 1923, Baker, ed., *Selected Letters*, 103.

14   Hemingway to O'Brien, November 20, 1923, Baker, ed., *Selected Letters*, 104.

15   Hemingway to Gertrude Stein and Alice B. Toklas, November 9, 1923, Baker, ed., *Selected Letters*, 101.

16   Ernest Hemingway, "The Blind Man's Christmas Eve," *Toronto Star Weekly*, December 22, 1923, quoted in Graeme Bayliss, "In Our Town: Ernest Hemingway in Toronto," *Torontoist*, March 7, 2012, torontoist.com/2012/03/in-our-town-ernest-hemingway-in-toronto/.

17   John Lorinc, "Once Upon a City: Toronto's Premier Italian Trattoria," *Toronto Star*, May 26, 2016, www.thestar.com/yourtoronto/once-upon-a-city-archives/2016/05/26/once-upon-a -city-torontos-premier-italian-trattoria.html.

18   Bayliss, "In Our Town: Ernest Hemingway in Toronto."

19   Burrill, *Hemingway: The Toronto Years*, 231.

20   Burrill, *Hemingway: The Toronto Years*, 234.

21   Ernest Hemingway, "Tackling a Spanish Bull Is 'Just Like Rugby'; Hemingway Tells How He Surprised the Natives," *Toronto Star Weekly*, September 13, 1924.

22   J. H. Cranston, *Ink on My Fingers* (Toronto: The Ryerson Press, 1953), 110.

4: PARIS

1   Ernest Hemingway, *A Moveable Feast* (London: Vintage Books, 2000), 11.

2   Hemingway, *A Moveable Feast*, 3.

3   Jeffrey Meyers, ed., *Hemingway: The Critical Heritage* (New York: Routledge & Kegan Paul, 1982), 2.

4   Hemingway, *A Moveable Feast*, 11.

5   Ernest Hemingway, unpublished fragment, Hemingway Foundation.

6   Hemingway, *A Moveable Feast*, 13.

7   Hemingway, *A Moveable Feast*, 27.

8   Hemingway, *A Moveable Feast*, 27.

9   Baker, *Ernest Hemingway: A Life Story*, 135.

10   Ernest Hemingway, "A Silent, Ghastly Procession," *Toronto Daily Star*, October 20, 1922.

11   Ernest Hemingway, *In Our Time* (New York: Scribner, 2003), 21.

12   Hemingway, *A Moveable Feast*, 63.

13   Michael Reynolds, *Hemingway: The Paris Years* (New York: Norton, 1989), 243.

14   Linda Wagner-Martin, *Ernest Hemingway: A Literary Life* (London: Palgrave Macmillan, 2007), 79.

5: CAYO HUESO

1   Stuart McIver, *Hemingway's Key West* (Sarasota: Pineapple Press, Inc., 2012), 11.

2   McIver, *Hemingway's Key West*, 112.

3   McIver, *Hemingway's Key West*, 112.

4   McIver, *Hemingway's Key West*, 14.

6: BIMINI

1   Ernest Hemingway, *Islands in the Stream* (London: Vintage, 2017), 17.

2   Hemingway to Sara Murphy, July 10, 1935, Baker, ed., *Selected Letters*, 416–17.

3   Hemingway to Murphy, July 10, 1935, Baker ed., *Selected Letters*, 416.

4   Ashley Oliphant, *Hemingway and Bimini: The Birth of Sport Fishing at "The End of the World"* (Sarasota: Pineapple Press, Inc., 2017), 99.

5   As quoted by Jan Fogt in *Anglers Journal*, "Fighting big fish with Ernest Hemingway," March 25, 2019, https://www.anglersjournal.com/saltwater/fighting-big-fish-with-ernest -hemingway.

6   Oliphant, *Hemingway and Bimini*, 47.

7   Baker, *Ernest Hemingway: A Life Story*, 439.

8   Baker, *Ernest Hemingway: A Life Story*, 439.

9   Baker, *Ernest Hemingway: A Life Story*, 480.

10   Hemingway, *Islands in the Stream*, 371.

7: MADRID

1   James M. Markham, "Hemingway's Spain," *The New York Times*, November 24, 1985, www.nytimes.com/1985/11/24/travel/hemingway-s-spain.html.

2   Ernest Hemingway, "Bullfighting is Not a Sport—It is a Tragedy," *Toronto Star Weekly*, October 20, 1923, ehto.thestar.com/marks/bullfighting-is-not-a-sport-it-is-a-tragedy.

3   Ernest Hemingway, *Fiesta* (London: Jonathan Cape, 1941), 251.

4   Dale T. Graden, "'The Earth Endureth Forever': Hemingway in Spain," *The Volunteer*, June 10, 2016, www.albavolunteer.org/2016/06/the-earth-endureth-forever-ernest -hemingway-and-the-spanish-civil-war/.

5   Ernest Hemingway, "On the American Dead in Spain," *The New Masses*, February 14, 1939.

6   Hilary Hemingway and Carlene Brennen, *Hemingway in Cuba* (New York: Rugged Land, 2005), 57.

7   Hemingway and Brennen, *Hemingway in Cuba*, 57.

8   Hemingway, *Death in the Afternoon*, 164.

8: CUBANO SATO

1   Hemingway and Brennen, *Hemingway in Cuba*, 131.

2   Hemingway and Brennen, *Hemingway in Cuba*, 12.

3   Hemingway and Brennen, *Hemingway in Cuba*, 59.

4   Hemingway and Brennen, *Hemingway in Cuba*, 60.

5   Hemingway and Brennen, *Hemingway in Cuba*, 131.

6   Hemingway and Brennen, *Hemingway in Cuba*, 68.

7   Nicole Jankowski, "The Cocktail King of Cuba: The Man Who Invented Hemingway's Favorite Daiquiri," *NPR*, April 25, 2017, www.npr.org/sections/thesalt/2017/04/25/525063025/the -cocktail-king-of-cuba-the-man-who-invented-hemingways-favorite-daiquiri.

8   Jankowski, "The Cocktail King."

9   Joy Lanzendorfer, "11 Facts about Hemingway's *The Old Man and the Sea*," Mental Floss, May 27, 2015, www.mentalfloss.com/article/64363/11-facts-about-hemingways-old-man -and-sea.

10   Lanzendorfer, "11 Facts."

11   Hemingway and Brennen, *Hemingway in Cuba*, 99.

12   Hemingway and Brennen, *Hemingway in Cuba*, 102.

13   Brian Gordon Sinclair, "The Nobel Prize Medal of Ernest Hemingway," Canadian-Cuban Friendship Association, Toronto, December 6, 2011, www.ccfatoronto.ca/articles-of-interest /178-the-nobel-prize-medal-of-ernest-hemingway.

14   Hemingway and Brennen, *Hemingway in Cuba*, 135.

9: LONDON

1   Ernest Hemingway, "London Fights the Robots," *Collier's*, August 19, 1944, www.billdownscbs.com/2015/08/london-fights-the-robots-by-ernest-hemingway.html.

2   Hemingway, "London Fights the Robots."

3   Hemingway and Brennen, *Hemingway in Cuba*, 84.

4   Noel Monks quoted in Fay Anderson, *Witness to War: The History of Australian Conflict Reporting* (Carlton, Victoria: Melbourne University Press, 2011), 168.

5   A. J. Liebling, *Mollie & Other War Pieces* (Lincoln: Bison Books, 2004), 96.

6   John Donne, *Devotions Upon Emergent Occasions*, 1624.

10: THE WOODS: PART II: KETCHUM AND SUN VALLEY

1   Hunter S. Thompson, *The Great Shark Hunt: Strange Tales from a Strange Time* (London: Picador, 2010), 372.

2   Baker, *Ernest Hemingway: A Life Story*, 695.

3   Baker, *Ernest Hemingway: A Life Story*, 695.

4   Baker, *Ernest Hemingway: A Life Story*, 697.

5   Baker, *Ernest Hemingway: A Life Story*, 706.

6   Baker, *Ernest Hemingway: A Life Story*, 824–25.

7   Baker, *Ernest Hemingway: A Life Story*, 851.

8   Thompson, *The Great Shark Hunt*, 375.

9   Jack Hemingway, *Misadventures of a Fly Fisherman: My Life with and without Papa* (New York: McGraw-Hill, 1986), 36.

10   Hemingway, *Misadventures of a Fly Fisherman*, 44.

11   Hemingway's Idaho Geographies, "Mapping Hemingway in Idaho," www.arcgis.com/apps /MapJournal/index.html?appid=8372c1acd90749a489cd937795d788a5.

12   Thompson, *The Great Shark Hunt*, 374.

INDEX

INDEX

INDEX